hONOR ANd ShAME ANd ThE UNITY of ThE MEdITERRANEAN

edited by DAVID D. GILMORE

a special publication of the American Anthropological Association

number 22

Published by the
American Anthropological Association
1703 New Hampshire Avenue, N.W.
Washington, D.C. 20009

Production Editor
Frederick Custer

Library of Congress Cataloging-in-Publication Data
Honor and shame and the unity of the Mediterranean.
   (A Special publication of the American Anthropological Association ; no. 22)
     1. Ethnology—Mediterranean Region. 2. Social values. 3. Honor. 4. Shame. 5. Med-
iterranean Region—Social life and customs. I. Gilmore, David D., 1943–   .II. Series.
GN588.H66   1987   306'.091822   86-26525
ISBN 0-913167-17-7 (pbk.)

CONTENTS

PREFACE

Over twenty years have passed since publication of the original volume on honor and shame in Mediterranean society (Peristiany 1965). Since then, a Mediterranean subspeciality has gained currency and legitimacy in some quarters of cultural anthropology, partly because of this pioneering work. But there remain nagging questions about the alleged uniformity, validity, and geographic boundedness of honor-and-shame, and of the correlative Mediterranean culture-area construct. These essays, originally presented at a panel at the American Anthropological Association's Annual Meeting in Washington in 1983, are all attempts to reexamine these questions and to reopen the issue of Mediterranean cultural unity and the relevance of the honor/shame model of this supposed unity. This symposium was organized by myself with the help of Sarah C. Uhl and Mariko Asano-Tamanoi, both of SUNY-Stony Brook.

The reader may notice that "Mediterranean" is sometimes used here in the nominative case, sometimes as a modifier, and that it is spelled with a lower case *m* by some of the authors. While I uphold a grammatical conservatism that consigns "Mediterranean" to adjective use—with a capital *M*—I have acceded here to the wishes of those who are trying to make a point with innovative semantics. Those who write "mediterranean" are apparently more convinced than others that it has enough proven empirical consistency to stand alone. I will let the reader judge; in any case I assume this grammatical ambiguity will be taken as a tribute to differing points of view rather than editorial inattention.

Most of the editorial tasks involved in this volume were carried out while I was a Visiting Scholar at the Institute of Latin American and Iberian Studies at Columbia University. I want to thank Lambros Comitas and Joan Vincent for facilitating my affiliation with the Institute. My thanks also go to SUNY-Stony Brook, which provided leave time, to the National Endowment for the Humanities, which paid my salary during that time, and to Dan Bates and Judith Tucker of Hunter College, who provided office space and other valuable support. Edward Lehman of the American Anthropological Association also deserves a word of gratitude for his perseverence and assistance under sometimes trying circumstances. Finally, the three anonymous reviewers merit praise for their valuable criticisms, and for responding so promptly.

David D. Gilmore

INTRODUCTION:
THE SHAME OF DISHONOR

David D. Gilmore

Like the other sciences, anthropology evolves through a dialectic of primary postulation, challenge, and revision. So much of this is based on presentation of new field data that it is sometimes hard to distinguish between description and deduction. This collection of empirically based essays has a dual and reciprocal purpose. The first is to provide new, comparable data on a standard Mediterranean paradigm, "honor and shame." The second goal is to reexamine fundamental assumptions about Mediterranean unity made on the basis of the original honor/shame model (Peristiany 1965).

This model is virtually coterminous with the birth of a Mediterranean focus in cultural anthropology. The earliest pathfinders in the Mediterranean Basin—notably British structuralists Pitt-Rivers and Peristiany—were struck by conspicuous affinities in the limited ethnography of the time. In response they conjured up a Mediterranean cultural archetype implicitly incorporating insights from the historical synthesis of Braudel (1972). Aside from obvious environmental and historical analogues, these pioneers saw the Mediterranean peoples as united by a pervasive and relatively uniform value system based on complementary codes of honor and shame. Peristiany (1965:10) called this value syndrome "supreme" in the secular consciousness of the region; and the other authors in the original volume acceded to this supposition and elaborated upon it, contributing ethnographic sketches of descriptive sparkle and literary grace. However, few questioned basic assumptions of consistency and distinctiveness. Nor did they broach questions of origin, diffusion, or causality. Their work provides us today with an invaluable prolegomenon, a kind of Ur-ethnography, but leaves the task of comparative analysis and integration open-ended.

Taking up the challenge, Jane Schneider (1971) inaugurated American Mediterranean studies by launching a vigorous analysis of considerable originality and muscularity. Regarding the honor/shame syndrome as an ideological displacement for underlying structural oppositions of the circum-Mediterranean societies, she added a historical-causal dimension to the study of implicit regularities. She also proposed a parsimonious thesis as to why the Mediterranean area as a whole differed from others in this regard. In linking causal variables to internal cultural consistency, Schneider's paradigm added substance to the emergent claim for Mediterranean distinctiveness. Her groundbreaking work is reflected in later studies by Black-Michaud (1975), Ortner (1978), and in original papers by Giovannini and Marcus in this volume.

Shortly afterwards, John Davis (1977) published a comprehensive critique taking earlier Mediterraneanists to task for naively assuming culture-area regularities without providing the necessary comparative framework. Like Schneider, Davis argues that the Mediterranean region is indeed a culture area, a bounded entity forged through millennia of contact, exchange, intermarriage, and mutual colonization. But he correctly warns that this unity must not be taken for granted but grasped through comparison and historical study. This volume is in part a response to Davis's challenge.

Most of the authors above have accepted the implicit assumption that the Mediterranean Basin represents a *cultural* unity; that it shows both an internal cohesiveness in moral-cognitive terms and a perspicuous trait enclosure in space. Further, there is general agreement that the honor/shame syndrome is diacritical to this coherence and differentiation. It is this dual notion, lying at the heart of Mediterranean studies, that has been questioned by some of the authors represented here.

In one of the first extra-Mediterranean comparisons (with Japan), Asano-Tamanoi breaks new ground by showing that this moral complex is not confined to the Mediterranean area. However, she observes that there are important—though subtle—structural distinctions having to do with sexuality and its control, subsumed under the concept of the "physical person" in Spain—a concept almost lacking in Japan. Similarly, Herzfeld continues his insightful critique of the presumed uniformity of the honor principle itself, first enunciated in a 1980 paper (see also Wikan 1984). Herzfeld, Brandes, Asano-Tamanoi, and I present fieldwork data which suggest that the original model of "honor" has indeed been prematurely nominalized, and that the Mediterranean region is dotted with societies where other moral principles overlay or overshadow an assertive "honor" as masculine ideals. Of course some of this may be due to rapid modernization and cultural accrual in the past two decades—a period of unprecedented regional transformation. All of us, though, would probably all agree that these "other" moral principles, which we call hospitality, respect, and honesty, are also specifically Mediterranean values which can and do complement the classic honor/shame system, however weakened it might be. Certainly the correlative emphasis on female chastity and the desirability of premarital virginity remain strong throughout the region despite modernization (Denich 1977; Giovannini, this volume).

At this point it would be worthwhile to summarize the seminal honor/shame model as originally postulated, and to outline its salience to the claim for culture-area distinctiveness. Afterwards, I will trace more recent refinements made in the model, its relationship to the culture-area idea, and presumed causal factors. Finally, I will make some preliminary remarks concerning neglected areas for comparative study on these issues, arguing the case for a crosscultural psychosocial perspective in Mediterranean studies.

Honor, Shame, and Mediterranean Unity

Honor and shame are reciprocal moral values representing primordial integration of individual to "group." They reflect, respectively, the conferral of public esteem upon the person and the sensitivity to public opinion upon which the former depends (Pitt-Rivers 1965:42). Since all face-to-face societies are moral communities where public opinion arbitrates reputation, all such societies may be said to have some form of honor and shame (Peristiany 1965:10; Wyatt-Brown 1982). However, what seems descriptively outstanding about the Mediterranean variant is the relationship to sexuality and gender distinctions:

It is the comparison of the male-female relationship and that of the roles of the sexes within these
societies that points . . . to significant analogies. . . . [Peristiany 1965:9]

Previously honor has been portrayed in the Mediterranean literature as essentially
male: it is the reward for successful power maneuvers in which a man's relationship to other men *through women* is the fundamental axis of evaluation (Dundes
and Falassi 1975:198). Honor is everywhere "closely associated with sex" (Pitt-
Rivers 1961:114). Its basic currency and measurement is the "shame" of women,
by which Mediterraneanists mean female sexual chastity. Throughout the Mediterranean area, male honor derives from the struggle to maintain intact the shame
of kinswomen; and this renders male reputation insecurely dependent upon female
sexual conduct. Men are responsible for the shame of their women "which is
associated with sexual purity and their own honor derives in large measure from
the way they discharge their responsibility" (Pitt-Rivers 1977:78). When men are
unsuccessful in this they are "shamed," that is, diminished in relation to other
men.

This conception of Mediterranean honor, then, posits a precarious inverse equation of moral obligations in which women become the "weak link" in the chain
of masculine virtue (Campbell 1964:199). "Dishonour is contagious, through
women" (Davis 1973:160). In a sense, then, one may regard Mediterranean
moral attributes as functionally linked to a particular kinetic notion of social sexuality. Sexuality itself is perceived through a competitive idiom by which men
jockey for control over women as objects to achieve narcissistic gratifications and
dominance over other men. Sexuality is a form of social power:

Successful claims on a woman entail domination of other men, both from the point of view of the
husband who jealously guards his wife, and of the adulterer, who shows himself to be more powerful than the husband. [Blok 1981:431]

The struggle for honor is not only erotic, though, for success has concomitant
economic implications (Schneider 1971). Patriarchal domination, once achieved
and defended, is instrumental in securing access to scarce resources. The latter,
of course, is facilitated by the acquisition of desirable affines, who in turn are
attracted by an honorable name (Boissevain 1976:7).

There are two logical consequences to this reciprocal conception of honor and
shame. First there is the rather unusual (ethnographically speaking) connection
between erotic and economic power, the latter being largely contingent upon the
former. This is "intrinsically interesting" as Davis remarks (this volume); but
what makes this different from other societies where affluence derives from control over women and their labor power? The difference is that in the Mediterranean lands women themselves are often nonproductive materially—ideally they
are "excluded" from nondomestic work (Davis 1977:43–44). Rather, they carry
an immaterial or conceptual resource, their chastity, arbitrarily elevated to central
position as an exchange value. This value is transmitted lineally through male
vigilance, enhancing the family patrimony. So as Schneider (1971) has argued,
female modesty is metamorphosed, almost in the manner of a fetish, into a pseu-
docommodity, or more accurately a capital good. The emphasis is thus on female
"labor" in reproduction rather than production. Second is that the masculine experience of sexuality becomes broadened conceptually to encompass a triad in-
volving two men—or groups of men—and a woman, who is reduced to an inter-
mediating object. Sexual relations are experienced as a measure of comparative

virtue, judged as "performance," among men. Necessarily, female sexuality becomes objectified, becoming not only a libidinal goal in itself, but a contentious and arbitrating social index for masculine reputation. The ensuing emphasis on male "sexual victory" (Dundes and Falassi 1975:203) has important affective and psychological consequences for males that I do not think have been sufficiently explored. I will discuss these later.

Since the honor/shame syndrome regulates both inter- and intrasex relations, it may be regarded as a total social fact. In this sense, Peristiany is probably right to call it morally supreme, if he means fundamental and pervasive. The syndrome accordingly has important homogenizing consequences in other areas of Mediterranean culture, although cause and effect are far from clear. For example, since women are thought vulnerable to a predatory male sexuality, they require masculine protection and tutelage; hence male domination can be morally justified as "for their own good," as Giovannini (this volume) shows for Sicily. From a Marxist perspective, then, honor/shame codes can be interpreted as an ideological mystification to oppress women, whose sexuality is thereby alienated and "domesticated" (Ortner 1978). Similarly, women must be physically secluded and segregated for their own protection: hence the physical and sexualized division of community space into a public and a private domain, and hence veiling. There are indeed few societies outside the Latin and Muslim worlds where women must not be "seen," as though this amounted to the provocative flaunting of a scarce resource.

This model presents a satisfying holocultural integrity and strongly supports the culture-area claim. Yet vexing questions remain. First, setting aside the question of historical accuracy, just how valid is it as a portrait of contemporary life under dramatically changed conditions? Second, how widespread and geographically uniform is this model? Last, is it spatially unique, or is it bounded enough to justify the culture-area construct? Recently, for example, some perceptive historians have suggested that Mediterranean honor and shame codes represent variants of a more universal moral system in Indo-European agrarian civilizations generally (Wyatt-Brown 1982:xiii).

To begin with, there has long been a suspicion among younger scholars that the sexual-contest perception of honor and shame distorts contemporary Mediterranean realities (Davis 1977:90). For one thing, it depicts a situation of unrelenting masculine contentiousness that accords poorly with recent field experiences (cf. White 1980:79). Left out of the picture are benevolent norms like generosity, honesty, and personal probity, which are by all accounts also vigorous masculine ideals in Mediterranean lands (Davis 1977:90–92; Herzfeld, this volume).

Pitt-Rivers himself (1965) made a fairly cunning attempt to resolve this incongruity by dividing Mediterranean "honor" into two nonexclusive moral categories. There is first an "honor of precedence" associated with elites. This derives from the "domination of persons" (1965:61). Its ultimate vindication lies in "physical violence" (Pitt-Rivers 1977:83). There is, second, a plebeian "honor of virtue" that is somewhat lamely described (1965:42) as "honesty, loyalty, a concern for reputation which involves avoidance of moral turpitude in general. . . ." The latter, significantly, is shared by both men and women. Peristiany (1965:189–190) seconds this dichotomy, distinguishing honor-virtue as "honesty." But he regards the two as opposed in some ways: while honesty breeds "passive conformity," honor-precedence promotes a touchy aggressiveness. A similar distinction is made by Caro Baroja (1965) for Spain in a historical treatise, and for some contemporary Muslim groups by Meeker (1976).

Still, there are problems. For one thing, there is nothing geographically specific about this composite honor-as-virtue conception: all societies have analogous notions and ideals. Also, most complex societies have elites whose moral standards differ from those of the masses in analogous fashion to Pitt-Rivers's model. So while these modifications improve our understanding of Mediterranean moral ambiguity, they also seem to weaken the claim for area distinctiveness, or at least they do not enhance it.

In reviewing the literature, Davis (1977) takes a slightly different tack. Minimizing a competitive sexuality, he stresses economic competitions in honor, demonstrating that in the Mediterranean region "everywhere honor is related to wealth" (cf. Boissevain 1979:82). Taking up the cudgels against Pitt-Rivers's (1977) notion of "sexual politics," Davis argues that Mediterranean honor is not directly cognate to sexual actions, but rather to the performance of economic sex roles, by which he means—in today's jargon—gender roles:

> Perhaps it should be said at the outset that honour is not primarily to do with sexual intercourse . . . but with performance of roles and is related to economic resources because feeding a family, looking after women, maintaining a following, can be done more easily when the family is not poor. . . . [1977:77]

Probably this is true. But then the question arises as to why this sensible observation has any special relevance to Mediterranean countries. Davis might well be talking about New Guinea or sub-Saharan Africa. There is, however, an implicit justifying assumption in Davis's remarks (which may or may not be true). This is that sex roles themselves, upon which economic motives and goals are ultimately based, are formally unique or unusual in the Mediterranean societies, that they are opposed or conjoined in some distinctive way—a theme adumbrated earlier in the work of Campbell, Pitt-Rivers and others. Again, while Davis has enlarged the scope of the discussion of honor by including economic variables, his claim for Mediterranean cultural distinctiveness falls back ultimately upon the archetype of documented sex and gender polarities. This widens the discussion, but there is a certain circularity in the argument that places Pitt-Rivers and Davis thematically closer than they appear at first glance.

One of the first anthropologists to tackle this apparent confusion head-on was the iconoclastic Michael Herzfeld. From an unabashedly ideographic perspective, he argues that the classic honor/shame model represents a premature conceptual imposition that conflates a rich ethnographic diversity. He believes (1980:349) the whole model-building enterprise to be counterproductive for a fledgling Mediterranean anthropology:

> Massive generalizations of "honor" and "shame" have become counterproductive; their continued use elevates what had begun as a genuine convenience for the readers of ethnographic essays to the level of a theoretical proposition.

Decrying the emphasis on sexual and economic aggression, Herzfeld (this volume) proposes another moral principle, that of hospitality. He offers this as both more valid empirically and more homogeneous geographically, and a better heuristic basis for future comparisons (see also Herzfeld 1984). There is much to commend this. I would certainly agree that the classic honor/shame model has been reified and that this has led to circularity and reductionism in some literature.

However, I would maintain that Herzfeld's hospitality is not opposed to "honor," but is a "layered" part of it (using the term introduced by Asano-Tamanoi here), and that Herzfeld is throwing out the fragile baby of correlations with the bathwater of reification by ignoring what appears an almost universal thread in the literature. This thread is the organic connection between sexuality and economic criteria in the evaluation of moral character. Particularism can be taken too far. What seems to unite the data so far is a moral idiom that might be called, in Hughes's (1978) terms, an "economics of shame," or perhaps a "fiscal sexuality." This refers to the conceptual identification of erotic with tangible resources and a correlative belief that sexual access represents a convertible or "marketable" commodity (Peristiany 1976:12).

Explanatory Modes: Globalist Approaches

The first and perhaps still most powerful analytic modality in approaching Mediterranean honor codes is that of the Schneiders (1971, 1976). Eschewing the community-study method, they espouse a globalist viewpoint that owes much to Wallerstein's world-economy thesis, though Jane Schneider's early work (1971) predates the influential Wallerstein volume (1974). In that paper, she argues persuasively that the Mediterranean honor/shame syndrome originated historically in a politico-economic complex in which small atomistic kinship units competed over scarce resources in the absence of effective state control. Given conditions of economic and institutional poverty, female chastity came to be considered a valuable component of each family's patrimony and hence a means of acquiring useful affines in the struggle for survival.

This intriguing thesis is later elaborated in the joint-authored book on western Sicily (1976). But here the Schneiders attempt something more ambitious: they want to reconstruct historically the origins of the conditions of scarcity and competition themselves. Using new insights garnered from the core-periphery thesis of Wallerstein (1974), they argue that these conditions have to do with exploitation and dominance by the core, by which they mean North Atlantic capitalism in league with hegemonic states and parasitic "dependency" elites. Thus the cultural unity of the Mediterranean area (Sicily being a convenient example) derives from a relatively uniform (peripheral) dependency relationship to the international forces of core capitalism, and previously, to Spanish and Roman mercantile hegemony.

This causal-historical model has a surface plausibility. But from the materialist viewpoint there are at least two internal weaknesses. First, the state is awarded causal primacy both for its hegemonic domination and for its institutional ineffectiveness. Second, a persistent historical phenomenon is explained on the basis of its hypothetical adaptive value sometime in the past when conditions were different. An example of the latter is the unsupported assertion (1976:97) that the modern seclusion of women in the Mediterranean area is a defensive response to wife-capture and white-slavery by the "center"—the metropole. Yet the seclusion of women continues today, hundreds of years after these phenomena have virtually disappeared. Are we to regard sexual segregation as a "survival?" There must be other, contiguous causal variables involved that mediate between exogenous and local factors.

The ambiguous role of the state is brought up again by Ortner (1978). Ortner sees the preoccupation with female chastity as an epiphenomenon of the state-

enforced code of masculine dominance. Both of these may be viewed as consequences of the political enthronement of the patriarchal extended family as a strategy of class domination in early state formation. In this view, female chastity
represents part of the cosmology of state religions which encourage submission
and self-effacement of women.

As Giovannini points out here, there is tacit agreement in Ortner's paper (1978)
with the Schneiders' view (1976) that virginity "came to be" regarded as a culminating expression of female virtue and thus "the" criterion in connubial selection; although again, why an arbitrary sexual purity should be cherished over
health, vigor, or industriousness is not readily evident. Also, it seems to me that
historical-materialist explanations that refer back to emergent state formation
have very limited usefulness in explaining ideological continuity under changed
and changing circumstances. Explaining origins is a far cry from explaining trait
persistence; the latter requires a different analytical approach because it is epis-
temologically a different question. As both Marcus and Davis show (this volume),
when historical conditions change, forms of honor get modified accordingly to
meet new challenges: superstructural adaptation is "negotiable" (Marcus, this
volume). Davis argues, also (this volume) that the state has too long been awarded
causal priority in the absence of supportive historical-ethnographic data. It is now
necessary to go beyond speculation, he urges, by illuminating the actual empirical
impact of statecraft, bureaucracy, and legislation upon family organization and
dynamics. He presents the somewhat anomalous case of Qaddafi's Libya as an
example of what can be learned by studying the impact of government interference in domestic, moral, and sexual relations.

Panoramic approaches like the Schneiders' seem to regard the Mediterranean
peoples as more acted upon than acting, and so award causal priority to external
stimuli. Congruent with this view, but bringing to bear a refreshingly concrete
perspective, is Delaney's conception (this volume) of the political role of the idea
of monogenesis in the state religions of the Mediterranean Basin. All three monotheisms, she notes, had their origin in the same general area of southwest Asia.
All teach and promote the creed of a specifically male God and male prophets,
relegating females to subsidiary roles and minimizing their contributions to reproduction. Delaney also regards the honor/shame code as reinforcing female
subjugation, but adds what I think is a valid scriptural-educational dimension to
sex role, previously overlooked.

Honor and Masculinity

Globalist approaches to Mediterranean moral codes are alike in one way. They
use a heuristic paradigm based on internal contradiction that emphasizes the
causal priority of conflict, defense, and compromise. This model is powerful because it is dynamic and accommodates history. However, conflict theory can be
applied usefully not only to history, but also to endopsychic development. Previously, I argued (1982) that many regularities in Mediterranean ethos stem from
psychosexual convergences in which internal developmental conflicts seem to be
resolved in similar ways. Here I would like to elaborate this observation by dis-
cussing the relationship among sex-role, gender identity, and honor and shame in
Mediterranean societies. It is first necesssary to make a few observations about
the cultural construction of masculinity in the Mediterranean area. This discussion
emphasizes the northern littoral, but I think it is relevant to the south.

Many anthropologists would probably agree that most cultures have concepts of a desirable masculinity that compromises a gender-specific role, a gender identity and sexual orientation (Hooker 1965; Stoller 1968). Gender identity and gender role are related, but different. The former is the self-awareness, either conscious or unconscious, that one belongs to one sex and not the other, the sense of "maleness" or "femaleness." The latter is the overt gender-specific behavior one displays in public according to cultural expectations (Stoller 1968:10). Frequently the construction of male gender role begins with a definition of manhood on the basis of a polaric separation of what is considered male from what is considered female. This separation is especially true of Mediterranean societies, but it occurs in many societies to degrees where sex differences are emphasized. As a result of this primary distancing of gender, a self-definition of masculinity often becomes perceived initially by males in "negative" terms, as the antithesis or opposite of femininity. As Chodorow (1974:50) puts it:

> A boy in his attempt to gain an elusive masculine identification, often comes to define his masculinity largely in negative terms, as that which is not feminine or involved with women.

Naturally there are other positive criteria that can vary a great deal, but these often demand a public demonstration of "manliness," as well as proof of its maintenance or "constancy" (Luria 1979). That is, masculinity is, first, often defined as the complementary obverse of femininity; and second, this differentiation encourages a male role which is problematic, controvertible, or "elusive" (Chodorow 1974:50). In the androcentric societies, masculinity must be won not only through internal and external struggle, but also through continual affirmation (Maccoby 1979:201). Manhood therefore is not only "created culturally" in these societies, as has often been observed (cf. Keesing 1982:8), but also culturally and publicly sustained. Inevitably both the conferral and maintenance of masculinity carry visibly competitive overtones, especially in societies which emphasize sexual distinctions, at least through invidious comparison. Conversely, femininity may depend more often on natural functions and is therefore often less problematical (Chodorow 1974:44).

This difference between the cultural construction of male and female can no doubt be exaggerated. To be sure, femininity is also competitive to a degree. Women's status varies on the basis of fecundity and relative compliance with repressive norms; but these rivalries are often emically construed as passive or acquiescent rather than aggressive. As a result of the uncertainty of masculinity, men often feel themselves under continual pressure to avoid appearing feminine in speech, dress, comportment, or affect. Women may feel such pressures less keenly and are less often subjected to the sanction of having their femininity called into question (Stoller 1968). The very paucity of terms and phrases that convey the gender converse of "effeminate," "unmanly," or "emasculated," express the difference in both social and psychological ramifications of male and female identities. In fact, women may be praised and admired for performing man's roles when circumstances so dictate. This often occurs in the Mediterranean countries, where strong masculine women are admired and are said approvingly to be like men except for anatomy:

> In the village where I stayed, lived a woman forced by circumstance to take care of many things which are usually men's affairs. She accomplished these tasks in a way which earned her wide approval. One male informant described her, favorably, as . . . "a woman who [only] lacked testicles [to make it as a man]." [Blok 1981:429]

It seems, therefore, that men in patriarchal societies frequently define themselves defensively as having something—achieving something—that women by anatomy or nature do not have and cannot have. This frangible extra something, which confers their social identity, their position, and their power, is precarious or arguable: since it has to be earned, it is also conceptually subject to loss. The achievement of an unqualified masculinity is therefore often perilous: manhood is "at risk" (Rochlin 1980:168).

These gender sensibilities are nearly universal to degrees. But they are particularly acute in the Mediterranean lands. One of the rare subjects to elicit almost universal agreement in Mediterranean studies is the identification of "honour" or alternative male ideals about virtue with defense of a beleaguered "manliness" (Davis 1977:95). For example, in Greece

a man is honorable when he meets certain exacting standards of manliness and is untainted by successful attacks on himself or his women. [Davis 1977:95]

This dogma of a contingent, exacting manliness, a "manly selfhood" (Herzfeld 1985:18), finds resonant echo in much of the literature of southern Europe. Even in anomalous cases where a violent honor-of-precedence is negligible (Gilmore, this volume), there nevertheless exists a direct correlation between ideals of masculinity and what passes for honor or male status. And in every case I know of, the exacting standards for this manliness include a separation or disparagement of women and of femininity, culturally defined, and a stress on virile display (Blok 1981:442). This virility, again, is suspect: it must be publicly demonstrated. It rests on visible proof of performance. For example, in Italy "only a wife's pregnancy could sustain her husband's masculinity" (Bell 1979:105). This also holds true for much of Spain (Brandes 1980). Most monographs on the area, in fact, contain similar qualifying statements about the need for incontrovertible male "performance." One may say confidently, therefore, that a common Mediterranean theme is the elevation of a demonstrated physiological masculinity, an ostentatious "indomitable virility" (Denich 1974:250) to paramountcy in the ascription of male social identity and reputation, whether we gloss this as "honor" or by some other term. The word does not matter much: what counts is the common sensibility.

From one point of view, this particular notion of masculinity, of "real" versus "effete" men (Marcus, this volume), provides a psychological key for gaining an appreciation of Mediterranean cultural distinctiveness. To be sure, competitive envy occurs in all societies: men are always rivals for material goods, for women, and for power; women are rivals for other things. But in the Mediterranean lands, masculine rivalries seem to be intensified by an erotic dimension, which, as I have said, triangulates the sexual relationship, bringing into play an essentially homoerotic aim along with a heterosexual object. That is, sexuality, whatever other meanings it conveys, also establishes symbolically an intimacy among men which can be interpreted as homosexual. For the man who is "dominated" sexually through his women, or who is bested in virile performance, is said to be "shamed" (Brandes 1980; Blok 1981; Delaney, this volume); and this sense of shame conveys very strongly the conception of diminishment, of feminization, of being placed in the passive position of a woman, and therefore conceptually subject to homosexual assault. This diminishment is symbolized by the near-universal Mediterranean image of disgrace: the horns of the cuckold. Among other things (Blok 1981), these represent an anatomical displacement tantamount to castration, and simultaneously the humiliating public garland of defeat in the shape of the victorious phallus of the aggressor. This widespread theme of an embattled masculinity and of homosexual triumph and ignominy is brought out clearly, if unintentionally, in Herzfeld's Greek material (this volume). There the rapist is said to "enter the father's house"; that is, to inflict outrage, most trenchantly, upon another man.

It appears then that sexual access in the Mediterranean area often involves an indirect threat to the masculine integrity of another man. This amounts to a symbolic "penetration" in rape or seduction, or a public display of potency (in marriage or other legitimate access) in which men are stratified through invidious comparison of phallic performance. Thus the stress on virility seems to belie a defensive or prophylactic strategy. This strategy is institutionalized in the particularly aggressive Mediterranean ethnomasculinities with their relentless, almost obsessive manliness—a feature found from the *machismo* of Spain and *maschio* of Sicily (Giovannini, this volume) to the *rajula* of North Africa (Geertz 1979:364) to cognate forms in the Balkans. Most of these, incidentally, have been likened explicitly to Hispanic "machismo" (Mernissi 1975:4–5; Simic 1969; Denich 1974).

Here we see the corollary affective significance of the Mediterranean concept of shame for men. Sexual shame is not only the arbiter of chaste femininity, but also, when lost, the negation of masculine identity. When a man is shamed through an erotic defeat or an equivalent social submission he is symbolically emasculated: his physical integrity is dissolved and he succumbs to the ever-present danger of sexual reversal, of feminization. In a sense, he surrenders his own masculine identity and *becomes* a woman who is victimized and penetrated. For instance in Crete, when a man is bested in a manly game of cards, this is felt not just as a defeat, but also as a "sexual attack on his person." Amidst cries of "Shame!" the looser is said to be "castrated" by the winner (Herzfeld 1985:160). So male dishonor implies more than loss of social prestige; it also implies loss of male social identity, of masculinity. Mediterranean honor, then, is a "libidinized" social reputation; and it is this eroticized aspect of honor—albeit unconscious or implicit—that seems to make the Mediterranean variant distinctive.

Underlying this Mediterranean unity from a motivational point of view are shared male anxieties about feminization. These fears are mainly couched in terms of being placed in a passive or vulnerable position—like a woman: actual loss of manhood. For example, in Turkey a man fears that

> if the boundary of what is his has been penetrated or broken by someone else, he is put in the position of a woman and therefore shamed. [Delaney, this volume]

In Morocco (Dwyer 1978; Crapanzano 1980a) men fear "entrapment" by dominant women who threaten their masculinity and reduce them to helpless thralls. That is, they fear being placed in the passive role associated with women; they fear sex reversal. In Spain, the adulterous wife will

> deprive her husband of his precious masculinity and even go so far as to convert him symbolically into a member of her own sex. [Brandes 1980:91]

These are common enough sentiments to anyone who has read the Mediterranean corpus. But why should this anxiety about sexual constancy be so strong in the Mediterranean societies? Why should men feel so threatened by passivity, and why should male status depend upon so fragile a manhood? Economic or political explanations which stress patriarchal domination or peripheral position in the world economy are probably relevant. But since a set of objective conditions can only be transformed into manifest motives through a process of intrapsychic assimilation, such explanations need psychological amplification. Here I would like to explore this issue briefly.

Normally obsessive fears about sexual integrity are not unidimensional, but reflect some degree of affective ambivalence. That is, sexual anxieties of the kind depicted in the quotes above often indicate internal conflict; or more specifically, they indicate both an intolerable unconscious wish and a defense against this wish. It is difficult from a psychodynamic point of view, for example, to accept a vehement abhorrence or disavowal of everything ''feminine''—a kind of ego quarantine of manhood—as not at some level reflecting repudiated wishes to be like a woman in some way, however remote. There is certainly exaggerated horror at homosexuality in many Mediterranean countries (cf. Maraspini 1968:182; Hart 1976:125–126; Brandes 1980). But we have no evidence beyond this that Mediterranean men are any more ''latent homosexuals'' than any others, and it is both impertinent and offensive to suggest this. I think the answer lies instead in the area of gender-identity ambivalence rather than in homosexual object-choice; that is, these men are defending, through honor/shame polarities and prohibitions, against unacceptable female identifications. The question then becomes: are there common developmental factors or liabilities which could be identified as promoting gender-identity ambivalence in Mediterranean males? Some of the recent work of neo-Freudian psychoanalysts (cf. Stoller 1968, 1973; Rochlin 1980) is helpful here as a starting point.

To summarize, this work holds that the primary (preoedipal) ego identification of children is with mothers, with nurturing parent. This view contrasts with Freud's supposition that the girl's preoedipal connection to mother is one of ''attachment,'' while the boy's is one of libidinal cathexis, that is, heterosexual object-love (see Chodorow 1978:115). The reason for this is the extended period of psychological dependency and consequent narcissistic psychic merging, or symbiosis, of infants of both sexes with nursing mother (Stoller 1973:244). Again, in contrast to Freud (1905a), this view holds that boys have to switch their gender identification to fathers during the oedipal stage while girls do not (Rochlin 1980:43). Thus masculinity is not the ''natural'' sex as Freud assumed: it has to be earned. Further developing this thesis, Greenson (1968:370) has postulated for boys a complemental developmental series of ''dis-identification'' from mother, followed by counter-identification with father. If true, the development of masculine core identity, like the achievement of gender role, is psychologically more problematic, more refractory, than the analogous process in girls since it involves repudiation of the original maternal identification. Furthermore this development is very likely impeded in the absence of available fathers or male surrogates who can act as counter-role models or psychic magnets, or when boys are raised under domestic arrangements excluding older males:

> An important factor in the development of a masculine orientation is the availability of the father, or another significant older male, as a discriminate male object. [Biller 1971:44]

This familiar notion that father absence impedes masculine identification is a hoary hypothesis in personality studies. True, it has never been conclusively proven (LeVine 1973; Pleck 1981). But it has received some credible crosscultural support in the work of the Whitings and others (J. Whiting et al. 1958; Burton and J. Whiting 1961; B. Whiting 1965). Even its harshest critics (Parker et al. 1975:690) admit the model's continuing plausibility. Is there any empirical support for its relevance here? I think there is, but it goes much further than a monocausal stress on father absence. The latter is but one variable among many situational contributants to gender-identity conflict in Mediterranean males.

First, there is the rather contradictory quality of Mediterranean masculinity cults themselves. Most Mediterraneanists have observed these hypermasculine syndromes in various guises and under various labels, of which "machismo" is simply the most famous. Their components almost always include both a distancing dread of the feminine and a phallocentric worldview, the latter perhaps best expressed in Delaney's account of the almost mystical appreciation of the penis in Turkey (this volume; but see also Belmonte 1980; Brandes 1980). A major theme in this attitude is its defensiveness: it is a panegyric to what is, the phallus, since this contributes the minimal anatomical definition of a cherished manhood. But it is also a prophylactic stance, reflecting a fear of loss, or impairment, or diminishment of the male genital through the hostile action and shaming of other men or domineering women.

Most of us are perhaps familiar with the popular interpretation of meretricious Don Juanism as a compensation against fears of inadequacy. Without supportive depth evidence, this may be a shallow notion; but its persistence no doubt reflects an intuitive popular understanding of sexual ambivalence. The Mediterranean masculinity cults are nothing if not ambivalent: they convey the notion that masculinity is at the same time both powerful and inherently fragile, that it requires constant vigilance and defense. Since this apprehension seems to carry with it a fantasy of feminization amounting to sexual reversal—organic emasculation—one may conclude that many Mediterranean men sense their masculinity to be at real peril, at least unconsciously, from a threat in the external world. But since there is no such emasculation threat other than that which is imagined, the danger to masculinity must have its origin endopsychically, from within. One plausible explanation is that this threat represents the residue of primary female identifications which have never been fully eliminated. That is, that the androcentric sexual ideologies, for which machismo may stand as a convenient label, represent a reaction-formation or "masculine protest" against unacceptable wishes *not* to have a penis, to be like a woman, to be dependent, to restore the early psychic merging with the mother. As Rochlin (1980:52) puts it in more general terms:

> The boy cannot expunge the early formed identification with women, and he remains haunted by it throughout his existence. It is this fear, and affront to masculine narcissism, which promotes his establishing himself in the role of the aggressor.

Hence the compensatory hypervaluation of the male genital and the almost priapic obsession with phallic assertion in the ethnomasculinities of the Mediterranean societies.

Evidence for gender-identity ambivalence among Mediterranean men comes from a number of areas of expressive or free-associative culture. First, there are rituals and forms of play and improvisational verbal literature, especially those featuring gender reversal or sexual inversion. Many Mediterranean societies have secular celebrations in which male transvestism is a major, or even paramount theme (Pitt-Rivers 1977:119). The transsexual dramas of Latin Carnival come at once to mind (DuBoulay 1974:60; Silverman 1975:158; Gilmore and Gilmore 1979; Counihan 1985). But other equally dramatic forms have been reported where men are placed—either voluntarily or forcefully—in the position of women by other men (Brandes 1980; Driessen 1983:128). For instance, in Andalusia, men are humiliated during public romping at harvest time by being homosexually raped (Brandes 1980:155). I recorded one Carnival song in which a male singer in drag threatens his mother-in-law with ''castration'' (Gilmore 1980:177), thereby assigning clinical masculinity to a woman and bemoaning his own impotence before so powerful a creature (see also Rodríguez Becerra 1985). Naturally all this is in jest, but as Freud argued (1905b), the momentary dis-inhibition allowed by such jocularity no doubt permits the release of forbidden wishes normally kept in check by repression.

There is further support for this hypothesis in certain areas of childrearing which seem to encourage mother-son intimacy and father distance. Unfortunately, we have yet so little data on socialization in the Mediterranean area that it is perhaps premature to make any claims at this point. Nevertheless, one may speculate about two related contextual features of male life cycle that appear relevant to this discussion. First there is the unusual degree of absention of Mediterranean males generally from domestic affairs, reinforced by the rigid separation of public and private worlds (Friedl 1967:97). Second there is the lack of institutionalized *rites-de-passage* from boyhood to a public conferral of masculinity in the Mediterranean cultures. I will examine each of these factors in turn.

A rigid spatial and behavioral segregation of the sexes and the consequent domestic division of labor is probably the most striking physical characteristic of Mediterranean community life. To be sure, it is a contributing factor in male political and sexual domination, but it also has important implications beyond questions of political and sexual stratification. The virtual absence of males from the home implies that boys as well as girls are reared until puberty in an exclusively female environment. In Cyprus, for example, a man who lingers at home is likely to have his manhood questioned: ''What sort of man is he? He prefers hanging about the house with women'' (Loizos 1975:92). In Algeria, ''men who remain much in the house . . . are suspect'' for the same reason (Bourdieu 1965:222). In Morocco, the father remains ''indifferent and external'' to childrearing (Brown 1976:102), even to the point of ''avoidance'' (Geertz 1979:333). In Yugoslavia, despite official state propaganda, men continue to resist the ''unmanly image'' associated with childcare (Denich 1977:229). In Italy, the father tends toward a ''formal and distant'' aloofness toward children (Cronin 1977); in Spain he is remote and ''evanescent'' (Gilmore and Gilmore 1979:297; see also Driessen 1983).

This male remoteness has two important ramifications given the other related factors described here. First is that boys, confined to a female-dominated space, are denied an accessible male figure with whom to identity at the precise time that the primary gender-identity formation process is going on (Luria 1979:173). Second is the consequent emotional closeness and affective ''symbiosis'' (Parsons 1969) of mothers and sons—a pan-Mediterranean trait (Saunders 1981). In Portugal the ''mother-son bond is thought to be the strongest possible bond between two human beings'' (Cutileiro 1971:112). In Italy this bond is the ''primary axis'' of family continuity (Parsons 1969:55); in Greece it is "indestructible" (Campbell 1964:168). Moreover, this uniquely powerful bond originates in a domestic scene in which the boy often perceives the mother—typical in Mediterranean societies—as dominant or "in-charge," or as the "primary handler of the family's financial resources" (Rogers 1975:734–735).

One may argue reasonably, therefore, that these widespread structural features impede a solid male gender identity and promote early psychic identification with the more accessible parent, the mother. As Parsons (1969:456) has argued for Neapolitan boys: there is never an autonomous same-sex ego identification with father; instead there is a "masculine identification with a set of cultural values identifiable as feminine." Even in the absence of such hypothetical liabilities, the boy must still at puberty—unlike his sister—make the hazardous spatial and behavioral transition from the female world to the homosocial world of men. In doing so, he must break forever the primary feminine association with home and mother that endangers his masculine image among his peers. This transition includes expunging past habits and inappropriate gender-specific patterns, for example avoiding "feminine speech" patterns, and suffering the sudden "trauma of removal from female society into the society of men" (Brown 1976:107). The traumatic quality of this rupture brings me to the second point, which goes beyond father absence to ritual and symbolism. This is the widespread lack of facilitating male initiation ceremonies or *rites-de-passage* in the Mediterranean area.

Again, most anthropologists would probably agree that all societies must provide some institutional support for the inevitable transition from childhood to adulthood (cf. Erikson 1950). Often this coincides with the conferral of an adult manhood and femininity—a sex role and gender assignment—through which a permanent social identity is forged (Young 1965; Shapiro 1979:282–283). Under the conditions described above—confinement of boys to the feminine domain—many androcentric societies compensate by subjecting adolescent boys to stressful or painful rites of passage by which they "become" men. Through these ordeals, membership in the male world is won through simultaneous testing and renunciation of female associations (Whiting et al. 1958; Herdt 1982).

What is most striking about the Mediterranean literature in this regard is both the emphasis on the elusive goal of masculinity and the relative absence of formalized rituals of transition to this goal. The maturational process of Spanish youths, for example, has been called an amorphous "riteless passage to manhood" (Murphy 1983). In Morocco, "puberty is socially recognized only in a tacit fashion, as in all Muslim society" (Hart 1976:124). The only Moroccan boyhood rite, circumcision, takes place well before puberty and reaffirms the mother-son relationship rather than severing it: during the ceremony "Mother and son are for the moment symbolically equated" (Crapanzano 1980b:28–29). In the resultant absence of a clear-cut consensual rupture with femininity, and without biological markers like menarche to signal manhood, each individual male must prove himself in his own way (cf. Parker et al. 1975:689). Since an abiding masculinity is neither conferred nor confirmed in the Mediterranean societies, this individual proof must be continual and unrelenting, because it is undermined perpetually by incredulity and suspicion from within and without.

Faced with these challenges to masculine autonomy and sensing peril in a world run secretly by women, Mediterranean men seem to fall back on the one unambiguous distinction between the sexes: anatomy. Thus they honor the penis as the repository of manhood and the mirror for the masculine ego. The proof of this precarious manliness is the demonstration of phallic potency through erotic triumph. In aggregate, this would explain the flamboyant virility complexes of Mediterranean males, the pressured need to prove and defend manliness, the rivalous conceptualization of sexuality, and the compulsion to denigrate and distance the female. Mediterranean sexual ideologies, along with their honor-and-shame derivatives, represent endless "rituals of manhood" (cf. Herdt 1982).

My goal here has not been to dispute existing materialist theories about Mediterranean unity or to propose a competing hypothesis. All present theories are good and useful up to a point; none stands alone. Rather, I have tried to point out the potential value of the classic Mediterranean construct by showing how cultural and psychological analogies may provide additional clues for comparative research into common life experiences. Despite the questions raised in the papers assembled here, and despite the anomalies and exceptions, the fact remains that there are some resonances about the Mediterranean cultures that invite comparison. I have argued that these "somethings" are characterological, deriving from parallel resolutions to universal psychosexual dilemmas of development.

In this volume other interpretations are offered: models are debated and deflated, paradigms lost. Mediterranean unity may itself remain problematical, as Herzfeld keeps telling us. But the "poetics of manhood," as he titles his recent book about Greek male "contests" (1985), would be most keenly appreciated by men in Sicily, or Andalusia, or Turkey, or Tunisia, rather than in other places distant from the Middle Sea. But if they have not yet forged a final consensus, the authors represented here have at least come to grips with these questions about unity and distinctiveness. They have broached the subject, made it accessible, overturned the sod. The final synthesis, the forging of new and more profound theories about that fascinating variant of human behavior known as "Mediterranean," must await the inspiration of those who read this book and are motivated by its failures.

Concluding Remarks

Finally then, as the Spanish philosopher Unamuno said, originality is a return to origins. In my opinion, the pathfinders, Pitt-Rivers and Peristiany, were right to look at the Mediterranean area as a unit of culture—though perhaps for the wrong reasons. This unity is at least partly derived from the primordial values of honor and shame, and these values are deeply tied up with sexuality and power, with masculinity and gender relations (cf. Davis 1977). Like competition and cooperation, honesty (or hospitality) and honor are not competing values. Rather they are compatible and necessarily correlative ones: obverse sides, or "layers" of the same coin. They are what Marcus (this volume) calls "the pacifist side of honor." Public esteem, success, respect in the Mediterranean lands are always imbedded in the process of proving oneself publicly a man or a woman, to an apparently greater extent than in other places. As Herzfeld (1985:16) says of the Cretans he studied, there is less focus attached to "being a good man" than to "being *good at* being a man." This felicitous phrase summarizes everything I have said above. But even so, if we have come this far towards identifying shared values, dialectically rather than circularly I hope, one last daunting question bulks large at a higher level of abstraction. If the Mediterranean lands constitute a culture area, then where do we go from there? In short, there is a big "so what" lurking about in the midst of all this that needs consideration. Aside from a self-appointed license to call ourselves "Mediterraneanists," what is the payoff to culture theory in the Mediterraneanist endeavor?

First, the comparative efforts here have implicitly conveyed some theoretical and methodological insights that may have more general application in area studies. In sum, these papers show the need for a fine-tuned eclectic approach in comparison: but not simply a haphazard, inorganic accretion of ideas. What is needed is an eclecticism that weds symbolic approaches to materialism (as Giovannini argues here), and that awards causal power to both endogenous and exogenous factors, and that sees culture as an overdetermined compromise between competing forces. Robert LeVine (1973) has called this the "two-systems" approach. This is fine, but the psychological anthropologists have not fully won acceptance for this model because of an overemphasis on endopsychic dynamics and a lack of appreciation of political and social class influences. Like all cultures, Mediterranean culture is an arbitrary symbolic system (cf. Sahlins 1976). But symbolic systems do not derive from nowhere; they *mediate* between internal and outside worlds. Sexual attitudes, ideas about procreation, childrearing, moral norms, and ego identity form a whole, but they are also adaptative devices for perceiving and controlling an inherited universe. If a gender-based honor-and-shame moral system defines a Mediterranean World, then this category emerges not simply as an example of butterfly collecting, but as a mutually intelligible framework of moral choices by which people communicate and gain an identity both with and within the group. Culture, which unites people into communities, is above all a moral system: culture makes a virtue of necessity. And morality is always connected at some level to sexuality and aggression and their control. In all this the importance of morality as *communication* is paramount. Honour-and-shame then may be seen as a "master symbol" (Turner 1969) of Mediterranean cultures.

Second, and following from the above, these papers show the critical importance of gender perceptions and gender roles in the etiology of symbolic systems. In the Mediterranean area we see gender polarities as a kind of "genetic code" for behavior and self-identity, as Delaney calls it (this volume). This genetic code produces a strictly dichotomous universe in which all things, even inanimate objects, are divided linguistically into male and female categories. (Dual nominal gender systems like those of the Mediterranean languages are relatively rare, as Brandes points out in his conclusions here.) But the generative power of gender to bolster cognitive and moral "dual structures" is only highlighted by emphasis in the Mediterranean societies, as Brandes also notes. The study of gender, of sexuality, and of variable concepts of male and female—a study inaugurated by Margaret Mead—may be the lost key to a deeper understanding of culture.

References Cited

Bell, Rudolf M.
  1979 Fate and Honour, Family and Village: Demographic and Cultural Change in Rural Italy Since 1800. Chicago: University of Chicago Press.
Belmonte, Thomas
  1980 The Broken Fountain. New York: Columbia University Press.
Biller, Henry B.
  1971 Father, Child, and Sex Role: Paternal Determinants of Personality Development. Lexington, MA: D.C. Heath.

Black-Michaud, Jacob
   1975   Cohesive Force: Feud in the Mediterranean and the Middle East. New York: St. Martin's
          Press.
Blok, Anton
   1981   Rams and Billy-Goats: A Key to the Mediterranean Code of Honour. Man 16:427–440.
Boissevain, Jeremy
   1976   Uniformity and Diversity in the Mediterranean: An Essay in Interpretation. *In* Kinship and
          Modernization in Mediterranean Society. J. G. Peristiany, ed. Pp. 1–11. Rome: Center for Med-
          iterranean Studies.
   1979   Toward an Anthropology of the Mediterranean. Current Anthropology 20:81–93.
Bourdieu, Pierre
   1965   The Sentiment of Honour in Kabyle Society. *In* Honour and Shame. J. G. Peristiany, ed.
          Pp. 191–242. London: Weidenfeld and Nicolson.
Brandes, Stanley H.
   1980   Metaphors of Masculinity. Philadelphia: University of Pennsylvania Press.
Braudel, Fernand
   1972   The Mediterranean and the Mediterranean World in the Age of Philip II. 2 Vols. Transl. by
          W. Collins Sons, Ltd. New York: Harper and Row.
Brown, Kenneth L.
   1976   The People of Salé: Tradition and Change in a Moroccan City, 1830–1930. Cambridge,
          MA: Harvard University Press.
Burton, Roger and J. Whiting
   1961   The Absent Father and Cross-Sex Identity. Merrill-Palmer Quarterly 7:85–95.
Campbell, John K.
   1964   Honour, Family, and Patronage. Oxford: Oxford University Press.
Caro Baroja, Julio
   1965   Honour and Shame: A Historical Account of Several Conflicts. *In* Honour and Shame. J.
          G. Peristiany, ed. Pp. 79–138. London: Weidenfeld and Nicolson.
Chodorow, Nancy
   1974   Family Structure and Feminine Personality. *In* Women, Culture, and Society. Michelle Ros-
          aldo and L. Lamphere, eds. Pp. 43–66. Stanford: Stanford University Press.
   1978   The Reproduction of Mothering. Berkeley: University of California Press.
Counihan, Carole M.
   1985   Transvestism and Gender in a Sardinian Carnival. *In* Sex and Gender in Southern Europe:
          Special Issue of Anthropology. David D. Gilmore, ed. Pp. 11–24. Vol. 9 (1 and 2).
Crapanzano, Vincent
   1980a Tuhami: Portrait of a Moroccan. Chicago: University of Chicago Press.
   1980b Rite of Return: Circumcision in Morocco. The Psychoanalytic Study of Society 9:15–36.
Cronin, Constance
   1977   Illusion and Reality in Sicily. *In* Sexual Stratification. Alice Schlegel, ed. Pp. 67–93. New
          York: Columbia University Press.
Cutileiro, José
   1971   A Portuguese Rural Society. Oxford: Oxford University Press.
Davis, John
   1973   Land and Family in Pisticci. London: Athlone Press.
   1977   People of the Mediterranean. London: Routledge and Kegan Paul.
Denich, Bette
   1974   Sex and Power in the Balkans. *In* Women, Culture, and Society. Michelle Rosaldo and L.
          Lamphere, eds. Pp. 243–263. Stanford: Stanford University Press.
   1977   Women, Work, and Power in Modern Yugoslavia. *In* Sexual Stratification. Alice Schlegel,
          ed. Pp. 215–244. New York: Columbia University Press.
Driessen, Henk
   1983   Male Sociability and Rituals of Masculinity in Rural Andalusia. Anthropological Quarterly
          56:125–133.
DuBoulay, Juliette
   1974   Portrait of a Greek Mountain Village. Oxford: Oxford University Press.
Dundes, Alan and A. Falassi
   1975   La Terra in Piazza: An Interpretation of the Palio of Siena. Berkeley: University of Califor-
          nia Press.

Dwyer, Daisy
1978   Images and Self Images. New York: Columbia University Press.
Erikson, Erik
1950   Childhood and Society. New York: Norton.
Freud, Sigmund
1905a   Three Essays on the Theory of Sexuality. Standard Edn., Vol. 7, ed. by James Strachey. London: The Hogarth Press (1975).
1905b   Jokes and Their Relation to the Unconscious. Standard Edn., Vol. 8, ed. by James Strachey. London: The Hogarth Press (1975).
Friedl, Ernestine
1967   The Position of Women: Appearance and Reality. Anthropological Quarterly 40:97–108.
Geertz, Hildred
1979   The Meanings of Family Ties. *In* Meaning and Order in Moroccan Society. Clifford Geertz, et al., eds. Pp. 315–386. New York: Cambridge University Press.
Gilmore, David D.
1980   The People of the Plain. New York: Columbia University Press.
1982   Anthropology of the Mediterranean Area. Annual Reviews in Anthropology 11:175–205.
Gilmore, Margaret and David Gilmore
1979   Machismo: A Psychodynamic Approach. Journal of Psychological Anthropology 2:281–300.
Giovannini, Maureen J.
1981   Woman: A Dominant Symbol within the Cultural System of a Sicilian Town. Man 16:408–426.
Greenson, Ralph
1968   Dis-Identifying from Mother: Its Special Importance for the Boy. International Journal of Psychoanalysis 49:370–375.
Hart, David M.
1976   The Aith Waryaghar of the Moroccan Rif. Tucson: University of Arizona Press.
Herdt, Gilbert H.
1982   Editor's Preface. *In* Rituals of Manhood. G. H. Herdt, ed. Pp. ix–xxvi. Berkeley: University of California Press.
Herzfeld, Michael
1980   Honour and Shame: Problems in the Comparative Analysis of Moral Systems. Man 15:339–351.
1984   The Horns of the Mediterraneanist Dilemma. American Ethnologist 11:439–454.
1985   The Poetics of Manhood. Princeton: Princeton University Press.
Hooker, Evelyn
1965   An Empirical Study of Some Relations between Sexual Patterns and Gender Identity in Male Homosexuals. *In* Sex Research: New Developments. John Money, ed. Pp. 24–52. New York: Holt, Rinehart, Winston.
Hughes, Dianne O.
1978   From Brideprice to Dowry in Mediterranean Europe. Journal of Family History 3:262–296.
Keesing, Roger M.
1982   Introduction. *In* Rituals of Manhood. Gilbert H. Herdt, ed. Pp. 1–43. Berkeley: University of California Press.
LeVine, Robert A.
1973   Culture, Behavior, and Personality. Chicago: Aldine.
Loizos, Peter
1975   The Greek Gift: Politics in a Cypriot Village. New York: St. Martin's Press.
Luria, Zella
1979   Psychosocial Determinants of Gender Identity, Role, and Orientation. *In* Human Sexuality. Herant Katchadourian, ed. Pp. 163–193. Berkeley: University of California Press.
Maccoby, Eleanor E.
1979   Gender Identity and Sex-Role Adoption. *In* Human Sexuality. Herant Katchadourian, ed. Pp. 194–203. Berkeley: University of California Press.
Marispini, A. L.
1968   The Study of an Italian Village. The Hague: Mouton.
Meeker, Michael
1976   Meaning and Society in the Middle East: The Black Sea Turks and the Levantine Arabs. International Journal of Middle East Studies 7:243–270; 383–422.

Mernissi, Fatima
1975 Beyond the Veil: Male-Female Dynamics in a Modern Muslim Society. New York: Schenkman.
Murphy, Michael
1983 Coming of Age in Seville: The Structuring of a Riteless Passage to Manhood. Journal of Anthropological Research 39:376–392.
Ortner, Sherry B.
1978 The Virgin and the State. Feminist Studies 4:19–33.
Parker, Seymour et al.
1975 Father Absence and Cross-Sex Identity: The Puberty Rites Controversy Revisited. American Ethnologist 2:687–706.
Parsons, Anne
1969 Belief, Magic, and Anomie. New York: Free Press.
Peristiany, Jean G.
1965 Introduction. *In* Honour and Shame. J. G. Peristiany, ed. Pp. 9–18. London: Weidenfeld and Nicolson.
1976 Introduction. *In* Mediterranean Family Structures. J. G. Peristiany, ed. Pp. 1–26. London: Weidenfeld and Nicolson.
Peristiany, Jean G., ed.
1965 Honour and Shame: The Values of Mediterranean Society. London: Weidenfeld and Nicolson.
Pitt-Rivers, Julian A.
1961 The People of the Sierra. Chicago: University of Chicago Press.
1965 Honour and Social Status. *In* Honour and Shame. J. G. Peristiany, ed. Pp. 19–78. London: Weidenfeld and Nicolson.
1977 The Fate of Schechem. Cambridge: Cambridge University Press.
Pleck, Joseph H.
1981 The Myth of Masculinity. Cambridge, MA: MIT Press.
Rochlin, Gregory
1980 The Masculine Dilemma: A Psychology of Masculinity. Boston: Little, Brown.
Rodríguez Becerra, Salvador
1985 Las Fiestas de Andalucía. Seville: Editorial Andaluzas Unidas.
Rogers, Susan C.
1975 Female Forms of Power and the Myth of Male Dominance: A Model of Female/Male Interaction in Peasant Society. American Ethnologist 2:727–756.
Sahlins, Marshall
1976 Culture and Practical Reason. Chicago: University of Chicago Press.
Saunders, George R.
1981 Men and Women in Southern Europe: A Review of Some Aspects of Cultural Complexity. Journal of Psychological Anthropology 4:413–434.
Schneider, Jane
1971 Of Vigilance and Virgins. Ethnology 9:1–24.
Schneider, Jane and P. Schneider
1976 Culture and Political Economy in Western Sicily. New York: Academic Press.
Shapiro, Judith
1979 Cross-Cultural Perspectives on Sexual Differentiation. *In* Human Sexuality. Herant Katchadourian, ed. Pp. 269–308. Berkeley: University of California Press.
Silverman, Sydel
1975 The Three Bells of Civilization. New York: Columbia University Press.
Simić, Andrei
1969 Management of the Male Image in Yugoslavia. Anthropological Quarterly 42:89–101.
Stoller, Robert
1968 Sex and Gender: On the Development of Masculinity and Femininity. New York: Science House.
1973 Overview: The Impact of New Advances in Sex Research on Psychoanalytic Theory. American Journal of Psychiatry 130:241–251.
Turner, Victor
1969 The Ritual Process. Ithaca: Cornell University Press.
Wallerstein, Immanuel
1974 The Modern World-System. New York: Academic Press.

White, Carolyn
   1980   Patrons and Clients: A Study of Politics in Two Southern Italian Communities. New York: Cambridge University Press.
Whiting, Beatrice
   1965   Sex Identity Conflict and Psychical Violence: A Comparative Study. American Anthropologist 67:123–140.
Whiting, John et al.
   1958   The Function of Male Initiation Ceremonies at Puberty. *In* Readings in Social Psychology. Eleanor Maccoby et al., eds. Pp. 359–370. New York: Holt, Rinehart, Winston.
Wikan, Unni
   1984   Shame and Honour: A Contestable Pair. Man 19:635–652.
Wyatt-Brown, Bertram
   1982   Southern Honour. New York: Oxford University Press.
Young, Frank W.
   1965   Initiation Rites: A Cross-Cultural Study of Status Dramatization. Indianapolis: Bobbs-Merrill.

FAMILY AND STATE IN THE MEDITERRANEAN

John Davis

The Unity of the Mediterranean

Many observers assert the unity of the mediterranean on various grounds, some of them more plausible than others. At a straightforward, noncausal level, anthropologists, tourists, even mediterranean people themselves notice some common cultural features: attitudes, elements of culture that are recognizably similar in a large proportion of mediterranean societies, and that are readily intelligible to other mediterranean people. "I also have a moustache" is the phrase happily recorded by J. G. Peristiany (1965:9). In an emblematic way, it serves to denote not only manliness, which is so common a concern around the mediterranean, but also a style of anthropological argument: feuding and vendetta, honor and shame, institutions of animal theft, certain kinds of political activity are all moustaches. They are cultural or social themes, recurrent from Gibraltar to the Bekaa Valley, which serve to identify a category of societies. Equally ahistorical, and rather less straightforward, is the suggestion that northern and southern shores of the mediterranean are in some way variants, even opposing variants, of a deep underlying structure. Gellner (1968) speaks of these two apparently diverse categories reflecting each other "as if in a mirror"; and although he is not very clear about the mechanics of this supposed reflection, it is certainly an aid to thought of one kind about the complexities of the mediterranean, and one which has echoes in other people's analyses (cf. Davis 1977:12).

Goody's recent work (1983) implies a history in which an originally homogeneous society diversified into the variety that observers can perceive today: the history of a "shattering of the unity" of the mediterranean world (Goody 1983:9). Perhaps this unity never existed, and some scholars dispute that it consisted of those elements that he discerns in it. Nevertheless, it is the basis of much stimulating and serious scholarship, related to the long-established tradition which explains the decline of civilization by the intrusion of religions, or Christianity in particular. Equally historical, but presenting a different line of argument, the work of Jane Schneider and Peter Schneider (1976) suggests that different societies have come to resemble each other because they have been subjected to similar historical processes: the societies exist on a "pastoral-agrarian continuum." And the processes are those of the world system: a progressive peripheralization.

Davis (1977:12–15) proposed a necessarily historical argument, without filling in the details: the people of the mediterranean have been engaged in conquest, commerce, colonialism, connubium, and conversation for about five millennia, and it is impossible to imagine that in that period they have not created common institutions. Finally, Herzfeld has suggested that the notion of Mediterraneanness is a construct of outside observers: it may or may not be justified, but cannot be assumed until ethnographers have done a great deal of very thorough fieldwork. His refreshing skepticism leads to an extremely particularist position (Herzfeld 1980:349) to which few people pay more than lip service, although they do admire the discriminating precision of his ethnography.

The Diffuseness of Moral Judgments

Honor and shame are fascinating because they are concerned with sex as well as with social status and importance, which are all intrinsically interesting topics. Although it is possible to overemphasize the part that sexual activity has in determining the honor of an individual, social and sexual potency in combination are essentially incongruous, affording prospects of elemental comedy, not always merely etically. But when you try to demonstrate the unity of the mediterranean by calling honor and shame in aid as a single criterion of inclusion, you compound the difficulties. As Gilmore rightly says in his introduction to this volume, no one claims that these elements of culture are specific or limited to the mediterranean, even though anthropologists take them to be characteristic of the area. Honor and shame are wide-ranging, taking whole persons into account, and in argument are therefore liable to constant revision, as Marcus notes here for the Moroccan tribesmen he studied: judgments of particular individuals are unstable. And honor and shame are in fact local values, some would say essentially so: the range of what is honorable or shameful in different societies is varied (within limits); so that the facile categorization of aspects of behavior can obscure variations that are important at any rate to the men and women concerned.[1]

Because honor and shame concern whole persons, moral evaluations seem to have a diffuse focus. You would expect the criteria by which people are evaluated to be ambiguous and multiplex: moral standards are characteristically imprecise; and people who argue about actions exploit that imprecision, invoking a variety of principles to evaluate actions in order to win arguments. But in addition it is not always a simple matter to whom the judgment attaches. A person's honor can be affected by other peoples' actions. Rules of thumb (e.g. ''All of a woman's close female relatives are affected by her behavior'') are usually inadequate. It is likely to be truer, for example, of misbehavior than of excellence; and people show considerable skill is dissociating themselves from taint. Indeed, in the Italian town of Pisticci, close kin were the quickest to dissociate themselves from disaster. These were the same people who might be tolerant and supportive to a friend or neighbor fallen on hard times. Similarly, a man who gained reputation seemed sometimes to have to insist that his kinsmen were more distantly related than they had begun to make out (Davis 1969). In the Libyan desert the focus of judgment is similarly diffuse, and the issue is further complicated by the fact that families are enclosed within a structure of families—that is, they are part of a lineage which is itself part of a structured series of lineages.[2]

Whatever the difficulties about focus, and the maneuvers people make to get themselves into or out of it, it is clear that evaluations of moral worth are preeminently local. Pitt-Rivers (1965) was the first to argue that within the same pueblo, different actions are judged honorable according to the overall standing of the person. It is a recurrent theme. Honor operates within a restricted social setting also because it requires intimate knowledge not only of persons, but also of their associates, their family and affines, and their lineage.

Honor, Shame, and the State

This restrictedness of moral evaluations, their negotiability, the way they are used for particularistic association and allocation of resources has led most anthropologists to contrast honor and the family with the universalism of the state and religion. That is implicit in Pitt-Rivers's (1961) account of relations between the pueblo and the wider society, and it is explicit in the work of most of the second generation of mediterranean anthropologists. The most powerful statement of this contrast is in the work of Jane Schneider and Peter Schneider (1976), culminating in the argument that

> The code of honor not only bolstered domestic groups in their rivalry against each other, but also defended the family against the hegemony of Church and State. [Schneider and Schneider 1976:96]

Their assertion that honor provides order, is an idiom within which people struggle for control of resources, protecting their own and threatening others', similarly links them to Blok (1974:91–96) and his discussion of the weak state, the state which is unable to arbitrate conflicting interests. Ortner (1978) also relates honor (the seclusion of women) to state-formation. She suggests (1978:31) that "the key" lies in "stressing the stratified nature of the state as a totality" and that the seclusion of women is the product of "interaction between elites and lower strata." The stratum that "started the whole thing" is the elite, concerned to domesticate and "juvenilize" the wild men of villages and deserts.

Each of these writers suggests a relation between certain kinds of family behavior and the state. It is a reaction of resistance, of defense; or for Ortner it is an imposition of dominant ideology. The fact remains, however, that the relation remains unexplored. Jane Schneider and Peter Schneider suggest that part of the reaction was to universalism in general; and another part was to the predatory capture of women by the center—an argument that Gilmore dismisses perhaps too readily in his introduction here. Blok seems to have in mind a vacuum theory of Mafia: if the state does not provide order, and if the landowning class goes to town and neglects its duties, something will necessarily fill the gap.[3] These are suggestive ideas, but rather imprecise. A finely tuned account might offer different reactions (from different domestic and lineage organizations) to these different manifestations of universalism. "The State" often appears universalizing because it makes general rules, applying to different local communities. But the mediterranean has many different kinds of state, and in each of them the general rules are made by people who themselves have traditions, customs, assumptions—they are members of particularistic communities. And if you regard the state not as an impersonal system of offices, but as a category or class of individuals in deadly combination, you might also say that the claim to universalism, when voiced by statesmen, is a way to brush off those who have no particularistic pull with state personnel. In short, the contrast between state and family or local community is almost certainly a real one. But its complexity does not seem adequately expressed by the contrasts between "universalistic" and "particularistic" orientations. It therefore seems sensible to try to take account of the varieties of tyranny, patrimonalism, and democracy that can be found in the mediterranean area, and their relations to different localisms.

How might this general topic of the contrast or opposition between state and local communities be studied? The Primordial State Intervention is irrecoverable, and so the plausible reconstruction proposed by the Schneiders remains just that: mind-capturing but undemonstrable (Davis 1980). It is true that the empires were literate powers, and the classical Roman historians, for example, are an important source of information about the domestic and kinship organization of the peoples they conquered. But—even if similar later sources exist in Turkish—the information can be polemical, gives only the picture from the center, and does not achieve modern standards of ethnographic reporting. Jack Goody's (1983) solution to this problem is what may be called inferential. He notes that the Church begins to regulate marriage and parenthood and the extension of kinship loyalties, principally by extending the range of prohibited marriages, but also by forbidding adoption, frowning on wet-nursing, and so on—all without scriptural justification. Then he asks: *cui bono*? There is not much else he can do in the circumstances, but the results are unconvincing. He has to make a connection between the legislation and the nearest observable interest, which he takes to be the Church's accumulation of property. The Church really wished to control strategies by which people assured themselves of heirs: if the claims of kin were fewer, the Church might step in to acquire land. In the eleven hundred years he covers, Goody finds not a single document from the interested party that establishes the link, although there were many complaints about mortmain and the canon regulation of marriage. Goody himself, clearly uneasy about his own procedures (see especially pp. 214–216), suggests that the interest may have been hidden from those who had it—hidden by an accumulated mass of precedents, so that an original interest is lost to view in concern for theology and the salvation of persons married improperly or to the wrong partners. Goody's work is important because it is the most detailed and scholarly work by an anthropologist in the area that Schneider and Schneider have identified as crucial. The conclusion must be that his central thesis (the Church was interested in its application of purportedly universal principles) is unproven; and therefore, further, that similar attempts to uncover early universalisms are likely to suffer from the same lack of evidence.

It seems that direct knowledge of the period in which universalizing principles first threatened mediterranean localisms is not available. Is there some way of acquiring indirect knowledge?—that is, of working by analogy on situations that might be taken as similar? Are there more recent and accessible changes that might afford the chance to speculate about the nature of the relation of state to family? Three areas of inquiry in fact suggest themselves. Remembering that states are not uniform, and in the mediterranean show themselves aleatory, it could be useful to examine changes in family law and reactions to them in conquests, in the creation of new states, and in revolutions. For example, Burns's (1975) work on the regime established in Spain by Christians for the subject Muslim population seems a fruitful area for investigation. In North Africa, colonial conquests and administrative policies of French, Spanish, and Italian authorities are a second and perhaps more documented area for inquiry. That is partly because in the later period of these empires it was considered appropriate to encourage ethnologists. For state-creation, the most obvious case is perhaps Italy. It is clear that at the eve of unification the different states of the peninsula had different marriage laws, and that the imposition of a unified regulation of marriage excited resentment and resistance: it is possible that is accessible.[4]

Contemporary Libya

Revolutions are also accessible. It may then be helpful to present some ethnography about the theory of family and state in Qaddafi's Libya.[5]

The question of honor and shame in contemporary Libya has a particular coloring, derived primarily from two sources. In the first place, marriage and chastity do not receive the same emphasis as they do in the Catholic countries. It is true that men kill, or threaten to kill those kinswomen or wives engaged in extramarital sexual affairs, together with their partners. And it is also true that they seclude women from strangers, as elsewhere in the mediterranean. But the seclusion of women takes on a different aspect when women commonly have more than one husband during their lifetimes: divorce is permitted, carries little stigma, and does not noticeably disrupt relations of cooperation and amity between the men-in-law. As an admittedly extreme example, one woman in Ajkharra had been married three times before she reached the age of twenty-one; another four times. It was indeed important that a woman should be married to her sexual partner; but it was not as important as in some Catholic countries that one husband should have permanently exclusive sexual rights in her. Muslims do not have the image of a Virgin Mother paraded before them. Moreover, in parts of Libya more than a quarter of the male population was killed or went into exile between 1911–44,[6] and perhaps that recent imbalance of the sexes had an effect on the attitudes of controlling men and women towards the marriages of their juniors. People say they preempt adultery with divorce, and that is not an option for Catholics.

Secondly, concern for honor seems to be much more directed to relations among men. A large part of the honor of an individual and of a lineage depends upon proper lineage behavior: it is a reflection on honor if guests at a wedding or funeral are insufficiently fed, if an old person lives in poverty, if an offense suffered at the hands of an outsider is not met with compensation. (And, conversely, if a lineage fails to compensate those outsiders who have been unjustly offended.) Men of outstanding wealth are expected, in the last resort, to ensure the honor of their group as a whole. Honor seems at any rate now to be chiefly concerned with relations between men and groups of men, and the shame or shyness between them in matters regarding women; much less with the control of women.

This emphasis is related to the contemporary importance of lineage and tribe in Libya, which, contrary to the general experience in other North African states, seems to be increasing.[7] The first cause of this discrepant change is oil-wealth: if that wealth is distributed as services and salaries in the population, people find it much easier to maintain a lineage structure. When lineages are scattered over a million square kilometers of territory, the members assemble more easily to solve a crisis if they have telephones and telegrams to notify each other of their need; and they assemble more quickly if they have airplanes and fast motor cars to travel in. The second cause is the ideology of the regime and its policies, which encourage family, lineage, tribe at the expense of the state. The essence of the Libyan revolution is that it includes an attempt to abolish the state altogether, and to introduce a form of social organization that is in some respects based on a folk-image of tribal solidarities. In effect that entails a tribalization of administrative politics, so that elections in all but the major cities, for example, are fought between tribal groupings voting for their own candidates. That is partly because all forms of rational association (as it might be, parties, policy groups, trade unions) are banned (Davis 1982a); and partly because the people elected have control of valuable state resources and can direct them, at the quite large margin, to their supporters: elements of the lamb-barrel exist in Libyan politics (Davis 1982b, 1987).

Qaddafi on State and Family

The Libyan leader Colonel Qaddafi perceives that all states involve representation. *Political parties* compete for the right to represent the entire population; or *The Party* claims to represent the true interests of the nation as in the Soviet Bloc; or a certain *Class* claims to represent justice or the valid interests of a population, and hence claims the right to exercise a dictatorship. All these ways of governance are wrong. Representation can never be right or just (Qaddafi says) because it necessarily requires the represented to surrender part of their personal sovereignty. It is always oppressive when one person or group dominates another: "Representation is fraud," says Qaddafi. Since states always involve representation, it follows that they are necessarily and inevitably unjust.

Most Britons or Americans would say it is necessary for citizens to trade off some of their personal sovereignty against the benefits that states bring (they say). And anthropologists might also agree with E. Colson (1975) that the autonomy of individuals in stateless societies is largely an illusion of the starry-eyed. What makes some part of Qaddafi's thought interesting is that he does not make this common move in defense of states. He says that since states are necessarily unjust they should be abolished; they have no saving graces. That conclusion would not be surprising from the pen of those students who led Colson to reflect on the social contract; it is perhaps unexpected to read it in a book "from the pen of" Colonel Qaddafi, the inspirer of what is often thought of as a particularly aggressive state.[8] However, Qaddafi has not only said that in his *Green Book;* he has also implemented measures that allegedly do abolish the state, eliminate representation and preserve individual sovereignty intact.[9]

Qaddafi does not expect society to collapse if the state is abolished. He says that politics are unstable when they are based on coercive and artificial solidarities: they are more stable when the bonds between citizens are based on nature and the natural sovereignty of individuals.

> Humanity, by its nature, is incarnated in the individual, in the family, and not in the state, which is foreign to it. The state is an artificial political or economic, sometimes military system, without relation to humanity. [III, "The Family"]

Individuals naturally live in families, which are incorporated into tribes, tribes into nations, nations into humanity:

> The tribe is a family which has grown by births. It follows that a tribe is a big family. Similarly, the nation is a tribe which has grown demographically. So the nation is a big tribe. Indeed, the world is the nation which has branched into different nations. The world is therefore a big nation. [III, "The Tribe"]

Qaddafi takes a Gellnerian view[10] of the relationship between these increasingly inclusive units:

> The bond which assures the cohesion of the family is identical to that which maintains the unity of the tribe, the nation and the world. However it gets weaker as the numbers grow larger. [III, "The Tribe"][11]

Unlike Gellner, Qaddafi insists that it is essentially a natural bond, not one that
results from an act of will, choice, decision: it is not a rational bond, for it devolves from an inescapable history of generation and nurture.[12] Qaddafi thus proposes a world that might be represented by a genealogy, with branches representing the major divisions of humanity, and then nations, then tribes, lineages
and families: present-day nations owing their existence to prolific ancestors. Although Qaddafi claims to have a universal message (the subtitle of *The Green
Book* is "The Third Universal Way"), it is clear that his schema does not im-
mediately apply to nations founded by immigrants from different parts of the
world, for instance,[13] and that he speaks principally to Libyans and others like
them.

There is one point to add. Qaddafi says, on the question of marriage:

> Marriage . . . can exercise a positive or a negative influence on social cohesion. In accordance with
> the natural law of freedom, men and women are free to accept the one they desire, and to reject the
> one they do not desire. Nevertheless, marriage within a group evidently reinforces the unity of the
> group, contributes to general development in harmony with the social factor. [III, (Introduction)]

In-marriage obeys the law of gravity which ensures the coherence of the sun and
planets and of every natural system.[14] Qaddafi's experience and knowledge of
tribes is that they recruit members by descent in the male line. As he strikes a not
very clear balance between natural liberty and the demands of the social factor,
he seems to assume a society (tribe, nation) which is patrilineal and frequently in-
marrying. The analogy is with those anthropological theories that account for the
definition of descent groups by invoking the application of a marriage rule. In this
case, Qaddafi says groups have greater cohesion when marriages are centripetal
rather than centrifugal. When the center is a man of authority, the pattern can be
presented as patrilineal and endogamous (but this is, of course, an image of social
order rather than a description of what happens). In summary, Qaddafi maintains
a political system that is in fact a military dictatorship and in which he aims to
abolish the hierarchy of the state in civilian affairs, preserving each individual
citizen's sovereignty intact. Some of the institutions of popular democratic control do approximate to that purpose.

So, Qaddafi answers the question "How do you propose to maintain social
cohesion without using an *apparatus* to adjudicate competing interests?" by in-
sisting on the strength of "natural" ties of family-tribe-nation. Nested patrilineal
and endogamous groups create "a sense of belonging and a common destiny"
(III, "The Nation") which is the sole basis of social justice, the sole source of
uncoerced order, and the irresistible natural force that breaks even the most powerful artificial states. "The motive power of human history is the social factor,
i.e. the national factor" (III, [Introduction]).

> To ignore the national bonds of human communities and to construct a political system which dis-
> regards social structure is to build a temporary building, which will collapse through the action of
> the social factor. [III, "The Nation"]

Qaddafi presents a model of the just society which corresponds in important respects to a widely diffused image of tribal organization. Tribes are natural groups
in which men are autonomous; nature will sooner or later undermine the artificial
creations of men's choices and acts of will. The only justice lies in obedience to
nature, and that will necessarily produce sovereign and hence egalitarian individuals. It does not seem necessary to comment much on this: it is a widely diffused

image of society both among Libyans and among ethnographers. If Qaddafi is novel, it is for his attempt to crystallize "the nation" as a significant and permanent level of segmentary action, and his attempt to create councils which take decisions for the nation without in theory detracting from individual autonomy: his attempts to assert that a modern society can be organized without representation of interests.

Qaddafi's attempt to abolish the state, to replace it by allowing full play to the "social factor" (at least in rhetoric) is an unexpected confirmation of general propositions to the effect that there is an opposition between family and state, that they represent contrary principles of organization and evaluation. *The Green Book* is particularly interesting to anthropologists for its attempt to adapt a Libyan image (folk-model) of a segmentary acephalous society to a modern society with high incomes, elaborated educational, welfare, and health services, and a heavy investment in public works and in economic development. Libyan reaction to it is mixed: sophisticates sometimes express the view that it is naive to expect them to believe that a bank, a post office, a water or electricity utility can be run by a version of tribal council, with no one giving orders, each person—staff and consumer—preserving his natural sovereignty. On the other hand, some others respond willingly enough to the notion that they will not be dominated by a state. Young people in particular do not know what acephalous tribal life was like and, having no practical administrative experience under any regime, they have no way to test what they are taught at school and university, that the Libyan is the most truly democratic polity since classical Athens.

Many Libyans notice the omissions from *The Green Book* and the institutions derived from it: no mention of the army or of the police forces, for example, nor of petroleum. The two questions you might ask first about any polity have no answer, and even Qaddafi's speeches carry scant reference to control of the army and of the national budget. That silence is most apparent when the army is engaged abroad, as it was in Uganda in 1978, as it has been in Chad on two occasions since then. It is apparent, too, when there is a radical change in internal policy. In 1975, when the first Libyan civilian was executed for what was widely understood as a political offense, people were shocked: "What did we fight the Italians for?" In short, Libyans are aware of the existence of a hidden state apparatus guaranteeing but exempt from the control of popular nonrepresentative democracy. And some of them resent it. In 1981, *Le Monde* carried an enigmatic report that a tribe from the Ajdabiya district had claimed blood money from the government for men fallen in battle in Chad. You should not assume (as the newspaper's correspondent did) that such "tribal" behavior was atavistic, an action betraying incomprehension of state systems. The tribesmen of that area are sophisticates, involved in petroleum and development, in banking and commerce. They did not misunderstand the claims of the state on the lives of citizens; rather they contested them. By demanding blood money for a group of fallen agnates they disputed statelike claims to ask citizens to sacrifice their lives; and they did so, invoking the traditional institutions of "the social factor." To receive compensation for offenses suffered is an essential part of the honor of a group; and in this case the assertion of honor against the hidden state takes official rhetoric at its word-value.[15]

Conclusions

When states change their nature, there should be corresponding changes in the forms of resistance by which local communities protect themselves from relatively universalizing interference. Qaddafi claims to abolish the state (but in fact hides an *apparatus* in silence), and to replace it with a family system of loyalties and claims on people's lives. Traditional notions of honor form a part of these ancient and supposed natural loyalties. He then calls this system "Universal." Perhaps there is a way to describe this that makes it coherent, but the immediate point is the reaction of Libyans. By and large they understand and respond to Qaddafi's partial abolition of representation and his alleged restoration of personal sovereignty; and they share his image of the autonomy of stateless families linked by lineage and tribe. They vote for tribal lists in elections, they settle disputes, make peaces, pay compensation and claim it, as men of honor should. To some extent that is an acceptance of Qaddafi's rhetoric, made easier by the telephones and Toyotas that oil-wealth affords. So Qaddafi has created a polity in which people's particularistic association and loyalties turn to serve the nation; and they have material incentives to participate in the new order. It is for these reasons that the institutions of honor among groups of men are resurgent in contemporary Libya, and nowhere else in North Africa, while issues of control over women are less pressing and less competitive. Note, also, that a nation that is organized by lineage and tribe is easier to control than one in which people associate on rational principles: lineages are much less dangerous to a regime than parties or labor unions, are no match for the hierarchies of command and central filing systems of a police force or an army. Even so, in extreme circumstances tribal loyalties and claims can be used against the government. Certainly in local politics administrative issues can quite easily lead to a mustering of lineage members to defend their interests against other lineages or tribes; and on occasion those solidarities have been invoked to contest the statelike actions of the regime itself. Honor and state exist in any uneasy balance.

The benefit that Jane Schneider and Peter Schneider conferred on the world of the Mediterraneanists was to direct attention to the historical origins of honor and shame, and to locate them in the confrontation of diverse local communities (on a pastoral-agrarian continuum) with universalizing states and religions. The Primordial State Intervention is inaccessible; states are not uniform nor perhaps especially universalizing. There are other problems with the Schneiders' model, as Gilmore points out in his introduction. Nevertheless, Schneider and Schneider (1976) made a real advance on the moustaches and mirrors of their precursors. In the first place, they directed attention to the confrontation of states and families. In the second place, they directed attention to history, to the origins of honor and shame. It must be the case that these primordial values have origins in the multiple choices of individuals with diverse interests to protect and diverse conventional ways of doing so; and it may be that by exploring the concomitant variation of states and of different honors and different shames, anthropologists and historians will be able to argue by analogy about the Schneiders' hypotheses. Confrontation of state and family is not the whole story: Libyan politics are strongly influenced by a colonial history—experience of other kinds of state—and by political movements, the exchange of ideas in the Middle East generally. Oil-wealth is also a factor that permits the discrepant strength of lineage honor in Libyan society. Nevertheless, these are matters of context, ones that explain (in this case) why Libyan families and lineages respond as they do to this particular threat to their autonomy: the general line of inquiry seems justified by its fruits.

Notes

[1]Arnold (1977) illustrates this point: Campbell's (1964) account of ideal manhood among Sarakatsani emphasizes male chastity; but in all other respects his description can be applied to the conventional *machismo* of men in the salon of a Peruvian brothel. Clearly, Arnold is right to make the link; but whether ideally men should be chaste or unchaste is surely a matter of quite considerable importance to men and to women in either society. Arnold's discussion is worth noting too because she gives more detail than is available for mediterranean countries about the range of sexual activity considered decent by Latin practitioners: it is perhaps rather limited. In default of evidence from mediterranean countries, that might be cited in support of the argument that "the gradations of honor are finely drawn, but the varieties of sexual behavior do not seem to be sufficiently great, nor sufficiently public, to account for the near absolute discrimination which Pisticcesi make between families" (Davis 1969).

[2]It should be said now that this is not the only structure available to contemporary Libyans—that is discussed below. It is probably true that within the last four or five centuries Libyans have always been able to invoke other support in addition to their lineage and tribe.

[3]In this regard, note the argument of Herr (1977) that the urbanization of a landed elite strengthens their position in the countryside: they are able to become socially more exclusive, and the opportunities they have for meeting permit them to consolidate practices in the management of their land.

[4]The chief descriptive sources readily to hand are the essays by Italian and French followers of Le Play. Their work has some defects (Rabbeno 1894), but nevertheless suggests variations in household composition, authority, and devolution. See: Peruzzi (1857), Mantovani (1898), Lombroso (1896), Chessa (1906), Santangelo-Spoto (1890, 1892), and Guerin (1890)—the latter reports that the Valmontonesi in 1887 complained about the imposition of Piedmontese intestacy laws. In addition the INEA series (Giusti 1931–40) which concludes with an index and summaries, may be useful. A general listing of diverse civil codes up to the mid 19th century is in ITALY (1845).

[5]This ethnography is derived from about two and a half years' fieldwork in the period 1975–79. The fieldwork was made possible by grants of leave money variously from the Social Science Research Council of the U.K., the University of Kent at Canterbury and the Gemeente Universitat van Amsterdam: their support is gratefully acknowledged. The fieldwork was limited to a part of eastern Libya. So the phrase "Libyans say" (or think, or do) means "Libyans in Ajdabiya, Ajkharra, Kufra, Rabbiana, Buzaima, Tazarbu say." You may accept that the shorter form is not intended as a claim to global representativeness, but is used for the reader's convenience. For more details, see Davis (1987).

[6]The figures are difficult to calculate and are politically charged. For a discussion, see Wright (1982:42 n.10). The losses were sustained in the colonial wars of 1911–32 (they were killed in battle, died, or were executed in concentration camps, went into exile) and in the fighting on Libyan territory in 1939–42 (as combatants with the allies, or as bystanders).

[7]That is an impressionistic statement. The economic basis of transhumant pastoralism was destroyed before exploration for oil created individual as well as national wealth, and led to extremely rapid urbanization. Any of those processes should lead you to predict a collapse of a tribal system, which has not happened. In Morroco, Algeria, and Tunisia, on the other hand, ethnographic reports suggest a decline of agnatic loyalty, its replacement by personally constructed networks, by social class and so on. Perhaps that has something to do with the dispositions of the ethnographers; but the impression is unmistakable.

[8]The book is *The Green Book, The Third Universal Way*. It has been published in various editions and translations, in several languages. It consists of three Chapters issued separately. Chapter I came out in 1973, Chapter II in 1976, and Chapter III in 1979. Since it has such a complex publishing history, and since the Chapters are really quite short, and are subdivided into sections no more than a few pages long, it is perhaps most convenient to refer readers simply to the Chapter and section, rather than to give years of publication and page references. The first section of III, however, has no title and so it is cited here as III (Introduction).

[9]"Allegedly" for two reasons. First, although his institutions achieve some degree of local devolution, they nevertheless involve representation. Second, Qaddafi maintains a fully-fledged military

dictatorship alongside his popular democratic non-state. The control of violence is not mentioned in his work. See Davis (1982a, 1982b) for further details.

[10]Like Qaddafi, Gellner assumes an economy of principle of organization: "The clan resembles the tribe of which it is a clan. It also resembles the minor clans and lineages of which it is itself composed. Groups are 'nested'; but the various levels of size or nesting resemble each other in function, ethos, terminology and internal organization" (Gellner 1982:39).

[11]Qaddafi's terms for social cohesion and for the social factor are *al-rabtah al-ijtima'i* and *al-aml al-ijtima'i;* he does *not* use *asabiya* (Ibn Khaldun's "group feeling").

[12]Qaddafi does say that people can become members of tribes, and hence of nations, by affiliating themselves. There is indeed a word for such people ("mukatibin": the written ones), and an instituted procedure for incorporating them into lineages and into the authenticating genealogy. Qaddafi's ethnography seems correct when he adds that people forget the rational origins of some of their fellow tribesmen. See III, "The advantages of the tribe." Naturalization into the Libyan nation is a more complex matter, and more contentious. See Davis (1987:Ch. 3). When Libyans pursue dissidents across their frontiers, killing them in Rome, London, or Manchester, it is justified essentially on these grounds. Law attaches to persons by birth, and is not an attribute of territories. Libyans cannot escape the consequences of their actions or thoughts by choosing to live in another place. The principle is not applied reciprocally (foreigners in Libya have to obey Libyan law).

[13]In fact he has occasionally denied the legitimacy of such artificial states—for example, offering Libyan protection to native American tribes against the federal government.

[14]Qaddafi uses analogies with nature at various points in his works. He compares crèches for children to battery-farms for chickens; and he describes people without families as being like plastic flowers. He also interestingly says that plants grow freely in nature, and that is how people should grow in society: states are like gardens or fields where they are restricted and constrained to grow in unnatural ways.

[15]"The tribe is a natural social umbrella . . . it offers a collective guarantee to its members for the payment of ransoms and compensation, as well as vengeance and defense: that is to say, it affords social protection" (III, "The Advantages of Tribes").

References Cited

Arnold, K.
　　1977　The Introduction of Poses to a Peruvian Brothel, and Changing Images of Male and Female. London: Academic Press.
Block, Anton
　　1974　The Mafia of a Sicilian Village, 1860–1900: A Study of Violent Peasant Entrepreneurs (Pavillion Series). Oxford: Blackwell.
Burns, Robert I.
　　1975　Medieval Colonialism: Postcrusade Exploitation of Islamic Valencia. Princeton: Princeton University Press.
Campbell, John K.
　　1964　Honor, Family and Patronage. Oxford: Clarendon Press.
Chessa, Federico
　　1906　Sulle Condizioni Sociali ed Economiche dei Contadini dell'Agro di Sassari. La Riforma Sociale 16:36–63, 266–298.
Colson, Elizabeth
　　1975　Tradition and Contract: The Problem of Order. London: Heinemann Educational.
Davis, John
　　1969　Honour and Politics in Pisticci. Proceedings of the Royal Anthropological Institute 1969:69–82.
　　1977　People of the Mediterranean. London: Routledge and Kegan Paul.
　　1980　Social Anthropology and the Consumption of History. Theory and Society 9:519–537.
　　1982a　Qaddafi's Theory and Practice of Non-Representative Government. Government and Opposition 17:61–79.

1982b   Principle and Practice of Government in Qadhdhafi's Libya. Al-Abhath 30:51–75 (American University of Beirut).
1987   Libyan Politics: Tribe and Revolution. An Account of the Zuwaya and Their Government. London: I. B. Tauris.

Gellner, Ernest A.
1968   Sanctity, Puritanism, Secularization and Nationalism in North Africa: A Case Study. *In* Contributions to Mediterranean Sociology. J. G. Peristiany, ed. The Hague: Mouton.
1982   Muslim Society. Cambridge: Cambridge University Press.

Giusti, U., ed.
1931–40   Monografie di Familie Agricole. Rome: Instituto Nazionale di Economia Agraria.

Goody, Jack
1983   The Development of the Family and Marriage in Europe. Cambridge: Cambridge University Press.

Guerin, Urbain
1890   Vigneron précariste et Métayer de Valmontone (Roma). Tenancier-Chef de Métier dans le Système des Engagements Momentanés. *In* Les Ouvriers des Deux Mondes: Etudes sur les Travaux, la Vie Domestique et la Condition Morale des Populations Ouvrières des Diverses Contrés. F. Le Play, ed. Pp. 385–432, Second Series. First Series, 5 Vols. 1857–75; Second Series, 5 vols. 1887–1899; Third Series, 20 fascicles, 1900–1912. Paris: Société d'Economie et de Science Sociale.

Herr, Richard
1977   Spain. *In* European Landed Elites in the Nineteenth Century. D. Spring, ed. Pp. 98–126. Baltimore: Johns Hopkins University Press.

Herzfeld, Michael
1980   Honor and Shame: Problems in the Comparative Analysis of Moral Systems. Man 15:339–351.

ITALY
1845   Collezioni Completa dei Moderni Codici Civili degli Stati d'Italia, Secondo l'Ordine Cronologico della Loro Pubblicazione, etc. Turin.

Lombroso, Gina
1896   Sulle Condizioni Sociali ed Economiche degli Operai di un Sobborgo do Torino. La Riforma Sociale 6:310–330.

Mantovani, Francesco
1898   Bilanci di Trenta Famiglie di Contadini in Provincia de Treviso. La Riforma Sociale 8:45–56, 134–156, 421–441.

Ortner, Sherry B.
1978   The Virgin and the State. Feminist Studies 4:19–36.

Peristiany, J. G., ed.
1965   Honor and Shame: The Values of Mediterranean Society. London: Weidenfeld and Nicolson.

Peruzzi, Ubaldino
1857   Métayer de la Banlieu de Florence (Grand-Duché de Toscane): Ouvrier Tenancier dans le Système des Engagements Volontaires Permanentes. *In* Les Ouvriers de Deux Mondes: Etudes sur les Traveaux, la Vie Domestique, et la Condition Moral des Populations Ouvrières des Diverses Contrés. F. Le Play, ed. Pp. 221–262, First Series. 5 Vols. 1857–75; Second Series, 5 Vols. 1887–99; Third Series, 20 fascicles, 1900–12. Paris: Société d'Economie et de Science Sociale.

Pitt-Rivers, Julian A.
1961   The People of the Sierra. Chicago: University of Chicago Press.
1965   Honor and Social Status. *In* Honor and Shame, J. G. Peristiany, ed. Pp. 19–78. London: Weidenfeld and Nicolson.

Rabbeno, Ugo
1894   A Family of Métayers of the Commune of Reggio Emilia (Italy). Economic Journal 4:545–551.

Santangelo-Spoto, Hippolyte
    1890   Mineur des Soufrieres de Lercara (Palermo, Sicilie). Ouvrier Proprietaire dans le Système
    des Engagements Volontaires Permanentes. *In* Les Ouvriers des Deux Mondes: Etudes sur les
    Traveaux, la Vie Domestique et la Condition Morale des Populations Ouvrières des Diverses
    Contrés. F. le Play, ed. Pp. 325–396, Second Series. First Series, 5 Vols. 1857–75; Second
    Series, 5 Vols. 1887–99; Third Series, 20 fascicles, 1900–12. Paris: Société d'Economie et de
    Science Sociale.
Schneider, Jane and Peter Schneider
    1976   Culture and Political Economy in Western Sicily. New York: Academic Press.
Wright, J.
    1982   Libya: A Modern History. London: Croom Helm.

SEEDS OF HONOR, FIELDS OF SHAME

Carol Delaney

Introduction

It may be questionable whether a village in the central Anatolian steppe can be considered a Mediterranean society or part of Mediterranean culture. Only a few people from the village have ever seen the Mediterranean, most have never seen a body of water larger than the small pond below the village. The Taurus mountains to the south raise a formidable barrier separating the temperate and benevolent climate of the coast from the severe as well as austere environment of the high inner plateau. The difference is as great as between southern California and Montana, and any person displaced from one to the other would no doubt agree that environment affects temperament. Anatolian Turks would be puzzled to think of themselves as a Mediterranean people, and indeed they possess few of the qualities popularly used to characterize them.

Nevertheless, the system of ideas, sentiments and practices related to honor and shame, long held to be a distinctive feature of Mediterranean societies, are as much a part of life in Anatolia as along the shores of that sea. Perhaps it is the honor/shame complex that gives shape to what is considered Mediterranean rather than the reverse. Still the fit is a loose one. Like the baggy *şalvar* that women in Turkish villages wear, not only is the outline of the body concealed, but there is much room for expansion. That is to say, it has been a little difficult to determine what is essential and what is extraneous to both the concept of Mediterranean culture and that of honor and shame.

The notions of honor and shame are not uniform and constant throughout the Mediterranean area. The use of the English gloss, "honor and shame," tends to fix them as if they were stable and unalterable, when in fact they cover a variety of terms, meanings and practices. This tendency to reification has led Herzfeld to raise the question of whether they are analytically useful or counterproductive (1980:349). At the same time, to dispose of them altogether when they appear to encapsulate something of existential importance is equivalent to throwing the proverbial baby out with the bathwater. The mistake has been to interpret the honor code somewhat like a dress code—as a set of rules and regulations—focused on superficial conformity. Instead, I propose that it is more like a kind of genetic code—a structure of relations—generative of possibilities. An analogy from botany may prove germane. In the way that genetically similar seeds sown in different soils produce phenotypically varied fruits, so do I believe that encoded in the honor/shame complex is a specific theory of sexuality and procreation that produces slightly different permutations in practice depending on the environment in which it takes root. They key to unlocking the code lies, I suggest, in an examination of sexuality and procreation.

Some contributors to this volume and to the literature in general would disagree that honor and shame are rooted in sexuality, but most would, I think, agree that sexuality is a prominent feature. Yet it is precisely this aspect of honor that is peculiar to and perhaps distinctive of Mediterranean societies (see also Gilmore, 1983). Honor in the sense of reputation, prestige, rank, or precedence has far more widespread, if not universal currency. "Honor and shame are social evaluations . . . the reflection of the social personality in the mirror of social ideals" (Peristiany 1974:9). Peristiany goes on to say that since "all societies evaluate conduct by comparing it to ideal standards of action, all societies have their own forms of honor and shame" (1974:10). On the other hand, honor and its obverse, shame, in relation to sexuality, is far more circumscribed. In this article I shall concentrate primarily on the restricted but not residual form of honor. In Turkish, the different forms of honor are specified by the terms *şeref* and *namus,* respectively. A man who is *namussuz* (without honor) cannot possibly have *şeref*; but a man who is *namuslu* (with honor) does not necessarily possess *şeref*. In other words, *namus* (honor related to sexuality) may be the more basic. The confusion or conflation of these interrelated but separable forms of honor has marred the discussion of this topic. This conflation has resulted in attempts to explicate the system of values, sentiments, and practices indexed by honor and shame by focusing on social structure, politics, economics, and ecology (e.g., Peristiany 1974; Davis 1977; Pitt-Rivers 1977; Bourdieu 1979; and Schneider 1971), rather than on sexuality itself.[1] All of these factors may contribute to an understanding of *how* the system works, but have yet to explain *why* it is that honor is primarily an attribute of men and shame of women, or why male honor is so inextricably tied to women.

Part of the problem is due, I believe, to the general or promiscuous use of the term *sexuality,* which has rendered any precise identification of meaning difficult, if not impossible. The way it is used also betrays the Western preoccupation with sex detached from the entire process of procreation. Implicit in much social science writing is an assumption that male and female, sexuality and reproduction, are biological givens rather than cultural constructions. Although the concept of gender has mitigated this tendency somewhat, sexuality and reproduction are more recalcitrant. Typically, reproduction is viewed as a natural process associated with women, and as a universal biological given, its relevance for any particular culture has seemed minimal. At the same time, it must be granted that while reproduction may be a universal physiological process, understandings of it are neither naturally determined nor universal. The way it is represented and understood varies considerably. In contrast, by procreation I mean the beliefs related to the question of how life comes into being, beliefs that, because they engage major categories of meaning, cannot be confined only to the physiological process. Sexual relations and reproduction always occur in a context of meaning. Whatever else they may be, they are also symbolic practice. In this article I am concerned with the way procreation is symbolically constructed, perceived, and embedded in a wider system of beliefs about the world. Briefly stated, I suggest that honor and shame are functions of a specific construction of procreation which, in turn, is correlative with the religious concept of monotheism. We are speaking of genesis at two levels.

The views presented here are the result of the conjunction of previous academic study of monotheistic traditions, training in anthropology, and almost two years of fieldwork in a Turkish village. Since it is the perspective from that village that will be described, some sense of place is necessary.

The Locale

There are more than 30,000 villages in Turkey varying in size from a few households to 2,000 people, after which it is no longer officially a village. Each village has its distinctive character and it is not possible, if even desirable, to find a typical or average village. Nevertheless, I believe the central ideas are generalizable, although certain specifics of practice vary as does the environment which is exploited. The village in which I lived and worked from August 1980 through June 1982[2] is located approximately 80 kilometers from Ankara on the skirt of one of the highest mountains in the province. Although relatively close to the capital, this area is one of the most sparsely populated in all of Turkey. Yet the village itself was relatively large, composed of about 850 people, evenly divided by sex.

Since the dirt roads leading down the mountain to the nearest highway 30 kilometers away can be treacherous at certain times of the year and occasionally impassable, no one from the village commutes outside of it for work. The few who work outside remain there for varying lengths of time and return to the village periodically. It is also not a village that has been decimated by the out-migration of men to Europe or urban centers in Turkey. With the introduction of tractors in the 1950s there was a brief period of migration out of the village. While this continues, the population has remained fairly stable for the past twenty years.

The inhabitants all profess to be Sunni Muslims and consider themselves true Anatolian Turks, descended from the original Turks who migrated westward from Central Asia. They are *yerli* (natives) as opposed to *göçmen* (immigrants, but to villagers, also ethnic minorities). Villagers think of their village as an interrelated and close(d) community. During the 1950s, when immigrants from Bulgaria were being resettled, a few families were placed in the village. After several months it become clear that they would not be absorbed, and like the foreign bodies they were, they were ejected from the community.

It is a viable village in terms of people and resources. The primary forms of livelihood are wheat cultivation and animal husbandry—sheep, goats, and cows. Wheat provides flour for bread, which is the staff of life both literally and figuratively. The surplus is sold for profit in government depots. Sheep and goats are raised for their wool and world-famous Angora (Ankara) goat hair, and to be sold as meat. Along with cows they provide villagers with occasional meat, but are valued especially for their milk, which is used in the forms of yoghurt, butter, and cheese. Milk products form the second major component of the village diet. In addition, most people have access to vegetable gardens and fruit trees; that is, those who do not own them have relatives who do. There is no market in the village—only a couple of small shops *(bakkal),* which consist of a room in a villager's house set aside for selling sugar, cigarettes, matches, thread, and cookies. There is a market each week in each of two towns about an hour away by village *dolmuş* (literally "filled," but meaning a shared vehicle, in this case a Ford or Chevy van).

The village is a prosperous one but not rich. While there is a considerable difference in wealth between the richest family and the poorest, the distribution of wealth forms a continuum, and most families fall in the middle. There are no real class divisions.[3] Similarly, there are status/prestige differentials, but these are relative and do not necessarily depend on wealth. The most important differences and divisions are those of sex.

Procreation: Monogenesis

In the village, male and female are defined by their role in procreation, and procreation, culturally understood, defines gender. Villagers understand and discuss procreation in terms of seed and soil and sometimes cite the Koran to support this view. There it is written: "Women are given to you as fields, go therein and sow your seed" (Sura 2.223). Note that this is a directive from God to men in an I-Thou relationship, women are objectified. This image of procreation should be familiar since it is common throughout the Old and New Testaments, and has also been the dominant folk theory in the West. What is not often recognized today is what this theory has implied.

The male role in procreation is to plant the seed; the female role is to transform and bring it forth. *Döllenmek* is the Turkish word that means "to inseminate," and it incorporates the word *döl,* which means seed, fetus, child. It is almost the exact equivalent of the English "inseminate" (literally, to put the seed in). *Döllenmek* does not mean to fertilize the ovum or to provide half the genetic contribution to the child, it means the whole thing. By way of the *döl yolu* (seedpath or vagina) the *döl* is inserted into the *döl yatağı (seedbed or womb).*

The child comes from the seed—*tohum'dan çoçuk gelir. (Tohum* is a more common word for seed.) The female body, like soil, is a generalized medium of nurture that any woman can provide, given that she is not barren. Barrenness *(kısırlık),* as in Euro-American culture, is a quality that describes both soil and women.[4] Blood in the womb and milk at the breast provides nutrients necessary for growth and development; they swell the being of the child but in no way affect its essential identity. That is a matter of seed. As another villager put it:

> If you plant wheat, you get wheat, if you plant barley, you get barley. It is the seed that determines the kind of plant that will grow, while the field nourishes the plant but does not determine the kind. The man gives the seed, the woman is like the field. [Meeker 1970:157]

It should be clear that men engender females as well as males.[5] Women do contribute to the substance of a person and their capacity to do so is valued. However, it is substance that derives ultimately from males and is, in any case, temporal substance applicable only to this world. It does not carry the essential, eternal identity of a person, nor is it generative. As we shall see, that is the quality of seed that allies men with the creative ability of God. The theory of procreation is what I have called "monogenetic," for there is only one principle of generation.[6]

Although women's function is to provide the fertile soil, villagers more commonly use the word *field* to describe their role. This distinction helps to clarify the meaning. A field is not a field merely because it is cultivated. It is still a field whether the soil has just been turned, whether it is fallow, or about to be harvested. The important distinction between soil and field is that a field is enclosed or "covered" by ownership. Analogously, the female soil must be enclosed if a man is to know unquestionably that the produce, that is, the child, is his own. The methods of "enclosure" will be taken up below. A woman's value, in Turkish village society, therefore depends not so much on her fertility, her intrinsic nature, but on whether she is able to guarantee the security of a man's seed. To focus on women's reproductive potential as a valuable resource over which men compete, as is argued in much of economic anthropology, Marxist or otherwise, is to miss this crucial point, and is analogous to missing the difference between soil and field. Fertility is not the primary issue, since all women are presumed fertile until proven otherwise. Similarly, if fertility were the most important issue one might expect less emphasis on the virginity and purity of women. The primary issue, I suggest, is a woman's ability to guarantee the seed of a particular man; it is because of this that she *becomes* valuable.

Within this construction of procreation, it is men who give the life, women merely give birth. It should be clear that a different construction of procreation would be associated with different values and different gender definitions. In this case, however, women are imagined as vessels through which life is made manifest. The life incorporated in seed is theoretically eternal, provided men produce sons to carry it down the generations. "A boy is the flame of the line, a girl the embers of a house." Seed is a kind of living torch that is passed from father to son, *ad infinitum. Sülâle,* the Turkish word for patriline is, according to Rahman, derived from Arabic and means reproductive semen. Rather than the spark that perpetuates the line, women are the fuel consumed in the process. If a man has no sons, it is said, *ocağı sönmuş*—his hearth has extinguished. It is a fate worse than death.

The penis is thus *the* generative organ, and it is an object of much attention. One ritual that concentrates and reinforces this is *sünnet* (circumcision) which, in Turkey, takes place between the ages of seven and twelve. *Sünnet* is considered the first test of manliness (see also Erdentuğ 1959:40). A boy who survives this ordeal without crying gains a sense of pride. Conversely, pride is focused on the penis.

Pitt-Rivers believes that the "private parts are the seat of shame . . . yet as a means of procreation they are intimately connected with honor, for they signify the extension of self in time" (1968:505). There is confusion here because Pitt-Rivers has not explored deeply enough the polarization of meaning of sexual difference in procreation. The female genitals, as we shall see, are the seat of shame precisely because they do not have the ability to perpetuate the self in time. In contrast, the penis, as source of the male's ability to do so, is a source of pride.

Much more than pride, however, is involved. One man pointing to his grandson's penis asked: "What is it that men can do that women can't"? The young boy answered correctly: "Go to the *cami,*" that is, to the mosque. Vividly expressed, the penis was explicitly denoted as the ticket of admission to the realm of the sacred. The possession of this member seems to be what qualifies a person for full membership in the brotherhood of Islam. Male generativity and the sacred are closely associated and mutually reinforced by such practices. But it is the theory of procreation that helps to illuminate the interrelations between "power, sex and religion; hierarchy, endogamy and the sacred . . . the three principles that come together in the notion of honor" (Pitt-Rivers 1977:viii), all of which shall be taken up in the following sections.

Honor

Minimally, the value of males derives from the social perception of their ability to engender; it is the foundation upon which honor is built. At the same time, this understanding of procreation engenders an extreme anxiety about the "legitimacy" of a child. "Legitimacy" here means not so much that a child is the product of a legitimate marriage, but that he or she can be legitimately attributed to a particular man. The entire structure is precarious for it can be shaken by the behavior of women. In other words, the ability to generate seed is a source of pride for men; however, a man's honor depends on knowing that a child is from his own seed. This assurance entails the control of women.

Meeker, who also worked in Turkey, has suggested that honor is essentially concerned with the legitimacy of paternity (1976:264) but he did not draw out its specific meaning. The concepts of paternity and maternity are so taken for granted, so commonplace in our own culture, that their implicit meanings have not been examined. Closer inspection reveals that the meanings in our own culture are not so different from what they are in Turkey. Maternity is not the equivalent but obverse of paternity. The images and associations conjured up by the simple phrases: 'to father a child' and 'to mother a child' convey the semantic differences quite clearly. Despite the close connection between mother and child, maternity has been associated with giving birth and giving nurture, while contrary to the evidence of the senses, paternity has meant the creative, life-giving role. Paternity is overdetermined, and in proportion so too are the social measures constructed to ensure the legitimacy of paternity. These have ranged from infibulation and clitoridectomy, harem and eunuchs, veiling and seclusion, early marriage and even murder, to less dramatic but no less effective psychological restrictions. The practices vary from region to region and even within one region, and their logic must be worked out within each society. At a more general level, however, they can be interpreted as various methods to enclose the human fields, like earthly ones, in order that a man be assured that the produce is unambiguously his own. Not surprisingly, a threat to the boundaries of either field provokes a similar response. (A man's honor is, thus, related to his power to protect the inviolability of what is his.)

Shame

Women, on the contrary, are, by their created nature, already ashamed; the recognition of their constitutional inferiority constitutes the feeling of shame. Shame is an inevitable part of being female; a woman is honorable if she remains cognizant of this fact and its implications for behavior, and she is shameless if she forgets it. A man's birthright is honor; he can lose it if he cannot protect the boundaries of "his" women. At the most reduced level, the boundary of a woman is her hymen. It is reserved for and is the possession of the husband. In breaking it, he possesses the woman. Once broken, only he can come and go as he pleases, as he, but no one else, may enter his fields with ease. If the boundary of what is his has been penetrated or broken by someone else, he is put in the position of a woman and is therefore shamed.[7] Thus, male honor is vulnerable through women.

Women's constitutional inferiority is attributed to a number of interrelated factors. Woman was created second. In the Garden, Eve's act of disobedience against Allah and her inability to resist the temptations of Satan are thought to have brought *pislik* into the world. *Pislik* means dirtiness, but here refers to metabolic processes such as urination, sweating, and defecation that signify the mutability, corruption, and decay of earthly life as opposed to eternal life. In addition, women were given menstruation to signify their deeper immersion in and identification with earthly life. While menstruation heralds the possibility of life in this world, it is also a primary symbol of mortality.[8] Menstruation is often regarded as the stigma of female impurity, a mark of inferiority and therefore shame. For example, Saadawi, an Egyptian physician speaking of her own experience but reflecting on that of the women she treats, says, "I was led to understand that in me there was something degrading which appeared regularly in the form of this impure blood, and that it was something to be ashamed of, to hide from others" (1980:45). At the same time, it must be noted that although women appear to accept the tenets of the dominant ideology, they do not have wholly negative views concerning menstruation. It is felt that it is a cleansing process that rids the body of accumulated impurities and leaves the womb an immaculate ground for the reception of seed.

In any case, the feeling of shame goes much deeper than menstruation. Women's shame, I suggest, is related to the theory of procreation in which she does not have the seeds of honor within her. That is, she lacks the power to create and project herself, she lacks a core of identity and autonomy, the possession of which is, according to Pitt-Rivers, the essence of honor (1968:506). A woman is not self-contained, her personal boundaries are diffuse and permeable, and these physical attributes take on moral qualities. The belief that female intelligence is thought to be less sharp than the male's suggests that she lacks the proper equipment to penetrate the ambiguities of life; her emotional lability makes her less able to discern the boundaries between right and wrong. Women's shamefulness is basically a kind of indiscriminate fecundity which can only be redeemed by constraining and putting limits around it.

Sex and Marriage

Mernissi (1975), among others, has argued that female sexuality in the Middle East is viewed as inherently insatiable and therefore needs to be restrained. However, this does not accurately capture village views. There, female sexuality is not so much insatiable, if indeed, women can be said to have a potent or agential sexuality of their own, but rather that it is indiscriminate. Left to herself, it is believed that a woman has no resistance, she is open to men. The externally imposed restraints are felt to be her only shield. For example it is believed that if a man and woman are alone together for more than twenty minutes they have had intercourse, and this constitutes reason for divorce. It is not just that the woman has been overpowered by the man or her own desires, but that she is thought to have no power of discretion or resistance. Thus, she must not be in a position where she is unprotected. "Independent, or unprotected women proclaim themselves defiled or defilable" (Douglass 1984:248). As one neighbor explained to me: "Women are as easily seduced as Eve was by Satan in *Cennet* (Paradise)." It is because women are thought to be so vulnerable, so open to persuasion, that they must be socially closed or covered.

Ideally, women should be enclosed in the house, but women's enclosure is also expressed by the voluminous clothing they wear and especially by the headscarf.

Female genitals, unlike the male's, are not a source of pride but a reminder of her shame. Instead, the focus of female sexuality is displaced to the head. A girl's luxuriant hair, symbolic of the entanglements by which men are ensnared, must be controlled. Around the age of menarche when sexuality ripens, it must be enclosed. The headscarf, which a girl dons at this time, covers and binds her hair and symbolically binds her sexuality, which is henceforth under the protection of her father and brothers until transferred to her husband upon marriage.

Marriage, as sexuality, is also under the overt control of men, though the covert negotiations are made by women. Marriages are arranged between the parents of the girl and boy, though it is unlikely today that a girl would be forced to marry a particular boy against her will. While the thought of an arranged marriage is greeted with horror by most American women, it does have the advantage, not often recognized, of leaving the girl (and to a lesser extent, the boy) emotionally free; she is not so identified with her choice. Under the mantle of men most women live full and satisfactory lives, and develop strong personalities quite separate from men. They are not isolated separately in their homes as are middle-class American women in suburbia. Instead, houses are the realm of women; there is much visiting back and forth and sharing of work and companionship. That is to say, these constraints and restrictions are not necessarily felt as such by women in the village. They are simply part of the accepted way of life. A girl who is not properly covered or about whom there are rumors of promiscuity loses her chances of marriage, if not her life. While no "murder of passion" occurred in the village, the newspapers frequently reported such cases. The "passion," it must be noted, is not that of love but of jealousy aroused because the male's right of "possession" has been usurped.

Most girls want to marry since it is the only means of achieving something like a social identity. Through marriage her existence is socially acknowledged; unmarried women are socially invisible.[10] Thus, most women participate in their own seclusion. A woman who wears the headscarf indicates she is *kapalı* (covered, closed), whereas a woman who walks about *açık* (open, uncovered) is felt to be openly inviting advances from men and is considered common property. This was made strikingly clear to me by villagers' remarks that men who allow women to go about *açık* must be communists, for they believe the latter to hold both land and women in common. (Note that the communist is assumed to be male.) This state of affairs is anathema to villagers, for it would confuse both the source of and the rights to the produce.

Sex is said to take place inside the woman but outside the man. "The innate vulnerability of women—defined in terms of their ability to be physically penetrated—is commonly cited to explain and justify their strict surveillence" (Giovannini 1981:411). But the surveillence and control of women involves much more than the capacity to be penetrated; it is related to the entire theory of procreation. Since seed carries the essential identity of a man, it leaves an indelible imprint which no amount of washing can erase. A woman who has sexual relations with any man other than her husband becomes physically polluted, and through her, her husband's honor is stained. She becomes permanently defiled, while a man, since he receives nothing from a woman is not so defiled[11] (Engelbrektsson 1978:137). It is sometimes assumed, retrospectively, that a woman who has had a series of miscarriages or given birth to a deformed child, has been defiled.

A woman's value is related to her noncontamination by men. The slightest shadow of a doubt causes suspicions about the security of a man's seed. Social intercourse between unrelated men and women is almost equivalent to sexual intercourse. The theory of procreation demands virginity before marriage and fidelity after marriage. The social recognition of a woman's purity, however, depends on and is exhibited by the men under whose protection she is. In the extraordinary case of the sultan and his harem of concubines, the control of fidelity was managed by the institution of eunuch guards who provided the assurance that the virgin fields were plowed only by the Sultan. In this way, he could be certain that the children were his. On a less exalted plane, legitimacy of paternity is assured by monogamy for women.

Endogamy

Given that monogamy, at least for women, is entailed by the theory of procreation, the question arises as to why there is a preference for and a practice of endogamy. This is another theoretical issue that has preoccupied the anthropology of this area. It is my belief that this too is intimately related to the honor/shame complex, which is grounded in the theory of procreation. Although it is generally assumed that marriage is for the purpose of legitimate procreation, rarely has a particular theory of procreation been examined for the light it sheds on specific marriage practices. In the literature on endogamy in Mediterranean-Middle East societies, the focus has been almost exclusively on patrilateral parallel cousin marriage, more commonly referred to as father's brother's daughter marriage (FBD). Indeed, calling it FBD misplaces the emphasis; father's brother's son (FBS) marriage would more accurately reflect the desire, expressed by all villagers, of keeping daughters within the group (see also Pitt-Rivers 1977:166; Bourdieu 1977:4; and Antoun 1968:693). In any case, patrilateral parallel cousin marriage accounts neither for most marriages nor for the more widespread practice of endogamy. Various explanations have been put forth about how that type of marriage helps to consolidate groups for political purposes or to keep land in the group (see Keyser 1974, for a review of this discussion). While it may serve these functions in some societies, it did not do so in the village where I worked. Patrilateral parallel cousin marriage is, I suggest, an exemplar of the more pervasive symbolic logic of sexuality, that is, the culturally perceived notions of male, female and procreation that are epitomized in honor and shame.

Those women whose purity a man can be most assured of are those who are closest—namely the daughters of relatives or fellow villagers. Secondly, I believe the practice of endogamy expresses a desire to keep the human fields and the fruits of thereof, as earthly ones, for the benefit of the group. It is not that women inherit land (which they rarely do), but that women *are* land. Both are sources of sustenance for the perpetuation of the group, both have been cultivated and the fruits of this labor are to be kept within the group. Endogamy ensures this and patrilateral parallel cousin marriage is the most perfect expression. Marriage between patrilateral parallel cousins is an attempt neither to alienate the female field nor to have an *el* (alien, outsider) as mother of the children; in this case both the seed and field have come from the same source.

In the narrowest sense, then, the group is the patrilineal kin. However, the same logic persists, albeit in widening circles of inclusion, until the boundary of the village group is reached.[12] Of forty-one marriages that took place while I was in the village, all were endogamous. Half were with relatives, a quarter with first cousins equally distributed, and the rest were with fellow villagers. The same pattern of marriages held for other years of which I was able to obtain records. It is as inconceivable for a villager to give a daughter to an outsider as it would be to give away a field; the alienation of either would diminish the livelihood and honor of the group. The honor of the group is enhanced by its ability to retain and increase its reproductive and productive resources for its own use.[13]

Because of the practice of endogamy for generations, villagers see the village as an interrelated and integrated group, as one body in relation to all others and symbolically female. Access to it is limited and under surveillence. The village, like a woman, is perceived as *kapalı* (closed, covered) and *temiz* (clean and pure), as opposed to the cities (as well as Europe and America) which are *açık* (open), *pis* (dirty) and *bulaşık* (tainted, contaminated). Those who protect and represent the honor and integrity of the village are men. In other words, the notions of honor and shame, grounded in the sexual nature of male and female, also apply to the way the house, village, and even the nation, are perceived. A transgression against the boundaries of any of these culturally discrete but homologous entities is an affront to the sense of honor of those whose duty it is to protect them. Endogamy itself is only one expression of the wider system in which it is embedded. As villagers say: "By thinking about procreation, one learns the order and meaning of Creation."

Creation: Monotheism

Intimate activities thus speak to ultimate realities. Procreation, it must be stressed, is not just the fact of physiological reproduction, but the way it is symbolized and understood. Nor can it be confined only to the symbolism of gender and the relation between the sexes, for it is felt to contain in microcosm something fundamental about the macrocosm.

The seed-soil theory of procreation encompasses the way both birth and death are conceived. While children are greatly desired, especially sons, and procreation is what male and female were created for, birth itself is a somewhat shameful affair. The entrance to life in this world is through the female genitals, which, as we have seen, are the seat of shame. But the shamefulness of birth must also be understood in relation to the second and higher order birth which is death.[14] The body buried in the earth's soil is likened to seed in the womb. After a brief period of incubation, it is born into the other world. Life in this world *(bu dünya)* is but a prelude to eternal life in the other world *(öbür dünya)*. In this cosmological system the material, unregenerate, and eventually perishable aspects of life and women associated with it are devalued in relation to and encompassed by the creativity and spiritual essence of men and God. It is not a relation of opposition and duality, for that would imply separate but potentially equal status; instead, it is a relation of hierarchy, dominance, and encompassment. As the world is dependent on and encompassed by God, so too are women dependent on and encompassed by men. In this world men are God's representatives.

Villagers say: "A man is the second god after Allah." The creative ability of men is compared to God. Allah is author of the world; men in their procreative roles are authors of children, and it is from this that their authority derives.

In monotheistic religions, there is not a god and goddess whose sacred marriage brings forth the world, as in ancient Near Eastern traditions. Instead, Genesis[15] inscribes the revelation that there is only one principle of creation, manifested on the human and divine planes, and only one god. The transformation from polytheism, in which the chief deity may be male, to monotheism is not merely mathematical, a reduction in numbers. It is a radical difference in kind. It is not just that there is only one God, but that divinity itself is creativity and potency and is defined as masculine. Women are perceived as lacking this power and ability. Women may be revered, as in the adoration of Mary, but it is precisely for the absence of potency-generativity. She is revered for her virginal and maternal qualities, that is, for her purity, succour, mercy, self-effacement, and as the vehicle through which divinity was made manifest. She is the reification of the female role in these systems. She is not revered for her creativity and perpetuation of self, nor for putting her stamp on things. God created things, Adam named them, and men give identity to persons. Although the more emotionally conspicuous forms of worship may sometimes camouflage the structure of patriarchal authority, they do not cancel or deny the existence of such a structure.

The male role in procreation is felt to reflect, on the finite level, God's power in creating the world. Between notions of conception and conception of the deity, a whole world is constructed according to similar principles. Creativity is a continuum in the male line. Because of the symbolic alliance between men and God, men partake of divine power so that their dominance seems natural and ordained in the order of things. At the same time, a structural and symbolic association between women and the earth is established; both are perceived as created material. Rather than creative beings, women are the soil or raw material, like the earth, to be utilized for the creations of men. Both the earth and women are fields to be explored and controlled; both are fields from which the products are abstracted and appropriated and used as tokens in the game of honor. Wealth, I suggest, is a kind of symbolic currency, the evidence of generative power. It is not the cause, but the manifestation, of honor.

Monogenesis and monotheism are two aspects of the same thing—an ideology that contributes to and supports men's superiority in all things social. The value of both men and women lies not in what they *do* but in what, culturally speaking, they *are* (cf. Peristiany 1974 [1966]:189; DuBoulay 1979 [1974]:100 ff.). What they *are* depends on their perceived role in procreation.

Conclusion

In summary, I am suggesting that in the lands that gave birth to monotheism, that is, the Fertile Crescent, procreation was already a source for the generation and expression of significant symbols by which the world was perceived, ordered, and reproduced. Monotheism continued the focus but changed the meaning radically. In turn, the embodiment of these symbols in the cosmological systems of monotheism perpetuates and legitimates male dominance and authority. At the same time, the honor/shame complex is not just a function of male dominance and authority. Rather it is a distinctive system in which power, sex, and the sacred are interrelated and seen to be rooted in the verities of biology. The "truth" of biology is, in this case, the particular (and peculiar) theory of monogenesis.

While the symbols of seed and soil may be used to describe the process of procreation in other parts of the world, one cannot assume identical meaning a priori.

It is necessary, says Lévi-Strauss, "to know the role which each culture gives them within its own system of significances" (1973:54). What is significant in this context is that they are utilized to portray a monogenetic theory of procreation that is consonant with monotheism.

While there are great differences between Judaism, Christianity, and Islam, the essential, central, and shared belief is that there is only one God who is Creator and who is implicitly or explicitly male. This is the pillar of faith on which all three monotheisms are staked and why attempts to change theological language, imagery, and institutions have met with such resistance. The cultures around the Mediterranean are united as much as separated by religion. As Muslims say: "They are all people of the Book." What they mean by this is that they all trace their common ancestry to Abraham, to whom God gave the convenant: "I shall multiple thy seed as the stars of heaven and as the sand upon the seashore" (Genesis 22:17).

From the shores of the Mediterranean these seeds have scattered far and wide, yet wherever they have taken root some notion of honor and shame have been the offshoot. Surely these were the terms in which the relation between the sexes was perceived and discussed during my own adolescence in the 1950s.[16] The difference was one of degree, not kind. The intense degree to which they remain in force in the Mediterranean area is certainly related to the political economy, social structure, education, and ecology of that area. These are not negligible factors, but are conditional rather than determinative. The significance and interrelationships between these analytically separate fields are, I believe, organized, animated, and reproduced at the symbolic level.

In this article, I have attempted to show how the specific theory of procreation is the key to unlocking the relations between the sexes that are encoded in notions of honor and shame. But, like Pandora's box, many other issues, unforeseen and unmanageable in the limits of this paper, have been released. The seed-soil theory of procreation has a generative logic that relates to far more than the small field of Mediterranean anthropology. But into this somewhat dry and unyielding soil, I hope I have been able to contribute a drop of a seminal thought to quicken the discussion!

Notes

[1]DuBoulay (1979), Pitt-Rivers (1977), and Gilmore (1983; this volume) give sex and gender relations a more primary place, but their analyses do not examine the way gender definitions inhere in and are constructed within the whole theory of procreation.

[2]The night I was finally settled in my own house in the village was the night the military took control of the government (September 12, 1980) after which all overt political activity was forbidden. Nevertheless, sex and religion are such intimate aspects of politics, the salient terms and issues in which formal political activity are cast are revealed by an examination of the micropolitics of everyday life in which honor and shame are integral parts.

[3]One could, of course, argue that within the political economy of the nation as a whole, villagers constitute a particular class.

[4]It is interesting to note the way sterility is differentially described for male and female. Males are impotent versus potent, females are barren versus fertile; one implies agency and power, the other a passive capacity.

[5]But the seed that engenders females has often been thought to be deformed or deficient. The theory that it is the male who contributes the generative and formal principle is as old as Aristotle; Galen held that the male as well as the female contributed substance, but male substance was still held to be generative and formative.

[6]This "monogenetic" theory of procreation is exemplified also in Aeschylus' drama *The Eumenides,* which states: "the mother is not the parent of that which is called her child, but only the nurse of the new planted seed." The parent is really the one who gives the seed (i.e., the male). One might also wonder whether the transformation of the Erinyes, who avenge crimes done to a mother, into the Eumenides, maidens of the hearth in a patriarchal household, are not also a sign of change of notions of procreation. See also Harris 1973.

[7]A man becomes shamed because he is no longer symbolically a man. Similarly, the passive homosexual is the most shameful, not so much because of homosexuality, but because he has allowed himself to be put in the position of a woman.

[8]These ideas are more fully discussed in my paper "Mortal Flow: Menstruation in Turkish Village Society."

[9]Mary Douglas's notion that the body is a rich source of symbols has been a rich source for theoretical elaboration. I cannot, however, agree with her that the "body is a model which can stand for any bounded system" (1966:115), for the female body in Turkish perception is one that is relatively unbounded. In other words, I believe that the meaning and definition of the body as well as the parts focused upon are themselves cultural constructions. In addition, all cultures make distinctions between bodies that are female and bodies that are male, and each type of body has different meanings and may even be related to the concept of bodiliness differently. For example, in our own and Turkish culture, the female body is more associated with and represents corporality more than the male. Thus to speak of bodiliness in general terms misses this crucial point.

[10]Women are concealed linguistically as their bodies are by their baggy clothes, veils, and seclusion in the house. When you ask someone how many children they have, the answer is usually given only in terms of boys. Similarly, the population of the village is given in terms of *hane,* usually glossed as household, but which means the number of married men, for there can be several *hane* within one household complex. In a general sense, women are always socially invisible, they never achieve full social identity as men do, but marriage provides the closest approximation.

[11]This statement must be qualified somewhat. Although intercourse is forbidden during menstruation, that doesn't mean it never occurs. A man who has intercourse with a menstruating woman becomes temporarily defiled. However, he can be purified by performing an *aptes* (ritual ablution). While a woman must also perform an *aptes* after intercourse, she will not be purified if she had intercourse with a man other than her husband.

[12]The boundary of the village group does not necessarily coincide with its physical boundaries. Villagers also marry relatives and fellow villagers who have moved to town.

[13]In this case, villagers control and benefit from their own resources, the relation between their labor and its fruits is direct. When this relation is severed, as it is among the wage-earning working class, men are then structurally and symbolically in the position of women. They control neither resources nor their labor; instead they are controlled. This, it seems to me, helps to understand why workers in Spain talk of themselves in terms of shame rather than honor. If a bull can be symbolically female in a bullfight, as Douglass (1984) cogently argues, then surely physical men can be symbolic women, as in the case of the passive partner in a homosexual relationship. At the symbolic level there is no contradiction.

[14]In Christianity, the second birth is baptism, which has different consequences for orientation in life. Nonetheless, physical birth from women, in both Christianity and Islam, is devalued in relation to the spiritual second birth.

[15]Islam, for Muslims, is not a separate religion, but the one true religion given in the beginning. The stories of Genesis are incorporated in the Koran and Islamic traditions.

[16]I too was taught the seed-soil theory of procreation, and I continue to hear it being used today. Although the ovum was discovered in 1826, its function was not understood until genetic theory was fully developed, knowledge of which did not become widespread in this country until the mid-twentieth century. I do not mean to imply that biology gives meaning, but since our notions of gender are so tied to biology, however conceived, changes in the understanding of biology are bound to affect gender definition. Rather than vessels for the male's seed, women learned that they are co-creators of a child. And, I believe, this awareness is closely related to women's demands for, among other interrelated things, reproductive autonomy.

References Cited

Antoun, Richard T.
1968   On the Modesty of Women in Arab Muslim Villages: A Study in the Accommodation of Traditions. American Anthropologist 70:672–697.

Bourdieu, Pierre
  1977   Outline of a Theory of Practice. Cambridge: Cambridge University Press.
  1979   Algeria 1960. Cambridge: Cambridge University Press.
Davis, John
  1977   People of the Mediterranean. London: Routledge and Kegan Paul.
Delaney, Carol
  1986   Mortal Flow: Menstruation in Turkish Village Society. *In* Blood Magic: Explorations in the Anthropology of Menstruation. Thomas Buckley and Alma Gottlieb, eds. Pp. 83–106. Berkeley: University of California Press. [In press.]
Douglas, Mary
  1966   Purity and Danger. London: Routledge and Kegan Paul.
Douglass, Carrie B.
  1984   Toro Muerto, Vaca Es: An Interpretation of the Spanish Bullfight. American Ethnologist 11:242–258.
DuBoulay, Juliet
  1979   Portrait of a Greek Mountain Village. Oxford: Oxford University Press. [1974].
Engelbrektsson, Ulla-Britt
  1978   The Force of Tradition. Göteborg: Acta Universitatis Gothoburgensis.
Erdentuğ, Nermin
  1959   A Study of the Social Structure of a Turkish Village. Ankara: Ayyildiz Matbaasi.
Gilmore, David D.
  1983   Sexual Ideology in Andalusian Oral Literature: A Comparative View of a Mediterranean Complex. Ethnology 22(3):241–252.
Giovannini, Maureen J.
  1981   Woman: A Dominant Symbol Within the Cultural System of a Sicilian Town. Man 16:408–426.
Harris, Grace
  1973   Furies, Witches and Mothers. *In* The Character of Kinship. Jack Goody, ed. Pp. 145–159. Cambridge: Cambridge University Press.
Herzfeld, Michael
  1980   Honor and Shame: Problems in the Comparative Analysis of Moral Systems. Man 15:339–351.
Keyser, James M. B.
  1974   The Middle Eastern Case: Is There a Marriage Rule? Ethnology 42(3):293–309.
Lévi-Strauss, Claude
  1973   The Savage Mind. Chicago: University of Chicago Press.
Meeker, Michael
  1970   The Black Sea Turks: A Study of Honor, Descent and Marriage. Ph.D. Dissertation, University of Chicago.
  1976   Meaning and Society in the Middle East: The Black Sea Turks and the Levantine Arabs. International Journal of Middle East Studies 7:243–270, 383–422.
Mernissi, Fatma
  1975   Beyond the Veil. Cambridge, MA: Schenkman.
Peristiany, J. G., ed.
  1974   Honour and Shame: The Values of Mediterranean Society. London: Wiedenfield and Nicholson, Ltd. Reprinted by Chicago: University of Chicago Press. Midway Reprint. [1964].
Pitt-Rivers, Julian
  1968   Honor. International Journal of the Social Sciences 6:503–511.
  1977   The Fate of Schechem, or the Politics of Sex: Essays in the Anthropology of the Mediterranean. Cambridge: Cambridge University Press.
Rahman, Fazlur
  1980   Major Themes of the Qur'an. Chicago and Minneapolis: Bibliotheca Islamica.
Saadawi, Nawal El
  1980   The Hidden Face of Eve. London: Zed Press.
Schneider, Jane
  1971   Of Vigilance and Virgins: Honor, Shame and Access to Resources in Mediterranean Societies. Ethnology 10:1–24.

"HORSEMEN ARE THE FENCE OF THE LAND": HONOR AND HISTORY AMONG THE GHIYATA OF EASTERN MOROCCO

Michael A. Marcus

Following John Davis's admonition that the anthropology of Mediterranean societies should be more historically minded (1977:Chapter 6), this article uses historical data in order to shed light on the conception of honor among the Ghiyata, a sedentary Arabic-speaking tribe of eastern Morocco. By this means I hope to demonstrate the utility of a historical approach for revealing the contextual meanings of honor among the different peoples with whom Mediterraneanists are concerned. A secondary goal is to contribute to the effort to shift analytical focus away from the study of Mediterranean communities as isolates, and "develop appropriate models to accommodate the impinging forces of the wider world" (Gilmore 1982:184). While not wishing to minimize the importance of the imputed "honor and shame" complex to Mediterranean male dominance and codes of sexual behavior, nevertheless in this paper its relationship to wealth and what Gilmore (this volume) felicitously calls "fiscal sexuality" will be emphasized.

While to outsiders the settlements of the Ghiyata may appear remote, their world was never a closed or unchanging one. Occupying well-watered mountain valleys on the northeastern flanks of the Middle Atlas, Ghiyata dominated the vital east-west passageway known as the Taza Gap. All tribespeople were affected by powerful economic, political, and religious forces originating in centers located not only elsewhere in Morroco but also outside its borders. Such centers as the ancient town of Taza, which today Ghiyati settlements entirely surround, often shifted in importance throughout Moroccan history as different tribes, ruling dynasties, cities, and foreign imperial powers made their influence felt. In these circumstances, the fortunes of individuals and groups could change rapidly and radically, particularly during periods of crisis which witnessed significant shifts in the loci of economic and political power. For this reason, it is important to examine the Ghiyati conception of honor in the context of tribespeople's involvement with social forces operating beyond their local communities but influencing systems of social stratification within them.

To cope with the exigencies of an unstable world, and with competition from other groups for access to the scarce resources of the Taza region, Ghiyata elaborated an ideology of honor that included an image of themselves as "artfully excellent" *(mfennin)* in the use of armed force. This image drew upon a heroic oral tradition through which Ghiyata traced their origin to the aid given the Arab Muslim conqueror of Morocco, Mulay Idris, by "the people of succour" *(hel ghiyath),* their purported eponymous ancestors. Because the Ghiyati sense of

49

honor cannot be separated from its original Islamic integument, the possibilities for fully comparing it with an imputed pan-Mediterranean cultural complex of honor and shame are necessarily limited.

To illustrate the heroic aspect of the Ghiyati self-image and its elaboration in the context of events that situated tribespeople historically in wider social processes, I will present a poem which was recited to me by an elderly tribesman and from which this paper derives part of its title. I was told that the poem had been composed around 1915 by a certain Qissisu, "master possessor of words" *(shaykh mula klam)*. It is ostensibly concerned with an incident of local history from the days of what Moroccans call the *siba,* or "anarchy" preceding the establishment of French colonial rule over their country in 1912. Like many other examples of tribal verbal art which I collected, the poem epitomizes the essence of *siba* and the conceptualization by Ghiyata of their history as one of "true men" *(tarikh fe-r-rejuliya),* standing ever ready to defend themselves against outside threats:

> The horsemen, the horsemen, O friends,
> They are the fence of the land,
> They appear in the distance.
> But where are the brave ones now,
> Whom I once knew,
> Who appear no longer?
> Riders of horses are excited:
> Love for the daughters of Idris[1] is almost
>   like their riding.
> O Ghiyata, we've not seen enough of you!
> For at Bab s-Sadat was turned white, O friend,
> The hair of he who was there.
> And I saw that stallion's rider, O friend:
> Whomever of the enemy fell,
> He wouldn't leave alive.[2]

In this poem, Shaykh Qissisu imagined the Ghiyata as "the fence of the land." Atop their mounts and armed with rifles, they unite in defense of their livelihoods and collective identity. Such men venture where they will: ruled by no one, Ghiyata are as Ghiyata do. This image conforms with accounts of local history given me by non-Ghiyata, who asserted that by the late nineteenth century the tribe had forcibly expanded its territory at the expense of neighboring groups (Miknasa, Tsul), begun extorting unreasonable fees for safe passage from urban-based traders whose caravans traveled the Taza Gap, and generally imposed their will over the inhabitants of Taza itself ("Tazi-s"). Throughout the century, Taza's commercial importance was in a state of decline. According to townspeople, this was because Ghiyata dominated them, but in reality the principal cause of Taza's decline was the reorientation of major trade networks toward the increasing European presence in the Mediterranean ports of Morocco and Algeria.

While nowhere in Shaykh Qissisu's poem is there any usage of a single Arabic word which might be glossed in English as "honor," it nevertheless appears to reveal the extent to which the Ghiyata perceived their self-image and collective honor as bound up with the pursuit of "strategic opportunities which involved aggression against other men" (Meeker 1979:32). However, this does not mean that in reality Ghiyata either consistently or as a whole engaged only in hostile relations with their neighbors. As Simmel noted, conflict does not inevitably occur over things that are scarce or highly valued, and every end can be attained by more than one means (1971:83). In Morocco, tribal leaders generally sought to maximize their relationship with one external center or force in order to resist domination by another. Maintaining such "peace" was a necessity if the sources of wealth, or "the fruits of the earth" (*l-khir;* literally, "goodness") were to be at least temporarily stabilized. When violence did occur, Ghiyata always justified their recourse to arms on the grounds that resources which should be either properly shared or equitably transacted had been unfairly monopolized or seized by others for their exclusive gain.

This is precisely what occurred in the incident that provides the background to the poem. My informant (himself a poet) explained that it recalls the victory in battle of Ghiyata over enemies belonging to the Hayayna tribe. At some indeterminable time early in the twentieth century, I was told, Hayayna intruded into Ghiyati territory and kidnapped the daughter of Kehhel d-Shawi, a rural notable. Thus, if it is read in terms of only one dimension of its full social, historical, and cultural context, Shaykh Qissisu's poem also seems to confirm the observation of numerous ethnographers that the cardinal foci of "honor" in Mediterranean societies include what one of them, referring to the Iqarᶜiyen of Morocco's Rif, has called the "forbidden domains" of women and land (Jamous 1981). Its documentation of the Ghiyata victory over the Hayayna seems almost to epitomize male honor and the "shame" or dishonor that females can bring about as a result of their liability to violate codes of sexual behavior and their resistance of men's control over them (Davis 1983:91,101). Seen in this light, interpretations of the poem and the events which it relates in terms of a generalized "honor-shame complex" seem plausible. However, other aspects of Ghiyati society and culture are at least equally if not more important to a correct "local" understanding of both the poem and the honor it appears to represent. Specifically, the primordial Islamic dimension of the Ghiyati warrior ethos, along with regional political and economic conditions obtaining at the time of the incident, must be taken into account.

Therefore I will not dwell on the text of the poem per se. It is sufficient to note that it reminds its hearers of a particular instance of violence between Ghiyata and non-Ghiyata, and for a specific reason. By recalling to them their past conduct, Shaykh Qissisu sought to shame his fellow tribesmen for a present defect which he perceived in their character. In his poem, he gives voice to the ideal image held by Ghiyata of who they believe themselves to be and what they stand for in the world. "Ghiyata did two things well," one informant told me. "They prayed and read the Qur'an well, and they fought well." These images are part of what, following Bourdieu, might be called the tribe's "official language" (1977:21). By asking his listeners whether or not such Ghiyata still existed (i.e., horsemen who are "the fence of the land") Shaykh Qissisu exhorted them to respond, not simply as honor demands but also as their religion demands, to the new crisis in tribal history beginning with the penetration of Ghiyata-land by French armed forces in the late spring of 1914. But unlike their reaction to the Hayayna intrusion, Ghiyata then were incapable of uniting in response to the infidel, European threat. In part, this was because many of their leaders—rural entrepreneurs whose principal sources of income had been regional trade and the taking of caravan tolls—were lost, between 1902 and 1909, to the cause of a failed rebellion against the Moroccan government.[3]

Kehhel d-Shawi was one such entrepreneur. As indicated earlier, Ghiyata told me that they rose against the Hayayna because his daughter (*bint;* a married female is *mra*) was "kidnapped." It is possible, however, that the girl carried out a willful act of rebellion against her father's authority and ran away from home. Perhaps she objected to the man her father chose for her to marry? Alternatively, she might have plotted to run away with a Hayayni "lover" whom she met by chance outdoors or at a weekly market. In any case, if she willingly ran away she was deliberately and consciously manipulating the only resource available to her: family ties. She would not have been seeking freedom, but a more acceptable means of relinquishing it to a man other than her father. Indeed, she would have been asserting a right to determine precisely how she would develop her own honor (i.e., that which derives from the respect that a Moroccan Muslim woman gains by fulfilling roles culturally available to her). According to the Qur'an, Islam's sacred text, "paradise lies at mothers' feet" (cf. Davis 1983).

While it is true that Moroccan women lend intensity to status-based modes of relationship such as those which give rise to segmentary tribal systems (Maher 1974:2), Ghiyata recognize that when a daughter leaves home to be married, "she empties her mother's house and fills that of another." Sons ideally stay with their fathers, while daughters inevitably transfer their allegiances to other men. The potential transitoriness and vulnerability of their relationships to men is one reason why women focus upon very specific social aspects of these relationships, while men view them through a more generalized cultural screen of "natural differences" between the sexes (Rosen 1978).

It seems clear enough that at one level, Shaykh Qissisu's poem is concerned with the challenge posed by Hayayna to Kehhel d-Shawi's personal reputation and to the integrity of either his family or a larger, property-holding group of agnates. But at another level, the poem's significance goes beyond such strictly personal considerations of honor. Ghiyata participated in Taza's regional economy by forming *ad hoc* alliances with other tribal groups and with the merchants of Taza (whom they considered unmanly and "effete"). Because of the region's relatively poor agro-pastoral resources, real wealth could be had only through commercial profits, caravan tolls, and contacts with Europeans—all of which originated outside tribal territory, notably in the port of Melilla, the Rifian market town of Tafersit, and in western Algeria. In the confrontation between Ghiyata and Hayayna, Kehhel d-Shawi's "honor" as subject to his daughter's behavior only appeared to be at stake; what was most threatened was his position in the political economy of eastern Morocco as it existed on the eve of the twentieth century.

At that time, Kehhel d-Shawi was a major figure in the conduct of a profitable cattle trade linking the pastoral economies of a number of Moroccan tribes east of Fez with French butchering interests in Oran, western Algeria. A chief *(Qaid)* of the Hayayna name Bizari was a prime mover of this trade, for it was among the Hayayna and their neighbors, the Wlad l-Hajj, that the cattle which were sold originated. The role of Ghiyata strongmen *(l-kobbar)* such as Kehhel d-Shawi was to guarantee, in return for money and goods, the safe passage of the herd as it made its way through the Taza Gap and eastward to the Algerian frontier. The Ghiyata who were involved in this trade refused to pay the taxes and customs duties demanded by the Moroccan government, and one historian has persuasively argued that these demands were among the principal causes of the aforementioned rebellion, in which the Ghiyata were major actors (Dunn 1981). The flourishing of such autonomous contacts between Moroccan tribes and Europeans posed a military as well as an economic threat to the central government *(makhzen)* for it enabled local leaders to continue in a state of *siba,* provide their followers with modern firearms, and thus strengthen their local power bases. This was the context in which a chevalier culture, and the man of arms, became focal expressions of Ghiyati affect and thought. Symbols of independence, force, and the active defense of honor were attributes of the ideal male, realized most dramatically—and perhaps exclusively—in the exploits of men like Kehhel d-Shawi and their armed bands of followers. The honor of these "real men" operated chiefly as a principle for governing the allocation of key, strategic resources. It is such Ghiyata of whom Shaykh Qissisu, our poet, has "not seen enough." And just as few tribesmen owned horses, honor did not inhere in every man.

In 1908 Kehhel d-Shawi was killed, along with a number of other Ghiyata notables, in a violent encounter with a Rifian tribe that marked the beginning of the end of the long rebellion.[4] Of the men who rose to take the place of these leaders, many quickly perceived the futility of a holy war *(jihad)* against the French when the latter arrived in the region six years later. The gains to be had through collaboration displaced whatever sense of tribal honor they may have had with a "spirit of calculation" (Bourdieu 1977:171). This new tribal elite submitted itself to central authority and, like European *colons,* began to center its commercial interests upon nonsubsistence agricultural production in the fertile lowlands of the Innawen River valley along the Taza Gap. This land was previously dominated by Ghiyata but was never fully exploited, because its produce could not easily be protected from theft (a problem which ceased to exist with the establishment by the French of military outposts at strategic points between Taza and Fez). While many tribesmen continued to resist the French, fleeing further south into the Middle Atlas and engaging them in sporadic guerilla warfare until 1920, colonial rule ultimately ended Ghiyati *siba.* It induced a series of radical transformations in the relations of tribesmen to one another, to the people of Taza, and to the central government. It is in the light of these impending changes, and the loss of Ghiyati autonomy, that Shaykh Qissisu asked, "where are the brave ones, whom I once knew?" To him their absence drew a curtain across the stage of a tribal history in which Ghiyata took matters into their own hands in a forceful and decisive way.

Shaykh Qissisu tapped tribesmen's knowledge of this local history as a source for the evocative power of the poetic images which he conveyed, but like anyone else whom they listened to or heeded, the position of a *shaykh mula klam* was socially ambiguous. His role as a poet often combined with that of the "student" *(taleb;* pl. *tolba)* who is learned in the Qur'an by virtue of having committed it to memory. For this reason, as Clifford Geertz has observed, in Morocco poetic language may be lent a quasi-sacred status. It emanates from an individual who freely "traffics . . . in the moral substance of his culture" (Geertz 1976:1488). Poets who were also students flourished among the Ghiyata: they led collective Friday prayers in rural mosques, taught children the rudiments of Qur'anic literacy and dogma, and transmitted to tribespeople generally the fundamental moral premises of Islam. These religious ideas intermingled with less formalized, implicitly held notions of virtue such as manliness and honor. Ghiyata see it as an expression of God's will that resources are scarce and men enter into conflict over them. Today, they interpret the enmities and *siba* of the past as simply the inevitable result of proximity to non-Ghiyata in a poor environment. To gain a competitive edge, tribesmen elaborated a warrior ethic, stressing, under certain circumstances, the violent side of honor.

Yet like other "feuding societies" Ghiyata also developed ideologies of egalitarianism and generosity as other concomitants to their perception of "goodness" as a scarce resource (cf. Black-Michaud 1975:179–180). These ideologies express the pacifist side of honor: men who are considered honorable by virtue of wealth (one of Mediterranean honor's "three vectors of competition," along with status and respect; Gilmore 1982:191), that is, those who possess (sing., *mula shi*), are obliged to share their bounty with those who have little or nothing. This dictum applied to the treatment of non-Ghiyata as well, as in the case of other tribespeople occasionally finding refuge among them. But when Ghiyata state emphatically that "all men are not equal in value" *(qima)*, they refer to a sense of general social worth that is not reckoned in material or monetary terms alone. The "egalitarianism" of the Ghiyata is analogous to what Herzfeld has argued is its characteristic form throughout the Mediterranean: "a *nominal* equality of access to moral resources" (1980:342; emphasis added). Oral accounts of past strongmen revealed that their achievement of honor entailed their shrewd positioning of both material and symbolic asserts *already at their disposal* to effective use. To read or translate Shaykh Qissisu's poem accurately, it is necessary to realize that honor was not the possession of Ghiyata in general, but the attribute of a minority of persons whose will prevailed in the social dramas in which its perceived loss could be invoked to justify the use of force to recover it—the "non-realistic prize" of feuding (Black-Michaud 1975:190). Of course, no such attempt could be made by individuals who were without the power necessary to make their threat of violence either credible or successful. But there has to be a realistic prize of aggressive interaction as well: in this case, Kehhel d-Shawi succeeded in recapturing his daughter. By doing so, he proved not only to the Hayayna, but also to potential Ghiyati rivals, that he remained someone whose "honor" must be satisfied if cattle were to freely pass through territory over which he had control.

In an earlier paper (Marcus 1985a) I was concerned with what ethnographers of North Africa often take to be honor's moral antithesis, the notion of *baraka,* or sanctity. Citing the case of members of holy lineages who today are deliberately contributing to the disintegration of Ghiyata as a "tribe," I showed how *baraka* is best understood as a flexible cultural construct that derives its meaning from the specific social and historical contexts in which it is recognized and put to use (in the Moroccan idiom, it is "worked"). Honor, too, ought to be seen in this way. It is the object of a game in which being recognized as having it or not having it is a matter of ongoing, active negotiation (cf. Eickelman 1976:136). Bourdieu pointed out that among the Kabyles of Algeria, this game has a temporal dimension that is constitutive of honor's meaning in any particular instance (1977:9). Within this time frame, actors leave room for themselves to maneuver in ways that are not only productive, but socially adroit as well. It is this freedom, and this history, that Shaykh Qissisu expressed by referring to Ghiyata as "the fence of the land." In the absence of effective state control over them, men like Kehhel d-Shawi stopped at nothing in pursuit of their interests. They lived "by their wits" in a world similar to the rural Sicily described by Schneider, Schneider, and Hansen, where alliances were *ad hoc* and temporary (1972:333).

Ghiyata today say that their "vital force" or power *(s-sula)* exists no longer, and attribute its loss to their "seizure by the *makhzen.*" The decline of their former relative autonomy from government gradually fostered new understandings both of honor and of what it means to be "Ghiyati." Today, tribesmen must devote enormous amounts of energy to working out a *modus vivendi* with the government's bureaucratic control over their lives. Many now discredit the past. Some tribesmen go so far as to refer to it as a period of "ignorance" *(jahl)*, using a term that implicitly condemns as un-Islamic the tribe's former, unyielding spirit of rivalry and arrogance (i.e., honor as epitomized in Shaykh Qissisu's poem; cf. Izutsu 1966:29 for the prophetic basis of this line of thought). Whereas precolonial *siba* and armed bands were outgrowths of the process by which the traditional Moroccan state expanded by coming to terms with local centers of power instead of obliterating them (Ayache 1979:164), today it is Ghiyata who must come to terms with the government. With their agriculture largely underdeveloped and insufficient to meet their needs, Ghiyata depend upon the goodwill of the state in order to receive the benefits of such new good things as paved roads, electricity, piped water, schools for their children, health care facilities, and passports for men to seek wage labor abroad. As tribesmen are increasingly proletarianized, previously solidary local groups fall apart. What is the fate of honor, when *siba*, feudal-like relations of production, and much of the basis for tribal social organization have disappeared?

David Hart has argued that among the Rifian Aith Waryaghar, labor migration to Europe has replaced feuding over honor both in importance and social function (1976:94). For the past two decades, Ghiyata have also been migrating in search of work, both to Europe and elsewhere in Morocco. Can these leave-takings, like the mobility and exploits of the horsemen of the past, be considered pathways to the achievement of honor? I do not believe so, although it is true that a worker's accumulation of earnings provides him with a certain measure of personal autonomy. He frees himself from agricultural toil and the necessity to defer entirely to the wishes of another person (for example, his father; cf. Eickelman 1976:143 for a discussion of this notion of honor).

It is also true that the experience of Ghiyata migrants conforms with Davis's observation that instead of severing ties with their natal communities, labor migrants generally tend to try to achieve prestige or other culturally defined goals within them (1977:30). But I do not believe that Ghiyata see honor as obtainable in this way. Wealth earned abroad may indeed be put to the service of such traditional ends as buying land, building a new house, getting married, giving feasts, and the like. These goals are within reach, but status and respect—which are moral, not material resources—are not so easily come by; they cannot be purchased with money. Nearly all of the Ghiyata who have gone to Europe find employment as unskilled workers. Discriminated against and largely illiterate, they are incapable of participating fully in an alien culture. Few, if any of them, become citizens of the countries in which they may live for many years. Ghiyata who settle in Taza upon their return to Morocco also suffer disabilities, although these are more subtly experienced (this is because Tazi-s see rural migrants to "their" town as an inalienable part of their "natural" tribal settings, and do not "forgive" Ghiyata for their violence of the past). Ghiyata are therefore still largely bound, by sentiment as well as by externally imposed pressures, to their rural places of origin. In Taza they create extensions of rural life through such means as their patterns of visiting and child-fosterage, and the shops and cafes they choose to patronize. Families of labor migrants speak of the time that the latter spend abroad as a sort of "vacation" (*fakans;* from the French, *vacances*), a state of suspended animation from the real life that can be enacted and resumes only among one's own people *(mn dyalna)*. Many returned migrants do try to become "somebody" by investing their earnings in projects that enhance their autonomy as individuals, such as opening shops or buying up land which, as patrimony, had previously been divided among relatives.

It is beyond the scope of this paper to consider in what ways this process of individualization might be the result of Ghiyata questioning the usefulness to them, in changed circumstances, of traditional ideas and practices pertaining to social relationships. Yet whether in Taza, or in the growing market centers that dot the Innawen River valley lowlands, Ghiyata are clearly developing notions of personal identity and community that are different from those obtaining in their lineage-based hamlets of origin. At Bab Merzuqa, for example, some fourteen kilometers from Taza on the east-west road, Ghiyata from different tribal areas and lineages live in the same place, build urban-style, neo-traditional houses, and open urban-style shops and cafes. In the shantytowns of Taza, Ghiyata encounter an even more heterogeneous world.

In both settings, there seems little place for the elaboration of honor as it may be thought to exist by anthropologists in the presumably closed and corporate peasant communities of the Mediterranean. In their daily lives Ghiyata now come into more direct and sustained contact with persons who are strangers to them. The latter evaluate tribesmen according to standards and criteria that have nothing to do with honor as Ghiyata traditionally conceived it; at least not in terms which stress its violent side. The only clear continuity between the past and the present lies in the fact that in order to survive, Ghiyata must participate in the world beyond the confines of their local communities. Horsemen of the past set their own boundaries; today the limits of the world have expanded to include the European labor market.

As I have indicated, labor migration has permitted more Ghiyata access to material resources, but a great deal of cultural ambivalence surrounds the practice of uprooting oneself so drastically. Parents fear that their sons will forget them and "turn Christian" in their attitudes and behavior. Unmarried migrants especially experience their stay abroad as painfully alienating. They say that they leave their land only "by force," because circumstances oblige them to do so. It is, after all, morally incumbent for a man to earn his livelihood, provide for his parents in their old age, and sustain a family of his own. One does not achieve honor by the mere fact of doing so. Nor, as one Moroccan pointed out to me, is it considered particularly manly to spend ten years "sweeping the streets of Paris." For these reasons I am not inclined to accept Hart's analogy between labor migration and feuding over honor, nor Davis's chiefly materialist argument asserting that honor is primarily "an idiom in which differences in wealth are expressed" (1977:89; cf. Herzfeld 1980 for a fuller critique of Davis's hypotheses).

How, then, may Ghiyata prove themselves real men in their altered social circumstances? Hart reduces honor to economic terms, arguing that "the values which formerly underlay the [bloodfeud] have since been integrally transmitted to [labor migration]" (1976:94). In other words, the kind of competition which in the past could provoke violence is now played out by men trying to outdo one another in displays of material wealth. But if we reject the contention that honor is what labor migrants gain, the question still remains of who, then, does have it, and of what precisely does it consist?

This question cannot be definitively answered, because honor is fundamentally an ambivalent moral conception: it "lays down opposing modes of conduct according to the social sphere" (Bourdieu 1966:228). Traditionally, it could be invoked by Ghiyata as an expression of either their peaceful or violent intentions toward others. In the absence of governmental control over their movements, the minority of tribesmen who were capable of doing so were free to mobilize their clients and take up the challenges which others posed to their control over resources. The successful riposte was one which not only restored a *status quo ante*, but somehow shamed the offending party. In the incident described earlier in this paper, Kehhel d-Shawi's men not only recovered his daughter in their raid against the Hayayna, but also captured three women of the enemy tribe, subjecting them to a mock wedding ceremony before releasing them from Ghiyata territory.

But the pursuit of honor through feuding is no longer a realistic option. If Ghiyata still consider the achievement of whatever it is that honor once entailed as a meaningful goal, they must recognize it as obtainable by means other than those which political change has made impossible. In any case, it is still not something that everyone actually has the means to pursue. However, Ghiyata today see virtue as bound up more with such exemplary, individual, and "pacifist" conducts as equity and probity *(nishan)* in one's dealings, showing hospitality and generosity without *apparent* ulterior motive (to say that one "gives bread" is a common compliment), not "enlarging" oneself or envying the good fortune of others, keeping one's word *(kilma)*, and the like. These ideal human qualities draw their moral force from Islam and, as tribespeople hasten to add, are actually possessed by only a select few. As for manhood, it is marked by an increase in "reason" *(ᶜqel)*, marriage ("completing half of one's religion"), and the expenditure of "vital force" in procreation. The world remains a place where all is God-given and where little—save for this premise alone—may be taken for granted: "as life comes, we go with it."

While the poem that I have discussed in this paper provides only one instance of honor's valorization earlier in this century, it is in terms of similar attempts by Ghiyata to define the boundaries of a moral community that what tribesmen present as their history must be read (Marcus, forthcoming). Shaykh Qissisu constructed meaning in his poem for an implicitly held conception of honor, which by its linkage with a unique historical event (the kidnapping and trespass), and the contexts in which it was composed and heard, was self-determined. The question here arises as to whether or not, in Mediterranean anthropology, we are comparing the same phenomenon when we examine honor in a number of different societies. My own conviction is that rather than emphasizing honor in some general sense, beliefs and practices in specific historical and cultural settings should be examined for what they might convey about a particular society's mode of thought and form of organization. Honor impelled Moroccan rural strongmen of the past to cooperate with one another as much as it impelled them to engage one another in strategic and violent contests. This duality of attitudes concerning honor coincided with ambiguities in social relationships which social change has not eliminated. In their affairs many Moroccans still leave room for indeterminancy, strategy, and choice—in a word, for gamesmanship.

Honor remains at the core of Ghiyata sociability, but it is in terms of generalized moral imperatives that it endures, not in terms of definite norms, rules, or roles. Above all, it still sanctions the subordination of followers to leaders, lending the latter an air of legitimacy. A Ghiyati Member of Parliament, for example, declares to his constituents that they must continue to support him because he "defends" them against what they consider the abusive intrusions of outsiders into their lives. He does so not by threatening others, as might have been done in the past, but "politically" *(be-siyasa),* which according to tribespeople's understanding of the term means having the sort of knowledge that enables him to maneuver shrewdly in their behalf when dealing with external authorities. The tradition of closing ranks behind honorable men—the "faces" of the tribe who resist outside forces of coercion—thus persists, but in a way different from how it was expressed in the days of *siba.* Changing historical circumstances have lent honor a new inflection, and it seems pointless to seek for all of the Mediterranean what cannot even be found for the Ghiyata; that is, a timeless and universally applicable definition of its attributes and modes of realization.

In addition to being shaped by material and environmental factors, social order and cultural forms are also the product of a range of possible meanings that culture itself makes locally available. Anthropologists—especially those who are alien to the society under study—are capable of discerning them only imperfectly and, in the process of writing ethnographies, endeavor to recreate them textually. In this paper, I have suggested that a reasonably correct reading or translation of an indigenous text is a prerequisite to crosscultural comparison. It follows that more interpretive and historically minded social studies in the Mediterranean need to be done. Above all, we require more work specifying, in each instance, the concrete social ends and purposes that Mediterranean peoples have represented to themselves as the pursuit of honor. In the case that I have presented here, probing beneath the surface expressions of a father's outrage at losing control over his daughter revealed some of the larger problematics of inter-tribal and tribe-state relations in a region of eastern Morocco on the eve of colonial rule. We can gain greater insight, I believe, into what precisely the Ghiyata men of honor were fighting for if, like the horsemen themselves, we look beyond "the fence of the land" to see more clearly what it was they were fighting against.

Notes

Acknowledgments. The field research on which this paper is based was conducted in Taza, Morocco and its rural hinterland between June 1979 and April 1981, and was made possible by an International Doctoral Fellowship awarded by the Social Science Research Council. The author alone is responsible for all opinions and conclusions expressed herein. This paper was prepared in the spring of 1983 for the AAA symposium on honor and shame organized by Denny Gilmore. In addition to Dr. Gilmore, I wish to thank Drs. Dale Eickelman, Michael Herzfeld, and William Kelly for their comments on an earlier draft. All transliterations of Arabic are from the Moroccan colloquial dialect.

[1]The reference is to Mulay Idris, the Arab conqueror of Morocco and a figure much venerated by Ghiyata. By "daughters of Idris" is meant also the daughters of the *shorfa,* i.e., recognized descendants of the Prophet Muhammad.

[2]The Arabic text of this poem is as follows:

l-khil l-khil a syadi
huma zerb le-blad,
fe-bᶜod yibanu.
yak fayn ṣ-ṣrata, di nᶜarf ana,
gaᶜ ma banu?

rkub l-khil ka-yihiyyej:
beḥra l-ḥobb be-bnat dris be-ḥalu.
a ya ghiyata, bi-kum ma skhina!
u-nhar bab s-sadat yishiyyib, a ya saḥbi,
l-ᶜamdah di hder fih.
u-hdit mul le-zrag, a ya saḥbi,
lli taḥ ma yikhellih.

³This was the famous "Bu Himara" rebellion, which contributed significantly to the collapse of the traditional Moroccan state and hence to the imposition of French colonial rule.

⁴Kehhel d-Shawi's death in this incident, and the treachery of the Rifian tribesmen who betrayed him (the Beni Bu Zgu), are the themes of another poem that I collected among the Ghiyata; see Marcus, forthcoming. The incident is also referred to by Seddon (1981:108–109), but without mention of Ghiyata.

References Cited

Ayache, Germain
　　1979　La Fonction d'Arbitrage du Makhzen. *In* Etudes d'Histoire Marocaine. Pp. 158–176. Rabat: SMER.
Black-Michaud, Jacob
　　1975　Cohesive Force: Feud in the Mediterranean and the Middle East. New York: St. Martin's Press.
Bourdieu, Pierre
　　1966　The Sentiment of Honour in Kabyle Society. *In* Honour and Shame: The Values of Mediterranean Society. J. G. Peristiany, ed. Pp. 191–241. Chicago: University of Chicago Press.
　　1977　Outline of a Theory of Practice. New York: Cambridge University Press.
Davis, John
　　1977　People of the Mediterranean: An Essay in Comparative Social Anthropology. London: Routledge and Kegan Paul.
Davis, Susan Schaefer
　　1983　Patience and Power: Women's Lives in a Moroccan Village. Cambridge: Schenkman.
Dunn, Ross E.
　　1981　The Bu Himara Rebellion in Northeast Morocco: Phase I. Middle Eastern Studies 17:3–48.
Eickelman, Dale F.
　　1976　Moroccan Islam: Tradition and Society in a Pilgrimage Center. Austin: University of Texas Press.
Geertz, Clifford
　　1976　Art as a Cultural System. Modern Language Notes 91:1473–1499.
Gilmore, David D.
　　1982　Anthropology of the Mediterranean Area. Annual Review of Anthropology 11:175–205.
Hart, David M.
　　1976　The Aith Waryaghar of the Moroccan Rif. Tucson: University of Arizona Press.
Herzfeld, Michael
　　1980　Honour and Shame: Problems in the Comparative Analysis of Moral Systems. Man 15:339–351.
Izutsu, Toshiko
　　1966　Ethical-Religious Ideas in the Qurᶜan. Montreal: McGill University Press.
Jamous, Raymond
　　1981　Honneur et Baraka: Les Structures Sociales Traditionelles dans le Rif. New York: Cambridge University Press.
Maher, Vanessa
　　1974　Women and Property in Morocco. Cambridge: Cambridge University Press.
Marcus, Michael A.
　　1985a　"The Saint Has Been Stolen": Sanctity and Social Change in a Tribe of Eastern Morocco. American Ethnologist 12:455–467.
　　1985b　History on the Moroccan Periphery: Moral Imagination, Poetry, and Islam. *In* Self and Society in the Middle East. Jon W. Anderson and Dale F. Eickelman, eds. Anthropological Quarterly 58:152–160.
　　Forthcoming　God's Bounty, Men's Deeds: Islam and the Moroccan Past Imagined.

Meeker, Michael
  1979   Literature and Violence in North Arabia. New York: Cambridge University Press.
Rosen, Lawrence
  1978   The Negotiation of Reality: Male-Female Relations in Sefrou, Morocco. *In* Women in the Muslim World. Lois Beck and Nikki Keddie, eds. Pp. 561–584. Cambridge: Harvard University Press.
Schneider, Peter, Jane Schneider, and Edward Hansen
  1972   Modernization and Development: The Role of Regional Elites and Noncorporate Groups in the European Mediterranean. Comparative Studies in Society and History 14:328–350.
Seddon, David
  1981   Moroccan Peasants. Kent, England: Wm. Dawson & Sons.
Simmel, Georg
  1971   Conflict. *In* Georg Simmel on Individuality and Social Forms: Selected Writings. Donald N. Levine, ed. Pp. 70–95. Chicago: University of Chicago Press.

FEMALE CHASTITY CODES IN THE CIRCUM-MEDITERRANEAN: COMPARATIVE PERSPECTIVES

Maureen J. Giovannini

Honor is a recurring theme in mediterranean ethnographies, where it refers to the cultural constructs used to evaluate social worth and to order social relations between individuals as well as kinship groups (Peristiany 1965; Gilmore 1982). In his seminal work, *People of the Mediterranean,* John Davis has even suggested that, because of its ubiquity, honor might constitute a mediterranean "social fact" (1977:13).

Not all scholars working in the circum-mediterranean area accept the notion of mediterranean cultural unity or agree with related interpretations of honor, however. For example, Herzfeld (1980) has criticized what he regards as circular reasoning, nominalism, and linguistic reductionism whereby qualitatively different cultural systems are reduced to a putative pan-mediterranean code of honor. To avoid these conceptual and methodological errors, Herzfeld opts for a kind of ethnographic particularism, with in-depth semantic and contextual analyses of moral-evaluative systems in specific locales.

Herzfeld's admonitions are valuable, for the ethnographic literature indicates that, in mediterranean societies, honor may encompass one or several of the following evaluative criteria: wealth, ancestry, physical strength and prowess, piety, and sexual comportment. Variation also exists within the same community—between classes, for example, or from one situation to another. This fluidity has led Gilmore (this volume) to characterize honor, at least in the Andalusian context of his own research, as a "chameleon-like construct."

Although I agree with Herzfeld's insistence on holistic ethnographic analyses, I believe that one can go too far in the direction of particularism. Despite considerable variation in the content of mediterranean moral-evaluative systems, some striking parallels exist which cannot be ignored. One of these is the cultural emphasis on female chastity as an indicator of social worth for individuals and their respective kin groups. Consistent with this pattern is male control over female sexuality since men are usually responsible for protecting the chastity of their female relatives (Peristiany 1965; Schneider 1971).

The cultural equation between female chastity and social worth may not be a mediterranean "cultural universal." Nor is it necessarily restricted to the mediterranean region. Yet, it is very pervasive in that part of the world where it is associated with institutionalized practices that both affect and reflect gender-based relations of authority, dominance, and coercion. These practices may involve female seclusion, the veiling of women, the "crime of honor" and ritual displays of virginity (bloody sheets, nightgowns) following the consummation of a marriage. Hence, for those of us interested in gender dynamics in the circum-mediterranean, the cultural emphasis on female chastity constitutes a promising area for comparative investigation.

In this article I attempt to further such inquiry by focusing on female chastity codes as a key dimension of gender ideology and related social practices in the mediterranean region. Rather than presenting an ethnographic account, my objective is to draw upon existing theoretical and substantive works to develop a model that will facilitate comparative analysis. By concentrating on one concrete evaluative criterion—female chastity—instead of the more nebulous concept of honor, I aim to avoid the reductionist pitfalls noted above. More important, I seek to contribute to our understanding of the social forces involved in the cultural preoccupation with female chastity along with the impact of this pattern on the women and men who live it.

Conceptual Approaches

I shall begin by outlining what I regard as some basic theoretical assumptions that should inform comparative inquiry into the codes of female chastity. As anthropologists, a fundamental aspect of our research is to reconstruct the shared meanings, beliefs, and values of our informants in all their richness and complexity. Thus, investigations of female chastity codes should give careful attention to local definitions of femaleness and maleness, to ideas about sexuality—both female and male—to specific categories of women and men, and to more general cultural constructs linked with the codes of female chastity (Giovannini 1981). Without such in-depth reconstruction, we run the risk of comparing and contrasting the codes of female chastity on but a superficial level.

Yet, if our goal is to explain rather than merely to describe differences and similarities in female chastity codes, we cannot limit our analyses to cultural meaning. For, in so doing, we would commit the error of circular reasoning by trying to explain culture in terms of itself (Gilsenan 1977; Asad 1979). Instead, we must attempt to uncover the actual material conditions and social relations associated with the equation of female chastity with social worth in specific mediterranean contexts. This does not mean "reducing" the codes of female chastity to reflections of the material world. Nor does such an approach overlook the significant impact of these codes on social behavior. However, it does acknowledge that the salient features of material and social life often supply the raw material for cultural codes. It also recognizes that evaluative cultural constructs like female chastity may be objectively possible and authoritative only under specific political-economic conditions (Asad 1979).

With this general framework in mind, I shall review existing conceptual models that have been used to account for the cultural codes of female chastity in terms of broader social and material processes. The work of Jane Schneider and Peter Schneider is particularly relevant here. In a path-breaking article, "Of Vigilance and Virgins," Jane Schneider (1971) argues that the pan-mediterranean preoccupation with female chastity arose from similar political-economic and ecological situations wherein kin groups competed over land and other scarce resources in the absence of effective state control. As an essential part of the family patrimony, women have been carefully guarded.[1] Correspondingly, their virginity has come to symbolize the family's ability to protect its material boundaries. Schneider suggests that the kin group's shared concern over female chastity may have the adaptive advantage of reinforcing intrafamilial cooperation in the face of potentially disruptive external forces (Schneider 1971).

In a more recent work, Jane Schneider and Peter Schneider (1976) reiterate the adaptive functions of the female chastity construct for competing kin groups in rural mediterranean contexts. They trace this endemic competition over scarce resources back to classical antiquity, when ancient empires began to put enormous strains on land ecologically ill-suited to feed imperial populations. The Schneiders also cite other features of the ancient mediterranean world that might have contributed to the formation of cultural codes stressing female chastity. These include attempts by both the state apparatuses of ancient empires and great religions (Islam and Christianity) to establish their hegemony over extended kin groups on the local level. Such efforts, particularly by Islam and Christianity, may have involved soliciting the support of women to undermine the solidarity of male-centered kin groups. Of additional relevance was the existence of a slave trade in the circum-mediterranean which preyed on women even more than men. The Schneiders conclude that, in such an environment, the codes of female chastity arose in response to and as a defense against these external threats to kinship groups. They further suggest that the cultural admonition to protect and control female kin reflects the idea that women were more vulnerable—emotionally and physically—to these dangerous external forces (Schneider and Schneider 1976).

These works make an important contribution to the study of mediterranean cultural constructs that equate female chastity with social worth. To begin with, they draw attention to the material conditions (ecological, political, economic) of possible relevance to the origin and functions of female chastity codes. Although speculative and even controversial, such models do pave the way for more in-depth comparative and historical analyses. In addition, by arguing that mediterranean cultural codes are rational responses to objective conditions and problems, they refute ethnocentric and distorted explanatory models, like Banfield's notorious "amoral familism" (Banfield 1958).

At the same time, these accounts can be faulted for the teleological fallacy of explaining the existence of a cultural phenomenon in terms of the functions it fulfills. Equally problematic is the assumption that the functions performed by the cultural preoccupation with female chastity are necessarily adaptive for competing kin groups. This approach tends toward reductionism, for it ignores the reciprocal, uneven, and sometimes discordant links between cultural constructs like the codes of female chastity and ongoing social relationships. Furthermore, it leaves little room for exploring the "dysfunctional" or problematic aspects of these cultural codes in specific contexts or for certain social groups.

In her essay, "The Virgin and the State," Sherry Ortner (1978) addresses some of these issues. Although Ortner's geographic scope goes beyond the circum-mediterranean, her arguments are relevant to the present discussion. Like the Schneiders, Ortner associates the cultural codes of female chastity with the historical emergence of the state. However, her theoretical assumptions and related analytical foci are of quite a different order. Rather than concentrating on the opposition between previously autonomous kin groups and hegemonic state processes, Ortner discusses the origin of female chastity codes in terms of increasing stratification in kinship forms, religious cosmology, and marriage alliances. She highlights the dynamics of gender in each of these institutional patterns, asserting that state formation was problematic not only for male relations but at least equally for female/male relations.

For Ortner, the most important change in kinship was the emergence of the family as an administrative unit with absolute authority vested in the father as senior male. For the first time in human history we can speak of patriarchy—that is, the institutionalized rule of the father. On a *de jure* level, women became legal minors subject to male control. Thus, with the emergence of the state, the legal-political groundwork was laid for male control over the sexual comportment of female relatives. But the cultural elaboration of female chastity cannot be explained in terms of changing family patterns alone. Ortner suggests that this cultural preoccupation was related to state religious cosmologies that emphasized ideas of purity and chastity while encouraging certain social groups—women, for example—to conform to the ideal.

Even more relevant, perhaps, were marriage alliances and the possibility for lower-class families to raise their status through female kin who "marry up." In this context virginity may have come to symbolize a woman's spiritual value, her inner worthiness for such a hypergamous union. According to Ortner, the situation was even more complex. For chaste women who were oriented upward represented their group's ideal (and often unattainable) status rather than its real position. Hence, the codes of female chastity were symbolically as well as functionally bound up with the ambiguities and contradictions of hierarchy and social change in early state societies.

Ortner's discussion is admittedly conjectural. But, as with the Schneiders' work, it offers new insights for comparative inquiry on the topic of female chastity. Most important, these models underline the need to take three interrelated features of the social and material world into account when comparing and contrasting the codes of female chastity in specific mediterranean contexts: first, the linkages between local community and more inclusive macro-level processes; second, class relations; and third, gender politics in the context of kinship as well as in wider social settings.

Micro/Macro Level Linkages

With regard to the first, most anthropologists have come to reject models of local level communities as static, closed systems. Instead, researchers are looking increasingly to the essential linkages between local-level social-cultural patterns and macro-level (regional, national, and even supra-national) processes (Boissevain & Friedl 1975; Cole 1977). This perspective has influenced mediterranean anthropology, where scholars are attempting to transcend the boundaries of the local community to study, among other things, industrialization, urbanization, migration, and patron-client ties (Blok 1975; Riegelhaupt 1979; Waterbury 1970).

The works of Ortner and the Schneiders suggest that a similar integrative approach be applied to analyses of cultural constructs like the codes of female chastity. Throughout the mediterranean region, the cultural emphasis on female chastity as an indicator of social worth and the corresponding male control over female sexuality have been intimately tied up with the legal/political system of the nation-state as well as with institutionalized religious forms. This has entailed much more than local-level reaction to the hegemonic processes of formal religion (Islam or

Christianity) and the state. Rather, over the years, state and religious institutions have formally legitimated, enforced, and symbolically justified the cultural codes of female chastity. This has taken the form of marriage and family laws emphasizing male authority, differential laws and punishments for female and male adultery, the "crime of honor" which condones by minimal sentencing any homicide committed to avenge the sexual transgressions of a female relative, and religious images like the Madonna, which glorify female chastity.

These macro-level structures and processes may have played an important part in the continuities as well as the variation in mediterranean codes of female chastity. Of course, we should not assume that mediterranean communities and their inhabitants have been merely passive recipients of macro-level political and symbolic processes. Indeed, ample evidence indicates that considerable diversity can exist among communities that are formally part of the same nation-state or institutionalized religious system. For example, Antoun (1968) documents the accommodations that occur between the Islamic norms of female modesty on the one hand and local conditions and beliefs on the other. Likewise, Silverman's (1968) comparative account of north and south Italy highlights the material and social factors that have contributed to south Italy's cultural preoccupation with female chastity along with its relative unimportance in much of north Italy. Therefore, a more useful analytical approach would concentrate on the dynamic interplay between supra-local institutions, sacred and secular, and indigenous codes of female chastity in specific mediterranean settings.

Class Relations

A second relevant analytical focus involves class relations and their implications for the cultural codes of female chastity. As integral parts of complex state systems, most mediterranean communities are stratified according to class (here defined in terms of control over material resources). Yet, the ethnographers doing work in the circum-mediterranean region have largely ignored both the existence of objective class relations and the implications of class dynamics for the content and usage of cultural constructs like the codes of female chastity. Rather than documenting existing material inequality, researchers have highlighted informants' statements to the effect that egalitarian relations prevail. And, correspondingly, analyses have concentrated on how evaluative constructs including female chastity codes serve to regulate relations among "near equals"—that is, among individuals (usually men) or kinship groups devoid of class content.[2]

Recently, however, this limited view of mediterranean social reality has been challenged by scholars attempting to document the relevance of class for the evaluative criteria used to assess social worth. Their works demonstrate that the culturally defined duties, obligations, and expectations involved in assessments of reputation and social worth are constrained by class position (Gilmore 1982). To begin with, one's place in the broader nexus of material resources and relations can set limits to what is perceived as possible, desirable, or pragmatically useful (Mouzelis 1976). Moreover, the historical unfolding of class dynamics may favor certain kinds of evaluative criteria over others, for example, the emphasis on male strength and prowess in the hostile and uncertain social climate of western Sicily (Blok 1981). As one author put it, "Social attitudes and moral orientations subsist and persist for good reason. They manifest real imperatives inherent in concrete configurations of power and production" (Aya 1975:2).

Hence, comparative inquiry into the codes of female chastity should investigate how the class positions and related experiences of social actors in diverse mediterranean contexts have contributed to the "common sense" ideational constructs underpinning these cultural codes. In addition, such an approach could be employed to shed light on the ways in which the codes of female chastity have entered into and have influenced class relations—for example, as modes of resistance or, conversely, accommodation to class domination. The former can be illustrated by my own ethnographic data collected in the Sicilian town of Garre. According to townspeople, when foreign lords ruled over their community, they often exercised the "right of the first night" with new brides. Local legend has it that one young woman, *la mala zita* (the unfortunate fiancée) threw herself off a mountain ledge just before her wedding to preserve her family's honor. By remaining a virgin—even at the cost of her life—*la mala zita* symbolizes and legitimates the resistance of family members to class-based oppression.

This is not the whole picture, however. Although cultural constructs are produced, conveyed, and interpreted in materially circumscribed social situations, they are not always accurate representations of the social and material world. Instead, these beliefs and values may serve to mask the real nature of social relations to the detriment of those individuals and groups who hold them (Silverman 1977). Such distortions can occur when evaluative criteria remain unchanged in the face of altered material circumstances (Gilsenan 1977). But distortions may also result when power holders promote certain evaluative constructs to further their own sectional interests. This might include emphasizing those values that contribute to the divisiveness of people who, objectively speaking, occupy similar class positions. For example, in South Italy the ideology of familism, supported by both Church and State, has had this effect. Conversely, as the following vignette illustrates, cultural strategies may be designed to obfuscate objective class differences.

In 1974, while I was conducting ethnographic research in the above-mentioned Sicilian town, the nationwide divorce referendum took place. At that time, north Italian Christian Democrat politicians visited the town and, in the context of a public debate, warned their male audience that, if divorce remained legal, they would all end up as *cornuti* (cuckolds).[3] I seriously doubt if these politicians really cared about the reputation of their Sicilian followers. But they were very much concerned with securing an important victory for their political party, a party which has consistently served the interests of the ascendent classes in both north and south Italy, often at the expense of most Sicilian women and men. Toward this end, the visiting politicians called up local gender-related evaluative constructs to gloss over regional and class animosities and align themselves with their listeners—all men equally threatened by the divorce legislation.

Gender Politics

The divorce referendum case highlights the need to analyze the ways in which female chastity codes have entered into class relations and have contributed to an existing order of class domination. But the vignette is important for another reason as well. It illuminates the politics of gender embedded in the codes of female chastity and demonstrates how gender issues can crosscut class affiliations in certain situations. Thus, instead of subsuming gender under class, we should make gender relations a key focus in comparative analyses of female chastity codes. This means that we should look at how the cultural emphasis on female chastity intersects with the following areas: the construction of women and men as gendered subjects; gender-based alliances as well as animosities; and the limitations, problems, resources, and privileges accruing to women and men on the basis of gender. These can be illustrated with references to my own field data collected in Garre.

For the Garrese, as for many mediterranean people, the shaping of gender consciousness was intimately bound up with the codes of female chastity. Gender segregation began during childhood when young boys had access to the world beyond the home, while young girls were obliged to help with the household chores and care for their younger siblings. Both girls and boys were socialized to act out the culturally defined personality differences believed to exist between the sexes. For example, young boys from infancy on were rewarded for aggressive and domineering behavior by laughs, claps, and shouts of *"che maschio!"* (what a man!). In contrast, similar behavior on the part of little girls was ignored or responded to by *"che vergogna!"* (how shameful!). At the same time, little girls might be praised for their gentle and obedient behavior—those qualities that would elicit ridicule if exhibited by a boy.

Children of both sexes were taught that women, being emotional, were inherently weak and thus in need of male protection. Young boys assumed this protector role early on when, at age eight or nine, they began to accompany female relatives who went out of the home after dark. Boys did not always relish their gender-based responsibilities, however. To illustrate, in one conversation that I overheard, a six-year old boy told his pregnant mother that he wanted a baby brother, because "if we have a sister, Carlo (his younger brother) and I will have to make sure that no one calls her *puttana* (whore) or our family will be laughed at. But if the doctor brings us a brother, then we will be able to call everyone else's sister *puttana* when we fight with them" (Giovannini 1981:409).

For their part, girls soon learned not to question the differential authority and rights held by males, in particular, their fathers and brothers. When little girls asked why they were not allowed to go in the piazza like their brothers, the answer was invariably limited to, "Because you are a girl and people will talk." Any further demands could be followed by a more physical response. In terms of positive reinforcement, young girls were socialized to accept the code of female chastity and value their virginity through numerous ritual ceremonies. Many of these ceremonies honored *la Madonna* (the virgin-mother) and were held at various times during the Church year. But perhaps the most powerful rituals involved the joint enactment of First Communion and Confirmation. At that time ten- and eleven-year old girls donned the symbols of purity (white dress and veil) for the first time and dramatically affirmed the ideal of chastity. This cultural theme would again be expressed at a later date when these girls appeared in church dressed in white as brides.

Female chastity codes not only influenced the construction of women and men as gendered subjects, but also entered into gender-based alliances and animosities. Much has been written about the unifying effects of female chastity codes for kin group members who share the common objective of safeguarding their women (Schneider 1971). But these codes can contribute to gender-based conflict within and outside of kin groupings as well. In Garre, for example, the cultural equation between female chastity and social worth along with the belief that all men are *ciacciatori* (predatory hunters) served to exacerbate the endemic conflict between unrelated men. In some cases male jealousy even prevented men in similar class positions from collaborating for their common good. To illustrate, while I was in Garre a cooperative farming venture between two peasants with adjacent land holdings failed when one became offended at the other for staring at his wife "with hungry eyes."

Turning to intrafamilial dynamics, there existed an implicit tension between male and female family members related to their identities and roles as gendered subjects. Consistent with the socialization process discussed above, *un vero uomo* (a real man) was defined by the strength, power, and cunning necessary to protect his women. Those men whose female relatives had been defiled were believed to lack these essential qualities and were viewed as being less than "real men." Unfortunately, a man's social worth was never secure in Garre. For, since women were allegedly weak by nature, their very existence constituted a living threat to the reputation of male relatives. One manifestation of this was the tendency for young Garrese men (perhaps not yet secure in their manliness) to be especially vigilant with their sisters and react violently when they felt threatened by the latter's behavior.

Female chastity codes also generated antagonism among women relatives, specifically unmarried sisters, within the family unit. This was more likely to surface if one sister was attempting to circumvent the norms of chastity—for example, by flirting or, even worse, meeting secretly with a young man. While in Garre I discovered that several young women were deviating from the norms in just these ways, but never with the aid of a sister. Indeed, their sisters would be the first to disclose such transgressions to other family members. To illustrate: in one case an older sister found out that her younger sister was secretly exchanging love notes with a boy in the neighborhood. She quickly informed her parents, who then stopped the correspondence before any real damage was done.

The "betrayal" of one sister by another begins to make sense once we examine the implications of having a female sibling whose reputation has been ruined. The Garrese believe that if one young women transgresses the norms of female chastity, her sisters will probably do likewise. The idea here is that even though all women are innately weak and vulnerable, some women have an inner sense of *vergogna* (shame) that helps them to avoid compromising situations. This quality of *vergogna* is said to be inherited through female lines. Hence, just as a young woman with a tarnished reputation (deserved or otherwise) would be shunned as a marriage partner, her unmarried sisters would also carry the stigma and, as such, find it very difficult to marry. This explains the length to which young women want to maintain the good reputation of their sisters, even at the risk of alienating them.

Quite a different picture emerged with regard to unrelated women in Garre, many of whom gossiped regularly about the alleged sexual misconduct of other females. This gender-based animosity can also be attributed to the codes of female chastity as they operated in Garre. Specifically, Garrese women derived much of their social worth through conforming to these codes. But within the Garrese cultural system the "virginal" woman could not exist without the corresponding image of her opposite, the *puttana* (Giovannini 1981). Hence, Garrese women who exhibited chaste and modest behavior had a vested interest in gossip. For each time that a female transgressor was discovered and condemned, the prestige surrounding the chaste woman was highlighted and reaffirmed.

Finally, perhaps the most important gender issue involves the extent to which female chastity codes have contributed to the subordination of women in historically and culturally specific mediterranean settings. By posing this question I am not negating the very real power and influence wielded by women throughout the circum-mediterranean region (Friedl 1967; Nelson 1974; Rogers 1975). Nor am I ignoring the problematic aspects of female chastity codes for men (for example, one of my Sicilian informants confided that he had not slept soundly since his daughter attained puberty). Rather, I am suggesting that the limitations and constraints experienced by women in societies that subscribe to female chastity codes are of a different order and greater magnitude that those faced by their male counterparts.

To illustrate, in Garre the codes of female chastity entered into and influenced the economic and political subordination of women in myriad ways. Until recently, Garrese women were secluded within the home where their sexuality and reproductive activities were strictly controlled by male kin. Confined to the domestic sphere, women had little access to the sources of power, wealth, and prestige in the wider society. For example, no woman in Garre has ever held public office, although ten years ago the wife of a local doctor ran for vice-mayor. She lost by a wide margin since, as one informant told me, ''We wanted to vote for her because she is the doctor's wife. But everyone knew that a woman would be too weak and emotional to handle the authority of vice-mayor successfully. So when it came time to vote, most of us chose other candidates.''

Hence, regardless of their class background, Garrese women were in similar structural positions of gender subordination. As in other mediterranean communities, this disprivilege was justified in terms of ''innate'' female characteristics. Indeed, women themselves were socialized to accept and even desire male protection because of their alleged vulnerability. Moreover, in order to secure the prestige accorded females who conformed to the chastity codes, women sometimes turned against each other. In so doing, they inadvertently contributed to the overall devaluation of the female gender in Garre.

Topics For Comparative Analysis

In the preceding pages I have discussed relevant conceptual approaches to the cultural codes of female chastity in terms of three sets of interrelated variables: the links between community and supra-local structures; class relations; and gender politics. Although analytically distinct, these features intersect in myriad ways to affect the form, content, and functioning of female chastity codes in diverse mediterranean settings. I shall now outline some specific research topics and questions that could form the basis for comparative analysis using the strategies outlined above.

Historical Research

The first of these involves the processes of state formation in the circum-mediterranean and their role in the emergence of female chastity codes. Notwithstanding real problems in data acquisition and interpretation (Davis, this volume) efforts should be made to gather the kind of information that would substantiate, modify and refine, or refute existing models like those put forth by Ortner and the Schneiders. At first glance their interpretations seem contradictory. But they could be focusing on different aspects of an enormously complex transformation. On the one hand, Ortner's alliance construct may be more accurate for those groups that experienced comparatively greater integration into emerging state systems. On the other hand, the Schneiders' model could reflect responses on the part of more geographically isolated and structurally autonomous groups. Clearly just as there was no "prime mover" in state formation, there was more than one path to the emergence of female chastity codes. Comparing and contrasting these paths in the mediterranean region and elsewhere requires detailed archaeological, historical, and ethnohistorical data on changing laws surrounding marriage, divorce, adultery, property rights, and so forth. Thus, multidisciplinary research efforts would be very useful in shedding light on the possible origins of female chastity codes and their functioning in early state societies.[4]

Other topics that invite comparative investigation relate to more recent historical transformations in the circum-mediterranean and the implications of such change for the cultural emphasis on female chastity. For example, one research focus might be the 19th-century abolition of feudalism and attendant commercialization of material resources that took place throughout the mediterranean (Gilmore 1982:188). Davis (1976:301) has noted that in south Italy these changes exacerbated economic competition while increasing the importance of family reputation, including female chastity, as a weapon in material struggles. Once this case is fully understood in terms of the variables outlined above, it could be compared with other 19th-century mediterranean contexts to see if similar processes unfolded and to explain any salient differences.

The qualitative changes associated with colonialism constitute an additional area for comparative research on the codes of female chastity. In some Arab mediterranean societies, the veiling and seclusion of women increased under colonialism as a form of opposition to external control. Correspondingly, colonial officials attempted to undermine such resistance by "liberating" women from alleged male domination. On the eve of the Algerian revolution, for example, French colonial leaders organized public unveilings (which, according to many Algerians, only prostitutes participated in).[5] These historical events raise important questions about the ways in which female chastity codes have served as an ideological device capable of generating opposition to an existing order of domination. Comparable research on colonialism in the mediterranean region can illuminate this issue by documenting the conditions and circumstances under which social groups and political processes have been shaped and moved by the codes of female chastity. Rather than assuming a homogeneity of interest among female and male colonial subjects, such inquiry should explore the extent to which gender politics entered into and influenced the ideological dimensions of female chastity codes under colonialism.

Contemporary Research

Perhaps the most fruitful area of inquiry is the contemporary mediterranean world, where female chastity codes can be studied through first-hand ethnographic data. Here one essential research question is the differential survival of these cultural codes in contexts of urbanization, industrialization, migration, and political change as well as in more stable settings. In some cases the cultural codes of female chastity have accommodated to new situations. For example, in Garre where I conducted research, a clothing factory was established in 1966 that employs one fourth of the adult women between the ages of 18 and 54. Initially, female factory employment did not challenge the local code of female chastity, since employees were doing ''women's work'' in a gender-segregated setting for the benefit of the family/household. Indeed, the factory was viewed almost as an extension of the domestic world of women. Moreover, factory positions were secured for women largely through the political machinations of male relatives. Therefore, in the eyes of most townspeople, men were still in control of the family and its members (Giovannini 1985).

Notwithstanding such continuity, certain changes as well as contradictions in gender-related values and behavior had become apparent at the time of my research. Although most townspeople still subscribed to the codes of female chastity, women had acquired more freedom of movement within the town. This was especially true for factory workers who had also gained in domestic decision-making power. In addition, new educational opportunities, a rising literacy rate, and access to television exposed younger Garrese women to alternative values and life-styles. Unfortunately, many young women felt ''caught between two worlds'' since their new aspirations could not be realized in Garre's restrictive social environment. Lutton (1980) reports similar kinds of tension in the Calabrian context of her own research, where the codes of female chastity were coming into conflict with the perceived economic and cultural benefits associated with higher education.

In other mediterranean communities female chastity codes have been imbued with new meaning and added significance. As a case in point, Schokeid (1980) reports that among Israeli Muslim Arabs, male control over the sexual comportment of female relatives has been intensified as a symbol of ethnic and religious identity in opposition to the hegemonic Jewish majority. Schokeid further states that, on a symbolic level, the cultural emphasis on female chastity serves to align Israeli Muslim Arabs with the wider Arab world where similar codes exist.

A third situation is one in which female chastity codes exert little authoritative or persuasive power in the dynamics of everyday life. For instance, Davis tells us here that in the Libyan desert, male social worth is rarely associated with female chastity today. Likewise, Gilmore notes that Pitt-Rivers's (1971) classic account of the cultural emphasis on female chastity in Andalusia no longer holds. Writing about a south Italian community, White (1980) remarks that ''honor'' (defined in terms of female chastity) is laughingly viewed by townspeople as an anachronism. Yet, she goes on to say that fathers still enforce strict control over their daughters' behavior. Also, her male informants agreed that a man whose wife was unfaithful was unlikely to be elected to public office.

White's account suggests that contemporary beliefs and values about the social importance of female sexuality may be ambiguous and inconsistent. Such a situation should not surprise us since cultural constructs do not come together as tightly integrated systems. Rather, commonsense views of the world, including ideas about sexuality and social worth, can be deeply contradictory, especially in situations of rapid social change. It is precisely these contradictions and displacements which must be unraveled if we are to understand the diminished importance of female chastity codes in some mediterranean contexts today, along with their continued and even heightened significance in others.

Conclusion

In this paper I have suggested that comparative analyses of female chastity codes in the circum-mediterranean region focus on three interrelated areas: community/supra-local linkages, class relations, and the politics of gender. Such a conceptual approach can illuminate the material as well as ideological dimensions of female chastity codes across time and space.

As a final point, I would emphasize that investigating the codes of female chastity necessitates a research approach that transcends the limitations of a "male" or "female" perspective. Instead, efforts should be made to incorporate the ideas, perceptions, behavior, and strategies of both women and men in the family and in the wider society. Unfortunately, the gender-segregated nature of many mediterranean communities places severe constraints on the female or male researcher working alone. For instance, in the Sicilian context of my own research I found it very difficult to gain access to the world of men. One solution to this problem would be for women and men working in the same mediterranean context to share research data or, better yet, to engage in joint research projects. Through such collaborative efforts, more complete pictures of mediterranean communities and their cultural codes of female chastity will emerge.

Notes

[1]See Blok (1981) for a similar interpretation.

[2]Detailed discussions of this issue can be found in Gilmore (1982), Davis (1977), and White (1980).

[3]The rally was held at 9 P.M., when all "honest" women including myself were at home. Fortunately, I was living with a family whose apartment overlooked the piazza where the rally took place. By crouching down next to an open window, I was able to hear most of the speeches. This paper is a substantially revised version of a work first presented at the 82d annual meeting of the American Anthropological Association, Chicago, 1983, in the symposium "Honor, Shame, and the Concept of Mediterranean Unity." I wish to thank Gerrie Casey, Sandra Joshel, and Paul Mishler for helpful comments on earlier drafts of the paper.

[4]Some interesting work is already being done along these lines. See, for example, Rohrlich-Leavitt's (1976) comparative study of state formation in Crete and Sumer.

[5]The Algerian case is particularly important because of the active role that women played in the revolution and, paradoxically, their relegation to traditional roles following independence. See Rowbotham (1974) for additional information on this topic. My own experience living in an Algerian oasis town in 1969 corroborates Rowbotham's account of the postindependence situation for women in Algeria.

References Cited

Antoun, Richard
    1968   On the Modesty of Women in Arab Muslim Villages: a Study in the Accommodation of Tradition. American Anthropologist 70:671–697.
Asad, Talal
    1979   Anthropology and the Analysis of Ideology. Man 14:607–627.
Aya, R.
    1975   The Missed Revolution: The Fate of Rural Rebels in Sicily Southern Spain, 1840–1950. Amsterdam: Papers on European and Mediterranean Societies. Anthropologisch-Sociologisch-Centrum, University of Amsterdam.

Banfield, Edward
  1958 The Moral Basis of a Backward Community. Glencoe: Free Press.
Blok, Anton
  1975 The Mafia of a Sicilian Village, 1860–1960: A Study of Violent Peasant Entrepreneurs. New
    York: Harper & Row.
  1981 Rams and Billy-Goats: a Key to the Mediterranean Code of Honour. Man 16:427–440.
Boissevain, J. and E. Friedl, eds.
  1975 Beyond the Community: Social Process in Europe. The Hague: Department Educational
    Science, The Netherlands.
Cole, John
  1977 Anthropology Comes Part-way Home: Community Studies in Europe. Annual Review of
    Anthropology 6:349–378.
Davis, John
  1976 An Account of Changes in the Rules for Transmission of Property in Pisticci, 1814–1961.
    In Mediterranean Family Structures. J. G. Peristiany, ed. Pp. 287–304. Cambridge: Cambridge
    University Press.
  1977 The People of the Mediterranean: An Essay in Comparative Social Anthropology. London:
    Routledge and Kegan Paul.
Friedl, Ernestine
  1967 The Position of Women: Appearance and Reality. Anthropological Quarterly 40:97–108.
Gilmore, David
  1982 Anthropology of the Mediterranean Area. Annual Review of Anthropology 11:175–205.
Gilsenan, M.
  1977 Against Patron-Client Relations. *In* Patrons and Clients in Mediterranean Societies. E. Gell-
    ner and J. Waterbury, eds. Pp. 167–183. London: Duckworth.
Giovannini, Maureen
  1981 Woman: A Dominant Symbol Within the Cultural System of a Sicilian Town. Man 16:408–
    426.
  1985 The Dialectics of Women's Industrial Work in a Sicilian Town. Anthropology 9:45–64.
Herzfeld, Michael
  1980 Honor and Shame: Problems in the Comparative Analysis of Moral Systems. Man 15:339–
    351.
Mouzelis, N.
  1976 The Relevance of the Concept of Class to the Study of Modern Greek Society. Transactions
    of the New York Academy of Sciences 268:395–409.
Nelson, Cynthia
  1974 Public and Private Politics: Women in the Middle Eastern World. American Ethnologist
    1:551–563.
Lutton, Susan
  1980 Women Servants in Southern Italy: Changing Patterns of Honor and Economic Constraint.
    Ann Arbor: Michigan Discussions in Anthropology 66–86.
Ortner, Sherry
  1978 The Virgin and the State. Feminist Studies 4:19–33.
Peristiany, J. G., ed.
  1965 Honour and Shame: the Values of Mediterranean Society. London: Weidenfeld and Nicol-
    son.
Pitt-Rivers, Julian
  1971 The People of the Sierra. Chicago: University of Chicago Press.
Riegelhaupt, Joyce
  1979 Peasants and Politics in Salazar's Portugal: The Corporate State and Village "Nonpolitics."
    In Contemporary Portugal: The Revolution and Its Antecedents. L. S. Graham and H. M. Mak-
    ler, eds. Pp. 167–190. Austin: University of Texas Press.
Rohrlich-Leavitt, Ruby
  1976 Women in Transition: Crete and Sumer. *In* Becoming Visible: Women in European History.
    R. Bridenthal and C. Koonz, eds. Pp. 36–59. Boston: Houghton Mifflin.
Rogers, Susan
  1975 Female Forms of Power and the Myth of Male Dominance: A Model of Female/Male Inter-
    action in Peasant Society. American Ethnologist 2:727–756.
Rowbotham, Sheila
  1974 Women, Resistance, and Revolution. New York: Vintage Books.

Schneider, Jane
    1971   Of Vigilance & Virgins. Ethnology 10:1–24.
Schneider, Jane, and Peter Schneider
    1976   Culture and Political Economy in Western Sicily. New York: Academic Press.
Schokeid, Moshe
    1980   Ethnic Identity and the Position of Women Among Arabs in an Israeli Town. Ethnic and
            Racial Studies 3:188–206.
Silverman, Sydel
    1968   Agricultural Organization, Social Structure and Values in Italy. American Anthropologist
            70:1–20.
    1977   Patronage As Myth. *In* Patrons and Clients in Mediterranean Societies. E. Gellner and J.
            Waterbury, eds. Pp. 7–20. London: Duckworth Press.
Waterbury, John
    1970   The Commander of the Faithful: The Moroccan Political Elite—A Study in Segmented Pol-
            itics. New York: Columbia University Press.
White, Carolyn
    1980   Patrons and Partisans: A Study of Politics in Two Southern Italian Communities. New York:
            Cambridge University Press.

"AS IN YOUR OWN HOUSE": HOSPITALITY, ETHNOGRAPHY, AND THE STEREOTYPE OF MEDITERRANEAN SOCIETY

Michael Herzfeld

Honor or Hospitality?

The renewed interest of anthropologists in the concepts of "honor" and "shame," and in their application to comparative studies of Mediterranean societies, suggests that the original formulations of this subject were both fecund with heuristic potential, and overstrained by new ethnographic insights and discoveries. The present article illustrates this double characterization. On the one hand, I propose here that the old label of "honor" might be usefully displaced by descriptively simpler and less ambiguous glosses such as "hospitality," in order to allow more precisely calibrated comparisons. On the other hand, the argument that I develop here is clearly dependent to a significant degree on the earlier discussions of honor and shame to which it is heir. Indeed, it makes those discussions part of its own object of analysis, by suggesting that the role of the ethnographer in the generation of such categories deserves critical attention.

While neither "hospitality" nor any other term can ever perfectly gloss the broader sense of "honor"—indeed, if it could, there would be no point to the substitution—a *group* of glosses of this sort might reasonably be expected to yield new insights. Essentially, my argument depends on four closely interwoven points. Since it will not always be feasible to deal with each one separately in the discussion that follows, it would be helpful to outline them before proceeding any further. First, as I have already pointed out elsewhere in more detail, the English language gloss of "honor" is both semantically and logically suspect as a demonstration of circum-Mediterranean cultural unity (Herzfeld 1980, 1984). I suggest here that concepts like hospitality, in which such clearly identifiable social phenomena as reciprocity and proprietary rights are entailed, might provide a more convincing basis of comparison, while at the same time forcing anthropologists to extend the scope of their comparisons beyond the circum-Mediterranean area. Second, while both "honor" and "hospitality" are tied to the historical development of a Mediterranean stereotype, the latter's more precise definition allows an easier escape from the clutch of well-worn generalizations about Mediterranean character and values. Third, hospitality can be studied not only at the level of village ethnography, but also at that of its national and regional transformations—as, for example, in the stereotyping of national attitudes to tourists ("our traditional hospitality" and the like). Fourth, since the anthropologist is a guest in both the local and national senses, this expansion of the focus of interest

forces us to consider our own part in the construction of the ethnographic generalizations on which all comparison necessarily rests.

The axis on which this set of interrelated points turns is the essential homology
between several levels of collective identity—village, ethnic group, district, nation. What goes for the family home also goes, at least by metaphorical extension,
for the national territory. Although many of the concepts that have been glossed
as "honor" and "shame" are clearly expressions of inclusion and exclusion, the
architectonic image suggested by "hospitality" brings this essential aspect into
much sharper focus. Evidence for the clarity to be gained thereby may be found
in indigenous discourse. For example, in the Rhodian village that I have named
"Pefko" (cf. note 4 below, and Herzfeld 1980) a man who had raped a young
woman was said to have "entered her father's house"—a metaphor that clearly
illustrates the saliency as a component in the definition of social relations. In
Pefko, again, the 1974 invasion of Cyprus was likened to a forcible entry into
one's "house." Such transmutations of level are not uncommon elsewhere: for
example, the Spanish *pueblo* as village is congruent with the larger *pueblo* of the
district (see Pitt-Rivers 1971:6–7). The Greeks' conventional distrust of *kseni*
(outsiders) from other villages translates easily into a comparable stance toward
kseni in the sense of "foreigners." Given that the moral boundary between in-
siders and outsiders thus seems to be formally similar at several quite distinct levels of social identity, ethnographers who study hospitality are necessarily forced
to examine the assumptions that undergird their own presence in the host community. For while it may not always be clear that they are honored guests, or what
it would mean if they were, it is at least certain that they are guests.

This demands a reconsideration of how far honor and shame—or hospitality,
for that matter—are the products of an anthropology embedded in its own cultural
and historical origins, rather than of a set of objectified "Mediterranean societies." Certainly, those who sell the images of their quintessence to West European
and North American tourists have rarely hestitated to exploit the image of a uni-
formly romanticized "Mediterranean culture." Ethnographers may have unwit-
tingly contributed to the creation of this stereotype (see Fernandez 1983a; Herzfeld 1984), which also serves the interests of the industrialized nations who patronize the Mediterranean lands; an apparently primitive and homogenous code
of honor includes the delights of one-sided hospitality. For the casual visitor, at
least, there is no obvious expectation of reciprocity, beyond the gift of a few snap-
shots to one's newfound exotic friends. No ideological or political clouds of self-
consciousness mar the southern sunshine.

Social and Ideological Implications of Hospitality

The anthropologist easily recognizes the tourist's pleasant experience as an instance of "honorable" behavior. Yet the notion of a pan-Mediterranean honor
code contributes to the very same kind of exoticism, and in a potentially damaging
way. By suggesting that whole populations may be rendered incapable of con-
certed industrial and economic development by their addiction to some peculiarly
agonistic form of self-promotion, it indiscriminately separates them from their
neighbors, who are often also their political patrons. It thus also interferes with
the critical evaluation of the ethnographer's own relationship with the host community.

Although the concept of hospitality can be equally misleading, and can suggest the host community's happy acquiescence in the burden which industralist, tourist, politician and ethnographer may impose upon it, its structurally unambiguous definition as the rendering of comfort to a visitor within one's own territory leads, in some cases, to a diametrically opposed impression. Certainly, the hospitality that one meets in any Mediterranean country may be altruistic, and given with genuine pleasure. At the level of collective representations, however, where personal sentiments are replaced by structural symbols, it acquires a significantly different import. It signifies the moral and conceptual *subordination* of the guest to the host. In this way, it "englobes" the visitor, to the substituting moral advantage for political subordination.[1] In Greece, the often heard expression of hospitality, "As in your [own] house!" *(opos sto spiti sou)*, reproduces a formula of exaggerated praise that actually foregrounds its own potential for ironic inversion.

The act of hospitality can thus become a means of expressing and reversing a pattern of domination at one and the same time. The stance the host takes toward the guest reproduces collective attitudes to the social or cultural group that the latter represents. Pitt-Rivers, for example, found himself labeled a spy, a characterization that he attributed to the fear associated with strangers. But spies, we should recall, constitute a rather despicable category. Offering him hospitality was indeed a means of shifting the ethnographer's identity to a more manageable level. Indeed, the *stranger* is a "shifter" in the technical sense: its exact meaning, and more particularly the exact level at which it represents a category of exclusion, depends upon the relationship between speaker and referent as well as upon that between speaker and audience.[2] Fernandez (1983b:324–325) has emphasized the "shiftiness" of the ethnographer, surely just a special case of outsiderhood in which the local role of the ethnographer shifts into national or regional significance if the context of interpretation should also change.

The stereotype of Mediterranean hospitality has a long and as yet not very thoroughly researched history. Its popularity soared in the nineteenth century—significantly, a period of resurgent nationalism in which the solidarity of emergent nations found expression in the resuscitation of ancient codes. The conversion of Victor Hugo's play *Hernani* into a Verdi opera *(Ernani)* gives us an Italian musical drama based on a French play about a Spanish rebel. Even the sinister character Silva, who eventually forces the hero to honor his pledge to commit suicide, appeals to the ancient virtues. When Ernani comes for succor, a refugee from the king they both hate, Silva refuses to hand him over; "hospitality," he says, "was always sacred to the Silvas, and [always] will be."

The emergence of the stereotype of "southern man" (cf. Fernandez 1983a) thus coincides with the theatrical exploitation of one of the great themes of Mediterraneanist ethnography: the extreme hospitality that forces a man to shelter his bitterest foe, even though he may slay the visitor as soon as the latter leaves the house (e.g., Black-Michaud 1975:139–140; 183–184). But what is significant, as Pitt-Rivers recognized (1968:19 n. 1), is that the visitor is a stranger; no co-villager could rely on such mercy, because, by definition, a co-villager never depends on one to any meaningful degree. The very clemency shown to the stranger is the mark of his total subordination.

The intensification of the rules of hospitality seems, moreover, to increase with the social distance of the stranger from the community. In Western Crete, a man who enters a coffeehouse will be treated by someone already seated there, and may not himself treat anyone who has arrived before him at least until he has first accepted this initial gift. It is clear from the requirement that the newcomer greet the assembled company first, before anyone speaks to him or treats him, that the newcomer is ritually seeking equal status; to be "sitting" and to be "inside" are symbols of possession and power, and his right to them must be formally claimed. A visiting *ksenokhorianos* ("stranger from another village") will reciprocate the drink he is offered when he first steps into a coffeehouse by then treating the entire clientèle. Here, the ritual is more complex because the stranger must prove himself to be a true Cretan, and so a *virtual* co-villager. The true foreigner is not allowed to reciprocate at all until a strong bond of familiarity can be established, although the local host acknowledges an entirely theoretical obligation on the part of the guest through the formula that "one day I may turn up in your place." Since, however, both parties usually know that such a development is in practice unlikely to occur, the possible irony—once again!—of the host's phrase reduces the foreign visitor to a state of still deeper moral indebtedness.

When I first arrived in the village of Glendi[3] to do fieldwork, I was not often allowed to treat villagers in the coffeeshops even after I had been duly incorporated into such gatherings, until I insisted that the villagers were "not treating me as a Glendiot." This challenge, which the villagers apparently saw as amiable, called the metaphorical bluff implied by the injunction to act "as in your own house," and won me vastly increased acceptance as a *kouvardas,* a man of liberal generosity. But the point here was not that I was *just* seen as good company. I was also credited with having learned and adopted the local "customs" *(sinithia).* When I visited a nearby village notorious for its inhabitants' lack of hospitality, I reported back that I had not been warmly received in the coffeehouse that I visited there, and that the villagers had seemed surprised when I attempted to treat the whole company after, eventually, being treated myself. The Glendiots' reaction was one of pleasure and amusement: "Mikhalis has learned the Glendiot customs!" Both villages are Cretan; but here the notoriety of the other community allowed the Glendiots to claim their particular style of generosity as their very own, and thereby to include me in their number.

Thus, the *act* of hospitality is a "shifter" in the same way as the term *ksenos,* "stranger": the level of social inclusiveness from which it derives its meaning depends both on the relationship between host and guest and on the nature of the audience to which the event is presented or related. Hospitality does not only mark the host as a person of goodwill. It also indexes a set of mutually congruent social boundaries, each of which reproduces the moral implications of all the others. The ritual incorporation of the guest through toasting and feasting reproduces the assimilation of the stranger who might tell otherwise disreputable stories about the village, or who might take home negative images of the entire country.

Hospitality and Reciprocity

Much has been made of the reciprocal character of *xenia,* the guest-host relationship of antiquity (see especially Pitt-Rivers 1968). In Greece, such reciprocal relationships have persisted into recent times. On Rhodes, for example, the slow pace of animal-droving obliged shepherds to establish such mutual relationships, and a powerful shepherd could boast, "There are forty-two villages on Rhodes, and I have a *yarenis* [reciprocal term meaning 'host/guest'] in each!" In such cases, hospitality is not a wholly disinterested institution, and the long-term benefits that it brings both parties are well understood.

On Crete, the situation is even more revealing, and deserves more detailed comment. The village of Glendi is one of a relatively small group of villages where animal-theft, largely defunct elsewhere, continues to be an endemic mode of establishing social relationships between local inhabitants and members of other communities (see Herzfeld 1985). The patterns of reciprocal raiding and subsequent alliance formation are paralleled, with some local variation, in several other circum-Mediterranean and Middle Eastern societies (see especially Di Bella 1983; Meeker 1977; Moss 1979). Many Glendiot men claim that the origins of the hospitality for which their village is famous (as is Crete in general) lie in animal-theft. Men would go in search of their missing livestock, or perform this errand on behalf of co-villagers and kin, and would need places to stay in the villages they visited. Usually, they would be entertained by their own spiritual kin, themselves perhaps the end product of some earlier raiding cycle, and would be expected to reciprocate the hospitality in due course.

The connection with raiding is laden with meaning. When Glendiots raid other highland villages, they do so on the clear understanding that this is likely to prove a reciprocal business and to entail considerable danger before a suitably daunting impasse causes the protagonists to accept mediation and eventually to become spiritual kin and allies. On other occasions, however, they raid the wealthier shepherds and farmers of the lowlands and plains. Here, they represent their activity as reciprocal in a different sense: the wealthy can only have acquired their riches through the exploitation of the poor, including the highlanders, so that raiding them is an eminently justifiable act of natural justice. It also serves to underscore a difference of identity between the raiders and their victims—between, in short, the brave highland fighters and the effete lowlanders who will never have the manliness to retaliate in kind.

The most extreme play on the theme of reciprocity is found when, as sometimes happens, animal-thieves invite their victims or the police to join them at a feast; all unaware, the guests then eat the stolen meat! This is structurally analogous to giving asylum to one's blood enemy. It confers superiority on the host in two registers simultaneously: it marks his respect for the sacred laws of hospitality, while placing his foe, however superior politically, at his mercy.

Finally, again because of the political disparity that they perceive between themselves and most foreigners, Glendiots see no contradiction between their truly lavish hospitality and the many requests that they make to strangers for material and political favors. I was asked for my radio, my tape recorder, help in securing the relocation of a nephew doing military service to a base nearer home, and help in arranging the import of a hunting gun. I was also drafted into attempts to sell woven goods to passing tourists, and was expected to buy a certain amount of these for my own family and friends. Sometimes, I noticed the same pattern amongst the villagers themselves. A friend who would generously treat one in his own home could be stopped as he went by in front of a coffeehouse and be forced to surrender his day's crop of wild artichokes as a tasty tidbit for the drinkers within.

The two situations are not as dissimilar as they appear. In each case, the "victim" is pressed to give up something of which he can reasonably be expected to have an open-ended supply. I was from a wealthy country, and classified as a "scholar"—a term that carries surprising connotations of wealth! Villagers therefore assumed that I could part with these luxury goods, or that I could use my (actually nonexistent) political clout on their behalf without incurring excessive political debts of my own. In this sense, the favors they asked of me were the exact reciprocals of their own, materially more modest generosity to each other with articles like wild artichokes. Each party gives up something of which he supposedly can at some point replenish his supply. Here, the logic resembles what we have just noted for animal-raiding: the *materially nonreciprocal* exchange is recast as an *ethically and virtually reciprocal* one.

Material inconsistency is thus transformed into a symbolic mutuality that conforms to local notions of social worth, or *filotimo,* an important component of which is the ability to recognize one's social "obligations" *(ipokhreosis). Filotimo* is shown by the old women who, having nothing else to offer, gives her unexpected visitors some water and olives (Herzfeld 1980:342). The rhetorical principle at play here is that of the limiting case: since *filotimo* is defined by the ability to match the social expectations commensurate with one's presumed wealth, education, and status, those of low standing in any of these respects may illustrate *filotimo* simply by appearing to be interested trying to achieve it at all— a truly limiting case. The *social* value of one's generosity is a balance of the material value of what one gives against one's presumed level of wealth. A woman engages in hospitality, which Glendiots regard as enhancing a *man's* prestige; she is poor, which means that she cannot provide the usual accoutrements of conventional hospitality; and she is old, which exempts her from the usual obligations of a host. But she still insists on doing what she can. This is the same rhetoric of *exaggeration by inversion* that we meet in the injunction to behave "as though in your own house," and in the admiring remark to the foreigner who speaks even halting Greek: "You speak Greek better than we do!" All devices have the same rhetorical structure: they compliment the disadvantaged person (the old woman) or outsider (the guest or foreigner) on *virtually* matching the speaker's own social worth *(filotimo). Filotimo* is displayed by those who do what seems to match society's best expectations of them, and this formally structural definition appears to transcend local variations in the material or pragmatic content of the term (Herzfeld 1980: 342–345).

The converse also applies: when an outsider fails to appreciate the implications of his dependent status, he may suffer. In Pefko, a person from another community who wanted to reply to an insulting verse *(mandinadha)* was told:

Dhen ekhoun to dhikeoma na traghoudhoun i kseni,
yati tous pernoun ti provia ke fevghoun matomeni.

Kseni [outsiders] don't have the right to sing,
because [i.e., and if they do] they get their hides
    stripped off and they leave covered in blood!

A visitor who engaged in verbal duels would be thought to have acted improperly, and would therefore merit a beating.

In the same way, a group of young Texans who showed up in Glendi and expressed ungrateful annoyance that they were not being looked after properly (there was a funeral in the household of their hosts at the time) were set upon and driven physically out of the village. They had failed to appreciate that the bestowal of hospitality is not only a privilege, but one that confers a reciprocal obligation to offer respect. Such is the logic of "englobing." The young Texans, moreover, were representatives of a powerful and, in Glendi, much disliked tutelary nation. Their behavior rejected a principle to which they were perhaps unaware of having to conform: *noblesse oblige*. Once their behavior became too intolerably over-bearing, they could no longer be symbolically contained; and so they were ex-pelled instead.

Their experience makes an exemplary parable for Cretin ideas about hospitality. They were not simply strangers to the village, but also guests in Crete and in Greece. Since their behavior violated the rules of local hospitality, it also violated those of the larger entities. Du Boulay (1974:38–39) has rightly pointed out that the fear of possible consequences is not the only reason why strangers are rarely turned away; there is also a strong desire to relate the household to wider social groups in a productive way. But to this picture we should also add that there is a point beyond which both the fear of the stranger and the desire for communion with the wider world give way to the reassertion of domestic, local, and national sovereignty—to control over the metaphorical "home" at all these levels.

This characteristic, moreover, enables us to link such local-level observations with the conventional attitudes toward foreigners to be encountered as a matter of course in the national newspapers. While Greek nationalistic rhetoric makes ex-tensive use of the notion of "national *filotimo*," the more specific image of the broken rules of hospitality seems to have risen to the fore as an apt metaphorical idiom for the discussion of how to respond to the uncouth behavior of various types of tourist. In the journalistic writing that has emerged, we find an agonizing tension between the desire to present a truly hospitable face to the hordes of strangers now arriving daily in Greece, and a deeply suspicious xenophobia that has hardly been alleviated by recent experience. For this tension, the moral am-bivalence of traditional hospitality provides an excellent model, and it conse-quently plays a major role in the journalists' rhetoric. That rhetoric, in turn, fur-nishes a new perspective on the central theme of this book, by showing how the traditional values of Greek village society, duly transformed, operate at national and international levels of social discourse as well. Journalistic writing serves as a grander version of village gossip, until now the major source of insight into the practical applications of local-level morality. Let us therefore now examine some specimens of the genre.

Hospitality and the Tourist: Fleas from "Europe"

The early travelers' accounts carry many detailed descriptions of Greek hos-pitality. As tourism became heavily commercialized, however, especially since the early 1970s, Greek reactions began to sour. One of the major sources of dis-may was the discovery that not all the tourists were wealthy, and that many of them were "hippies" *(khippidhes)*—in Greek, a generic term for young people with long, unkempt hair and casual, scanty clothes. But here the question of re-ciprocity became crucial. What could these undesirables give the Greeks in return for the hospitality of the land? As the mayor of one island community (Sifnos) expressed the increasingly prevalent attitude:

We're used to men of letters—architects, artists, who come to us every year. Not these [back]pack-carriers who go and swim in the sea as though in their own bathtubs! The other day an old woman came close to giving up the ghost from the shock she had when she saw one of them naked as the day he was born. *Pa-pa-pa!* Sifnos has a tradition of tourism and isn't about to give it up. [*Apoy-evmatini*, Aug. 30, 1976, p. 3]

The attitude seems, on the surface, blunt enough. Hairy foreigners with no money are dirty; therefore, they should be kept out of the country. There is certainly an audience for this attitude, which is endorsed with notable warmth by some sectors of the church hierarchy.

But there are also those who argue that to refuse the "hippies" the right to enter the country violates the spirit of free movement among the nations; that it argues a disturbing intolerance of cultural differences; that it places wealth above a desire to learn; and, most significantly of all, that it constitutes a violation of the traditions of Greek hospitality. Once again, newspapers are a valuable source of conventional responses. Compare two statements, of which the first is a bitter attack on the offending foreigners, and on those Greek officials who defend their right to "Greek hospitality":

> Then again, it is time that the traditional spirit of Greek hospitality was adapted to the prevailing international conditions so as not to provoke through its excesses the ironic responses of the usually cold and stingy foreigners. [Th. Papakonstandinou, *Akropolis*, Oct. 5, 1975, p. 5]

Foreigners, most of whom come from the industrialized countries of the frigid north, are thus recast in the terms of a symbolic opposition—Mediterranean generosity and warmth vs. the calculating avarice of the North—that may indeed have originated in their own condescending stereotypes (cf. Herzfeld 1984, for a fuller discussion). These foreigners are stingy—a complaint that is echoed by the Rhodian villager[4] who objected to the youthful tourist couple who shared a single omelette in his café rather than buying one apiece. The stingy stereotype may also imply an analogy with the Gypsies: the latter group is stigmatized for its nomadic habits, as are the "poverty-tourists," and *yiftos* (a derogatory name for "Gypsy") is also a common synonym for "miserly." By assimilating the poor representatives of the dominant powers to one of the Greeks' own most despised minorities, the villagers can exploit the despised visitors to assert a sense of their own moral superiority.

For the Rhodian villager, the sharing of the omelette contrasted with the generosity of the *kouvardas*—the man who expansively treats all his friends without a thought for the damage to his pocket. An outstanding instance in his own community was furnished by a co-villager who returned from a long period of residence in Australia, distributing handfuls of his newfound wealth as widely as he could. In the same way, the author of the newspaper article just quoted objects to the presence of the "unwashed beard-wearers," accusing them of bearing every evil from venereal disease to drug peddling, and contrasts them to the almost simplemindedly generous Greeks.

But there is another dimension to his diatribe that deserves comment. It appears especially in a caustic reference to these "poverty-tourists" as "tomorrow's generation of scholars and tomorrow's ruling class of Europe, America, Asia, and Australia, which will also be the herald of Greek tourism." The bitterness apparently stems from the notion that the youthful spongers are actually the true heirs of their exploitative societies. The wealthy tourist can at least be exploited. The "hippies," on the other hand, take everything, but own nothing that can be taken from them. Their presence is somehow an abuse of the system, because it subverts the balance of reciprocity between foreign exploitation and local cunning that tourism of the grander sort has helped to create. The *alitotouristes* ("layabout-tourists") represent the *inversion* of a symbolic system in action: they are poor, in a frame of reference that opposes the poverty of the *Greeks* to the wealth of the *foreigners,* while at the same time their evident marginality and their stereotypic association with sexual and other forms of depravity fuels the sense of moral superiority that the writer feels toward the west.

But not all Greek writers (or villagers) respond to the hirsute hippie in the same way. The title of another, very different piece parodies a classical proverb, an injunction to give hospitality to strangers; such irony at the expense of the ancient heritage would hardly ever find a place in the more self-serious rhetoric of more aggressively conservative writers (P. Paleologos, *To Vima,* Aug. 18, 1976, p. 1):[5]

> The tourists to whom I refer do not belong to the luxury class. They are those whom the Athenians' sense of propriety has named "poor tourists," "layabout-tourists," "lice-tourists" *(ftokhotouristes, alitotouristes, psirotouristes),* and those who [take it upon themselves to] interpret public opinion demand that the country be ringed about with barbed wire so that entry may be permitted only to those who bring foreign currency.
>
> I see them with their backpacks on their shoulders, with indications of poverty in their faces, with discrimination in their glance, and I think about the fate of a word, the word *filoksenia* ("hospitality"). The registered trademark of antiquity, Zeux Xenios ("the Zeus of Guests"). The simplest, the truly divine title of the father of the gods.
>
> The heir of the ancient world is the modern Greek one. If you deny this, people get mad. We put hospitality forward as one of our virtues.
>
> But the [proverb] "give hospitality to your hosts" (*ksenous ksenize* [the phrase parodied in the title of the article]) is tending to get restricted to those who can pay for their presence in [foreign] exchange.

In short, this argument is actually a negotiation of the meaning of hospitality. Is hospitality possible under conditions of commercialization? The National Tourist Organization, which used the name *Ksenia* (the ancient word for the reciprocal host-guest relationship) for its hotel chain, clearly thought it was. But the author of the more liberal of the two newspaper articles under consideration took an idealistic stance that would have delighted Marcel Mauss: why should we reject these youthful voyagers and seekers after knowledge simply because they are poor? We have turned the very father of the gods into a commercial emblem, a "registered trademark."[6] Greek hospitality, with its echoes of antiquity, has become a commodity.

The more liberal article is revealing in another sense also. Rather than attempting to imply that the Greeks with their ancient heritage are the natural allies of foreigners of the respectable kind, it suggests that the more *scruffy* tourists have something to teach the *Greeks*. It thus challenges one of the basic tenets of neoclassicism: the ruling classes of "Europe" have always been inspired by fundamentally Hellenic moral principles. It points out that these poorer tourists set an excellent example that Greek schoolteachers would do well to bring to their young charges' attention: they expend much effort and learning on studying the monuments of antiquity that the Greeks themselves ignore.

Newspapers are a valuable source of data about the symbolism of national identity; their wide distribution makes it virtually certain that the schematized discussions they carry represent popular discourse on a scale far greater than that conventionally addressed by ethnographers. Moreover, there are some striking echoes in this material of voices already heard in the established ethnographic accounts; for example, the allusion to Zeus Xenios recalls the proud boasts of the villagers studied by Friedl: "the villagers associate certain qualities with Greek ethnicity . . . [including] the hospitality extended to strangers often at the expense of the family—they cite *Ksenios Zefs* (Zeus, the patron of strangers) and the sheltering of individuals during the German occupation" (1962:105–106). Whether a community is *literally* hospitable or not is immaterial; its claims to Greekness presuppose that it is at least formally possessed of the ancient virtue.

The basic gestures of hospitality toward the western stranger are a means of containing the danger that the latter represents through a conflation of outsider-hood and presence within the community (cf. also Simmel 1971:146; Pitt-Rivers 1968): he may be a spy, a government agent, or an exploitative developer. The formal gestures of hospitality not only contain the stranger *qua* person, moreover, but also signify encompassing levels of interaction: the stranger in one's house is also perhaps a foreigner in the land.

Perhaps the most extreme illustration of this is an insistence, common on Rhodes (Booth and Booth 1928:147), that Turks should be entertained with especially lavish attention: once the representatives of the dominant political and religious group internally, they still represent a potent external threat on Rhodes, where incidents of suspected Turkish espionage are far from uncommon. By inviting a Turk (or any foreigner) into one's home, one simultaneously incorporates the potentially dangerous representative of a feared foreign power and expresses pride in the national virtue of hospitality. The house, the village, and the very land itself have become so intimately linked that the act of inviting the stranger in for a meal is no longer *simply* a matter of kindness, or of personal pride, but a characteristic demonstration of Greekness. At the same time, the operation of reciprocity is raised to a correspondingly larger level. When I protested that villagers were treating me too kindly, they would almost invariably respond that I could repay them when they decided to show up at my far distant home (cf. also Pitt-Rivers 1968:24). Such assurances delicately reaffirmed the existence of infrangible boundaries. The villagers, not I, were at home; and the level at which the mutual obligations were now set also defined the salient level of identity as that of *nationality*.

Such uses of reciprocity to signify something other than itself are ethnographically far from uncommon. Schwimmer, for example, has demonstrated how the intensification of Australian tourism in Orokaiva has resuscitated the older patterns of exchange as signs of local identity, in contrast to that of the foreigners (1979:283). In the same way, the influx of tourism in Greece has intensified a process already begun by the educational establishment, whereby the very idea of hospitality has come to signify being Greek. This process can perhaps best be seen in negative instances: Peristiany (1968:80 n. 1), for example, reports that a politically left-wing visitor to the Greek Cypriot community he studied was told that the expression of his views "betrayed the hospitality" of the village. Since, until recently, left-wing ideologies were actually labeled as "anti-Greek," one can see very clearly in this example the operation of congruence between national and local levels of collective identity, and the deployment of the idiom of hospitality as a means of defining both.

The emphasis on hospitality developed in these examples shows a clear demarcation between attitudes that can be simply *entertained* toward certain categories of stranger, and attitudes that can and are directly *expressed* to them. Except in extreme cases like that of the Texans who were thrown out of Glendi for their insolence, Greeks rarely if ever actually show the *alitotouristes* the contempt they feel for them. They simply regard the poor behavior of the latter as confirming what they already know, namely that these extremely dependent beings are *ipso facto* morally inferior.

A Patras restaurateur told me (1984) that he did not want such "barefoot" *(ksi-politi)* customers in his *de luxe* establishment. His ambivalence toward foreigners was reproduced in the décor of the restaurant: he claimed to have only popular *(laiko)* Greek food, but the restaurant itself was decorated in markedly "European" fashion, with Italian ceiling moldings and an enlarged French engraving of a bourgeois gentleman treating his guests to champagne, on the wall separating the (entirely Greek) kitchen from the dining area. Moreover, despite his talk, he repeatedly ran after *alitotouristes* to get them to sit down in the outside area in front of the restaurant even though he must have anticipated poor takings from them.

His expressions of contempt for these lowly tourists were nevertheless not necessarily duplicitous. They expressed the strains inherent in his experience of the tourist "invasion." He needed the small pittances the poorer tourists brought him, since during the daytime at least they were far more numerous than the well-heeled local customers he claimed as his true constitutency. At the same time, it must have been galling to him that the only constant representatives of the "European" culture to which he aspired could pay him so little, and yet still be so essential to his survival. His attitude thus represents a way of dealing with this humiliating situation. "Europeans" (and in context this term includes North Americans) are englobed as morally base, stingy ingrates, whose behavior violates the expectations of the local businessman—whose own morality thereby comes to seem more "European" and "respectable" than that of his foreign customers. (The point of the French engraving seemed to be that it symbolically converted the Greek kitchen products into "European" dining.) The category of "Europeans" is ambivalent in Greek: it both includes and excludes the Greeks themselves. Thus, the restaurateur was conforming, in his own fashion, to a deeply rooted sense of ambiguity about the correct approach to strangers whose own behavior violates the local idealization of both "Europeans" and "Greek hospitality." The importance of this kind of ambivalence emerges most strongly when we recognize the political inequalities that generate and nurture it.

In general, the representatives of the Greek tourist industry continue to purvey traditional Greek hospitality. Again, this is not so much hypocrisy as a response to global political realities. As such, it reproduces at an international level the sometimes painfully ambiguous attitude that the traditional concept of hospitality represents. Local entrepreneurs may genuinely want their clients to enjoy themselves, and may take true pride in their work. But this does not preclude an inbuilt assumption, easily decoded from the tourist industry's advertising, that the visitors are morally beholden to their Greek hosts for the simple joys of life—a fair exchange, the implicit argument goes, for the economic dominance of the tourists' national cultures over that of Greece. Since the wealthier visitors have indeed come to learn such Zorbaesque enjoyment from the Greeks, while their poorer counterparts are charged with introducing such undesirable horrors as bugs, drugs, and nudism, the Greeks experience a symbolic reversal of the reciprocal obligation that accompanies traditional norms of hospitality. Now, while the wealthier strangers are seen as receiving the commodity for which they came, the apparently poorer ones (who nevertheless still come from rich countries) are thought to violate the norms of hospitality by their supposed stinginess.

These perspectives do not so much represent the collapse of some ancient idyll of generosity as the symbolic transformation of its material terms. The modern rhetoric appears to justify the more exploitative aspects of the tourist trade, transforming the entire relationship from an informal to a bureaucratically regulated one; the point is nicely made by a cartoon in which, under the general caption "Are tourists bringing us fleas?" a stern-faced customs officer is seen admonishing an obviously foreign couple, "Of course, the import of weapons, hashish, and bugs is prohibited!" (Skoulas, in *Apoyevmatini,* Aug. 30, 1976, p. 14). Under the new circumstances, the Greeks—who reject all the evils that the *alitotouristes* bring—always end up giving of their spiritual heritage; they are the ones who open up their collective home to these dangerous strangers, never to receive more than a banal, financial return at best, but just as probably nothing more than disease and corruption. As unilateral givers, then, the Greeks are enabled to use the moral implications of reciprocity to reverse the historical and political dependence of their country upon the West. Hospitality is the social format that permits Greeks to englobe the dominant cultures of Europe.

Conclusions: Hospitality and Ethnographic Comparison

Hospitality is thus able to mediate between different but congruent levels of social and cultural identity: household, village, island, nation, and—more recently—the geopolitical entity known as "the Mediterranean." As a component in the stereotypes of all these levels, it has become a symbol for ever larger forms of collective identification. It is actively *constitutive,* rather than simply a *component,* of the stereotype of Mediterranean culture. This leads to much the same conclusion as my earlier discussions of honor and shame and the evil eye: that "the Mediterranean" deserves should be treated as an ethnographic datum for analysis, rather than exclusively as an analytical category. Whether it can *also* be used effectively in the latter sense is dependent on how far we can disembed it from its ideological matrix within the cultures whose characteristics we study and whose hospitality we receive.

Two main themes seem to emerge from the foregoing. First, the presence of lavish hospitality in Greek villages is an expression both of the moral superiority of the host and of the political potential of the guest. Second, and consistently, both sides have an interest in maintaining these implications. The hospitality I have described reproduces in an active, spatial, and symbolic frame the ideological structure of patron-client relations (see especially Campbell 1964): it is the moral englobing of political asymmetry that allows the client to maintain self-respect while gaining material advantage.

Most of the circum-Mediterranean nation-states have experienced the humiliation of international tutelage, and most of them also reproduce the same pattern in class relations within their own local social systems. Is it pure coincidence that these countries should both promote and resent the stereotype of their "hospitality" as presented to foreign tourists? And what does the emergence of such a pattern contribute to our understanding of the role of the ethnographer in such a society? For once we focus on hospitality, we see more clearly what closer attention to the problematic of honor ought to have taught us long ago: that the ethnographic phenomenon that we are making the basis of our comparative research is also a *condition* of that research. One hopes that anthropologists are well past the stage of interpreting hospitality as signifying nothing more than the friendliness of the natives. But if the relationship is indeed a more complex and ambivalent one, and is merely a part of that more diffuse complex glossed by the phrase "honor and shame," we will get nowhere by simply matching it to Mediterranean stereotypes. To do so, moreover, undermines the goals of comparativism by turning a highly productive heuristic concept ("hospitality") into an *a priori* conclusion ("Mediterranean hospitality").

"Honor" itself can of course be used heuristically. Indeed, had it never been cast as a first approximation, the insights resulting from its progressive deconstruction would perhaps never have been gained; but its reification, by the same token, renders those insights inaccessible. Let me illustrate with a final ethnographic example. Like most anthropologists working in Greece, powerfully influenced by what I had read, I was anxious to collect whatever materials I could find on the subject of *filotimo*. Glendiots often told me, in response to my direct questioning, that *"filotimo* was hospitality *(filoksenia)."* For a long time, I simplistically assumed that this theoretical statement of equivalence made hospitality a single—if notably clear—illustration of *filotimo* as entailing the recognition of social obligations. But why make *filotimo* rather than *filoksenia* the primary category? Perhaps the other instances of what we have called honor for so long might more appropriately be treated in terms of hospitality, obligation, and so forth? The Glendiot's response to my questions showed that awarding honor logical priority over hospitality meant potentially violating the indigenous hierarchy of moral concepts.

The obvious next step, then, is to see how far the *equivalence* implied by the copula *("filotimo is* a [*sic*] hospitality") corresponds to other evidence. Next, we need to find out how far Glendiot usage is idiosyncratic within the larger Greek linguistic context—emphasizing *filoksenia* rather than *filotimo* as the common point of comparison this time (cf. Herzfeld 1980). To those who would complain that this places excessive reliance on purely linguistic evidence, I offer two answers. First, the linguistic evidence need not (and should not) be treated in isolation from the social context from which it is derived; it merely serves as the most accessible point of entry into a more all-embracing social analysis. Second, if we reject linguistic evidence altogether, it becomes all the more important to abandon vaguely defined concepts in favor of crisper ones for the purposes of comparative analysis. By narrowing the semantic range of our own analytical vocabulary, and perhaps concomitantly increasing the number of terms available to us, we increase both the precision and the heuristic power of our comparisons. All of these considerations advance the claim of a constellation of descriptive and analytic terms like hospitality over those of the broad and ambiguous notion of honor.

Honor, moreover, has become so strongly associated with Mediterranean anthropology that the very use of the term discourages comparisons with other lands. When arguments do stray beyond the Mediterranean littoral, they usually apply to preemptively labeled "Mediterranean" cultures such as those of Latin America—as striking an instance of cultural expansionism and Eurocentrism as one could hope to find, and a self-fulfilling prophecy to boot. Analytical discourse should begin with a critical perspective on the entire presuppositional framework that permits assumptions of Mediterranean unity. The cultural implications of *Ernani* may not be so far removed from those of the division, in current geopolitical symbolism, between "north" and "south."

The thoroughness and clarity of the ethnographies written during the heyday of anthropological Mediterraneanism are the very source of whatever critical response we can muster. If we now focus for a while on "hospitality" and related concepts, rather than on their conflation as "honor," this should not lead us to view hospitality as the principal definiens of Mediterranean society. On the contrary, it should lead to a more critical inspection of the notion of "Mediterranean society" itself. As a result, we may expect a dual redeployment of emphasis— toward more localized comparisons on the one hand, and toward a more global formulation of the key concepts on the other. In that case, we may one day be able to look back on "Mediterranean anthropology" much as we already do on *Ernani,* as a culturally, politically, and historically localized discourse. This is the direction in which the logic of comparativism now beckons.

Notes

Acknowledgments. This paper is essentially a continuation of the argument developed in two earlier studies (Herzfeld 1980, 1984), the second of which was presented at the Washington panels on which the present volume is based but had already been committed for publication. The brief remarks that constitute the present paper develop an argument that I sketched on that occasion, to the effect that "hospitality" might make a more useful basis for comparative analysis than "honor and shame" because of its more clearly defined formal features. I am grateful to David Gilmore for providing me with this forum for some further exploration of these issues, and to Roger Just and Akis Papataxiarchis for their critical responses at a later stage in the development of this essay. I would also like to acknowledge the benefit of grants-in-aid from Indiana University (Office of Research and Graduate Development, Russian and East European Institute, and West European Studies Center), which, in the summer of 1984, enabled me to reconsider the problematic of this paper in the light of ideological tensions between different national self-images in Greece.

[1]"Englobing," a term originally coined by E. Ardener for the process or condition of dominance whereby "one structure blocks the power of actualization of the other" (1975:25) is as applicable to informal levels of mutual representation as it is to intellectual interactions on a national or international scale.

[2]On "shifters" in this sense, see especially Silverstein 1976.

[3]"Glendi" is a highland pastoral village in the Mylopotamos district, Rethimni nome, western Crete (population approximately 1,400), where I conducted fieldwork for a total of over 15 months between 1974 and 1981. See Herzfeld 1980, 1985.

[4]From "Pefko," a small (population 160), depopulated agricultural village on the west coast of Rhodes, where I conducted six months of fieldwork during 1973–74 (see also Herzfeld 1980).

[5]The two articles under discussion are coded as ideologically distinct from each other. The diatribe against poor foreign tourists appeared in a conservative newspaper, and is written in a version of the neoclassical register of Greek *(katharevousa)*. The article to which we now turn, by contrast, appeared in a more liberal newspaper, and is written in a demotic Greek very close to everyday speech. It is also much more critical of Greeks' attitudes to their own culture, whereas the previous article attacked only those policymakers whose decisions contradicted the author's ideological preferences. In short, the two articles jointly represent the complementary opposition between extroverted idealizations of Hellenic culture and the more introspective image that permits irony and collective self-deprecation— self-views that have a complex history in modern Greece.

[6]"Registered trademark" *(sima katatethen)* is an ironical phrase here, neoclassical linguistically *(katharevousa)* and brutally commercial in its implications. The use of the formal language here is a way of rather bitterly suggesting a close association between ideological conservatism, cultural formality, and political and economic exploitation.

References Cited

Ardener, Edwin
1975   The 'Problem' Revisited. *In* Defining Females. Shirley Ardener, ed. Pp. 19–27. London: John Wiley.
Black-Michaud, Jacob
1975   Cohesive Force: Feud in the Mediterranean and the Middle East. Oxford: Blackwell.
Booth, C. D., and Isabelle Bridge Booth
1928   Italy's Aegean Possessions. London: Arrowsmith.
Campbell, J. K.
1964   Honour, Family, and Patronage: A Study of Institutions and Moral Values in a Greek Mountain Community. Oxford: Clarendon Press.
Di Bella, Maria Pia, ed.
1983   Dossier: Les Représentations du Vol de Bétail dans les Sociétés Méditéranéennes. Production Pastorale et Société: Bulletin de l'Équipe Écologie et Anthropologie des Sociétés Pastorales 13:4–83.
du Boulay, Juliet
1974   Portrait of a Greek Mountain Village. Oxford: Clarendon.
Fernandez, James W.
1983a   Review article: Consciousness and Class in Southern Spain. American Ethnologist 10:165–173.
1983b   Afterword: At the Center of the Human Condition. Semiotica 46(2/4):323–330.
Friedl, Ernestine
1962   Vasilika: A Village in Modern Greece. New York: Holt, Rinehart and Winston.
Herzfeld, Michael
1980   Honor and Shame: Some Problems in the Comparative Analysis of Moral Systems. Man 15:339–351.
1984   The Horns of the Mediterraneanist Dilemma. American Ethnologist 11:439–454.
1985   The Poetics of Manhood: Contest and Identity in a Cretan Mountain Village. Princeton: Princeton University Press.
Meeker, Michael E.
1979   Literature and Violence in North Arabia. Cambridge: Cambridge University Press.
Moss, David
1979   Bandits and Boundaries in Sardinia. Man 14:477–496.
Pitt-Rivers, Julian
1968   The Stranger, the Guest, and the Hostile Host: Introduction to the Study of the Laws of Hospitality. *In* Contributions to Mediterranean Sociology. J. G. Peristiany, ed. Pp. 13–30. Paris: Mouton.
1971   The People of the Sierra. 2d edition. Chicago: University of Chicago Press.
Schwimmer, Erik
1979   Reciprocity and Structure: A Semiotic Analysis of Some Orokaiva Exchange Data. Man 14:271–285.
Silverstein, Michael
1976   Shifters, Linguistic Categories, and Cultural Description. *In* Meaning in Anthropology. Keith H. Basso and Henry A. Selby, eds. Pp. 11–55. Albuquerque: University of New Mexico Press.
Simmel, Georg
1971   The Stranger. *In* Georg Simmel, On Individuality and Social Forms. Donald N. Levine, ed. Pp. 143–149. Chicago: University of Chicago Press. [1908]

HONOR, HONESTY, SHAME:
MALE STATUS IN CONTEMPORARY ANDALUSIA

David D. Gilmore

"But why should honor outlive honesty?"
—*Othello*, V, ii.

All moral communities may have some form of honor and shame (cf. Peristiany 1965:10). But in the Mediterranean area these moral twins have been portrayed in a particular light. First, both honor and disgrace are said to be acquired by men principally through women, specifically through female sexual misconduct (Pitt-Rivers 1977:78). In southern Italy, "impropriety is said to be a character trait acquired through women" (Davis 1973:69). In Greece, women are the "weak link" in the chain of honor (Campbell 1964:199). Thus women are paradoxically powerful because of their potential for collective disgrace: "Women hold in their hands the power not merely to put pressure on their menfolk but actually to 'ruin' them" (Pitt-Rivers 1977:80). Second, shame is mainly the property of women. Mediterranean men become dishonored through their women: shame governs the moral relations between the sexes (cf. Brandes 1980:87–91).

Third, honor tends to be viewed as a zero-sum contest. Men achieve honor by taking it from others; the existence of an honor code leading to "quarrels among equals" (Davis 1977:98). Pitt-Rivers (1977:92) says: "the honour you strip from others becomes yours." Mediterranean honor therefore involves "the domination of other men" (Blok 1981:431), and "the claim to excel over others" (Pitt-Rivers 1977:3). Hence honor is nothing if not "aggressive" (Pitt-Rivers 1977:78);[1] and it follows logically that achieving honor involves defeating or deceiving other men, often in erotic contests. Hart (1976:125) reports for Moroccan Berbers: "How to be a man involves cuckolding others."

This "pecking order" model of honor (Pitt-Rivers 1965:23) is useful, but it easily leads to distortion, because it excludes a broad range of less contentious male virtues that are also typically Mediterranean. To his credit, Pitt-Rivers (1965) perceives the problem and attempts to resolve it by introducing the contrast honor = precedence vs. honor = virtue. This arbitrary division is probably logically valid, but it begs the question of what Mediterranean honor is by dividing it up into contrasting categories and by calling different things honorable. So we are left with the question as to how a conciliatory honor = virtue integrates with the aggressive ideals and demands of a competitive masculinity.

More recently other anthropologists have addressed this issue. Davis (1977), Herzfeld (1980), and Blok (1981) have shown that principles of male status comprise many elements other than a minatory phallic dominance. Equally important are economic success, physical prowess (however also related to manliness), and family autonomy. But they also recognize less aggressive criteria like hospitality, integrity, and generosity. While these other values are certainly compatible with honor, they do suggest that it is more complicated and variable—in effect, richer—than the pioneers suspected.

Yet it is perhaps no exaggeration to say that a quintessential sameness still pervades descriptions of shame. As a social and psychological phenomenon, shame has yet to receive an analytic treatment comparable to the concern for honor. Being "inexorably" associated with female virtue (Luque Baena 1974:147), shame retains an undiluted, almost monolithic meaning of passive sexual chastity or modesty. It is not earned, but innate; it can only be lost, not gained (Pitt-Rivers 1977:29). It is inherited matrilineally as is the stigma of its loss. This leaves the impression of an androcentric perspective in which male virtues are relative, based on variable cultural accomplishments, while female attributes are genetic or "natural." Thus the latter need no further explanation. And despite the refinements described above in the study of honor, the impression lingers that honor is a "system of stratification" entailing "acceptance of superordination and subordination" (Davis 1977:98) based largely on female shame.

Honor and Male Status in Contemporary Andalusia

Southern Spain (Andalusia) is a typically Mediterranean society, both culturally and ecologically. Occupied by the Moors for seven centuries, Andalusia retains many of the classic features of the so-called pan-Mediterranean culture type (cf. Davis 1977; Boissevain 1979), especially in concepts of male and female, and in associated symbols and ideologies. Here I would like to describe notions of male virtue in one Andalusian town and in conclusion to offer some trial postulations about these findings and their relevance for Mediterranean ethnography.

My argument here is this: male status in Mediterranean societies is based not only on a rivalrous sex-linked "honor," but also on cooperative norms of intrasex conduct. Obviously this is not an entirely original idea. Nor is it incompatible with the pecking-order model. As mentioned above, many authors have alluded to the ambivalence of honor and of other male status criteria in passing. But perhaps in keeping with the emphasis on flamboyant sexual rivalry, few have explored the implications of the plebeian honor = virtue conception. Two who have done so are Michael Murphy (1983a, 1983b) and Michael Herzfeld (1980; this volume). Herzfeld (1980:344) notes that Greek male self-esteem *(filotimo)* consists largely of living up to expectations and obligations to peers. Rather than exacerbate tensions, *filotimo* instead acts "as a break on aggressively competitive behavior." (A more recent work [1985], though, goes back to masculine "contests"—so one wonders.)

Likewise, Murphy (1983a:651) notes that male position in Seville is involved with norms of sociability, especially trustworthiness and deference. Caro Baroja (1965:118) points out that dishonorable men in Spain are not only cuckolds, but also cheats and frauds and those "who possess unpleasant habits in money matters." Peristiany (1965:181) also notes that in Greece a man's prestige depends largely upon filial respect; dishonor stems not only from sexual shame, but also from "neglect of duty." Pitt-Rivers (1965:57) too, briefly getting off the subject of "affront" and "challenge," observes that male reputation in Spain can involve reciprocal fiscal responsibilities. Noting the value attached to "honesty" *(hon-*

radez) in money matters, he remarks (1965:39): "Reputation is not only a matter of pride, but of practical utility. Where free associations of a contractual kind govern the forms of cooperation and enterprise, a good name is the most valuable of assets." Perhaps we might systematize these observations by adding the following proposition: where male dependencies are consciously recognized in the form of socioeconomic obligations, one will find codes of male status which elevate compliance in contract to equal place with erotic one-upmanship. I do not mean to argue that cooperative norms *replace* the competitions of a narcissistic masculinity where men recognize mutual needs, but rather that these sublimated courtesies can soften these ever present competitions to a greater or lesser degree or can rechannel their energies.

The Local Setting

The social context is the agrotown of Fuenmayor (a pseudonym).[2] Today with about 8,000 inhabitants, the town is located in the midst of the alluvial Guadalquivir River Basin—the "Great Valley" (Wadi-al-Kabir) of the Moors. The fertile municipal territory comprises about 15,000 flat hectares, virtually all of it arable. The vast majority of the town's economically active population makes its living at agriculture, mainly the dry cultivation of wheat, olives, and other Mediterranean cultivars. Farming has been heavily mechanized since the 1960s, and extensive: the large estate, or latifundio, worked by day laborers predominates. However, there are many smaller extensions, including postage-stamp "minifundios."

People engaged in agriculture today are divided, by both objective indexes of wealth and subjective criteria of categorization, into three main social classes: big landowners (called "señoritos in the Andalusian fashion); peasants called by a localism, "mayetes"; and semi-migratory farm workers—"jornaleros" or "peones." The señoritos, who are mainly educated and well connected, comprise about 1% of the town's total population, but control about 52% of the arable land. The mayetes make up about 22% of the population. Although controlling about 44% of the land, they had little access to political power during the Franco Regime (1936–76) when the municipal government was firmly in the hands of the elite. The workers, who have barely 2% of the resources, make up the gross numerical majority of the pueblo. Even more than the peasants, they were excluded from political affairs during the Dictatorship. Since the turn of century, both workers and peasants have maintained strong political and trade union traditions, reflecting a history of radical class consciousness. Today, the freely elected mayor is a Communist.[3]

In many respects, Fuenmayor fits the familiar Mediterranean pattern of structural and psychological atomism (Gilmore 1978, 1980a). The nuclear family predominates; the economy is poor and undercapitalized; agrarian wage work is scarce and declining; and outside of farming there are few opportunities for advancement. In 1975, the average unemployment rate for farm workers was over 25%, but in the "dead times" of summer and early spring the absolute majority of workers were idled by lack of work. Laborers in Fuenmayor as in most Andalusian agrotowns suffer greatly therefore from penury; typically the answer for them, as for many poorer peasants, has been cyclical emigration (Gilmore 1980b).

At first glance Fuenmayor's society of scarcity seems to nourish a model of south European competitive familism. Men and women compete daily for land and bread, for jobs, for suitable spouses in a dwindling pool, and of course for personal and family reputation. The cumulative ethos is what Pitt-Rivers (1977) calls agonistic, that is, fractious. Yet these structural oppositions can be exaggerated if viewed out of context. For the very conditions of economic insecurity and familism, combined with the lack of elite patronage, also create secondary dependencies and needs that serve to mitigate open strife among peers. For example, the consciousness of job scarcity and of class struggle has led many workers to a recognition of mutual need and to an awareness of the desirability of class solidarity. These historical understandings have, in turn, produced a measure of reciprocal employment and other social assistance. Among farm workers, any man who undercut his fellows in the job market or who concealed information would soon acquire a deplorable reputation. This might hamper his chances later in finding work, since workers depend often upon a grapevine mutuality in finding jobs. A man who freely shared such information, or who aided comrades in getting work, would find his own chances immeasurably improved.

Similarly, because of simple propinquity there is an unstated understanding of at least minimal mutual obligations in crises or emergencies. Too poor to acquire formal bank credit, and lacking stable elite patronage, workers and peasants depend upon one another for loans, child care, and for other forms of neighborly back-scratching. Unlike what is described for Sicily (Schneider and Schneider 1976), stealth, cunning, and deceit are neither particularly admirable nor workable strategies in Andalusia. Although these things happen more than occasionally, they are always deplored by everyone. Naturally there are tensions and rampant suspicions, but their open expression is confined to gossip, backbiting, and mutual avoidance. As in Greece (cf. Herzfeld, this volume), generosity is a celebrated virtue which can conceal a multitude of secret animosities.

Male Status: A Bundle of Virtues

Any discussion of honor-and-shame in Fuenmayor begins with the recognition that the Castilian terms *honor* and *honora*,[4] both roughly equivalent to the old-fashioned English "honor," are virtually obsolete. The operative evaluative conception for both men and women today—at least that which bears a linguistic label—is *vergüenza*, or shame. For most people in Fuenmayor, except perhaps the most traditional latifundists, "honor," in the sense of claims to excellence, suggests a vestigial aristocratism, as quaint and archaic as "cuckold" would sound to modern American urbanites. Not that being cuckolded would not be fiercely resisted in Spain, but the state of being such no longer forms a social *category*. In this way Andalusians have approached northern European sensibilities in the past few decades.

If you mention "honor" to a local man, you may get a bemused response like, "Ah yes, we know about that; it's in the plays of Lope de Vega, Spanish pride of the Siglo del Oro," that is, the seventeenth century. A man may puff out his chest a bit if you are a foreigner, especially in bars, and sometimes educated people make proud references to the romantic traditions that every schoolchild learns as heritage to the supposed amaranthine national glory. Others may comment philosophically on the collapse of the chivalry of the past, with perhaps a little rue or whimsy in their tone. But a personal "honor" contrasts almost comically with modern morality and everyday concerns, especially among average men. Acutely aware of the decline of a prideful Spanish "honor," many workers and peasants like to recite a favorite motto that expresses their disinterest in the ancient ideal: "Somos todos honrados hasta que dejamos de serlo," roughly "We're all honorable, that is, until we stop being honorable." The ideal may be there, but when put to the test, it evaporates like the ephemeral Andalusian dew in midsummer.

A classical honor-of-precedence then is not a serious concern for most Andalusians today. But townsmen do speak often of another moral formality, a central concern. This is what they describe as being *honesto,* or honest. For example, when I asked if a certain man was "honorable" *(honrado),* I was informed that if I meant honest, then yes, this man measured up: he paid his debts. The nature of this honesty is communicated simply in this casual summation: it means being trustworthy or reliable in the society of peers, in this sense differing little from the ethical standards conveyed by the businesslike English "honest," for which my dictionary gives "trustworthy and credible" as alternate glosses. This honesty has little to do with the conduct of one's women, although there is an important connection with sexuality that I will discuss later. Rather honesty is social *ethics,* demanding scrupulous compliance in social commitments: simple quotidian virtues, what Brandes calls "estimates of personal decency" (1980:48; see also Lison Tolosana 1968). Its yardstick is shame (vergüenza). If a man has shame, they say, he acts honestly, he complies to expectations. The unethical, dishonest man is shameless and "brazen-faced"; he callously ignores obligations and thumbs his nose at public censure.

This Andalusian honesty may be elaborated further. Its internal mechanism and its social (thus measurable) manifestation is a punctilious—though implicit—reciprocity, usually balanced and predictable. Obviously, a comparison can be made here to Herzfeld's "hospitality": both rest on reciprocal obligations. The evaluative arena is not only the bedroom (but it is that too, as we shall see) but also the marketplace, the social locus being various material and social exchanges among men and women. Moreover, as townsmen insisted, honesty and shame, and the obligations they entail, vary depending upon the wealth of the man and upon context. What is honest or shameless among workers is often different from what is honest or shameless between workers and their employers, since different objects or values are being exchanged. Even among peers, honesty is measured in relative terms, for it depends upon preexisting forms of dyadic relationships and upon the specific corresponding expectations that these entail at particular stages of unfolding. First, let us take a look at how this criterion of propriety is measured in peer contexts. Then we will briefly examine interclass behavior.

Male Exchange

Townsmen recognize three different forms of male sociability (Gilmore 1975). The first is a casual comraderie that takes place in the public places, especially bars and taverns, where the men from the same neighborhood meet at night for good fellowship. These bar regulars spend the evening hours amiably chatting, exchanging jokes and stories, and with the contagious conviviality that outsiders find so seductive, treating each other to rounds of drinks and cigarettes. These hospitable small prestations seem disinterested, but they are governed by a subtle but iron etiquette. While no man would ever say so publicly, it is a gross solecism to accept more than a few drinks without "inviting" one's hosts. The underlying principle is an almost immediate material reciprocity by which everyone makes out more or less evenly in the long run. What counts of course is the show of disinterested generosity. For a man to withhold, to appear miserly, or to respond grudgingly or cheerlessly, is to earn the consensual deplorable label *sinvergüenza*, or shameless. Conversely, men who reciprocate appropriately are considered honest and reliable. They are worthy of at least minimal trust. Flagrant and open violation of the reciprocity principle earns a man the label *sinvergüenzón*, literally a big shameless, a crassly offensive manipulator. Given the pervasiveness of gossip, such labeling quickly leads to public censure, even ostracism. Most workers and peasants therefore abjure an exploitative calculus that is sure to backfire and can lead to social isolation and economic handicap.

A deeper form of masculine sociability ensues when two long-term friends escalate their exchanges to more important things like loans of money or tools. This mature friendship involves the two men's families in exchanges of services and group favors during life-crises and emergencies. Friends or neighbors who recognize such mutual obligation are said to have "commitment" and to be bound by rules of support beyond mere neighborliness. Again, the obligations are balanced, but now they have become delayed and involve both social and economic services.

Beyond commitment, there is a best-friend bond called "trust" *(confianza)*. It is the ideal of every man and the goal of all. When two men have beome trusting friends, their mutual obligations reach a higher level where daily assurances are no longer needed, as indeed the term trust implies. The establishment of trust both transcends and obviates the need for immediate display of honest intentions. Naturally honesty and shame still operate here, but they intensify, shifting to the affective realm. A man who betrays a trusted friend, for example by divulging a confidence, is a sinvergüenzón of the worst sort, one who has shamelessly exploited a trusting nature. Here the dishonesty represents an emotional deception and a psychological exploitation, both of which probably have homoerotic elements, given the unparalleled, almost romantic intensity of the tie. But in every case, we see the importance of "honesty," measured on the basis of mutual obligations or gifting, and its correlative shame: the failure to reciprocate some object or symbol of male bonding. Shamelessness is accepting something of value with no intention of reciprocating, the mainspring of masculine honor or reputation.

Occasionally, when an informant is asked to summarize his thoughts, he will portray the sinvergüenzón as follows: He is a man who is not "open"; he venally cheats others; he betrays a trust; or simply, as one informant put it, trying to condense: he is two-faced, a liar. A man may also be sinvergüenzón in relation to a woman. One who is not a "caballero," a gentleman, but who is false to a good woman, who betrays a sexual commitment, is also shameless. This is true, however, only if an erotic experience has been formalized by marriage or by an official courtship *(noviazgo)*. For example, a man who betrays his wife openly, or has two serious girlfriends *(novias)*, or who callously abandons a good woman after making a serious commitment, is considered dishonest and shameless. This moral opprobrium implies a model of sexual decorum somewhat divergent from Pitt-Rivers's wanton libertine (1965:46) whose amoral seductions strip "honor" from his victims. Here the deceitful Don Juan may be envied and even admired by men with stronger inhibitions or less opportunity, but he is not perceived as honorable. As informants say of extramarital affairs and false courtships: both parties "lose something," both reputations suffer, although naturally only the woman's is irrevocably reduced.

At this point, I should point out that integrity in contracts is only one ingredient among many which confer a man's social status. Ultimately the operative principle is the broader inclusive concept, "reputation." This is sometimes conveyed by the expression *fama*, literally "fame," which we may depict as a dramatized public image or persona. Usually one has either *buena fama* or *mala fama* with little intermediary shading. Aside from this honesty of duty, buena fama results from the following virtues, mostly having to do with projecting a manly image.

Manhood

First, and of central importance, is virility, the Andalusian ideal of the *macho*. This means being sexually potent in a physiological sense. For married men this includes fathering many children (preferably boys), in the process satisfying one's wife, frequenting brothels, and publicly displaying lecherous intentions (though not necessarily actions) toward nubile women. Mistresses, if they are discretley maintained, are appropriate. For young bachelors, this would naturally include actual attempts at seduction, frequent masturbation, a sexual bravado (usually more impressive in word than deed), and generally, as men say, obeying the peremptory commends of the testicles *(cojones)*. A "macho" (that is, a real man) is a "guy who thinks with his balls."

Since the requisite adolescent displays are unavoidably comparative, they are also always competitive; and I would argue that a sexually aggressive "honor" of precedence therefore seems most relevant, at least at the conscious level, among bachelors and young husbands seeking proof of their manhood in potency (see Murphy 1983b:387). With both bachelors and older attached men, however, a logical relationship does exist between a desired masculinity and female sexuality. But for mature married men this relationship is not quite the predatory and hostile type described by Pitt-Rivers and others, although it is still pressured and competitive. A man whose wife takes a lover is scorned and suffers a loss of prestige. But this is not necessarily because a hypothetical irretrievable "honor" has been "defiled" and stripped away (Pitt-Rivers 1965:47) by some local sexual rival. Rather the hapless cuckold is shamed in his *machismo* and criticized for sexual weakness, for effeminacy, for impotence. The distinction is subtle, but critical. In the eyes of the watchful, judgmental community, the cuckold's most trenchant defect is his failure to meet the masculine obligations of the marriage bed: he has grievously broken the contract to satisfy his wife and to provide her with children—services for which she in turn has contracted an honest fidelity. Otherwise why would she need a lover?

To illustrate from Fuenmayor: the childless Manolo "Matapollos," a chicken vendor, lost his spirited wife in 1973 when she ran off with an itinerant pottery salesman from Seville. Shocking though it was, her defection came as no surprise to those in the know. There had been long-standing gossip concerning Manolo's sexual performance, spread possibly by his irate mother-in-law who longed for grandchildren. Ultimately the wife's absconding was attributed not to innate female shamelessness but to Manolo's contemptible impotence, and her behavior was generally excused, if not condoned, on this basis. Manolo had failed resoundingly to meet her sexual needs (and some said the need of Spain for many children) and he was clearly unworthy to keep her. So here is an example of female virtue resting insecurely on male sexual performance, not vice versa. Sexuality, whatever else it involves, is also a matter of complementary obligations.

Male reputation is also based on *hombría*. Technically this means manhood, but it differs from the macho virility discussed above. Hombría is physical bravery or valor—not, however, in the sense of violent confrontations with other men, as this term is sometimes used in northern Mexico.[5] Andalusians strongly devalue physical violence and have no love of fighting, which they deplore as uncivilized. Nor does it mean taking advantage of others through superior cunning, as apparently is the case in southern Italy (Schneider and Schneider 1976; Belmonte 1980; Blok 1981). Rather hombría means a courageous and stoic demeanor in the face of adversity or threat, not necessarily local, and not even necessarily mundane. For example, a group of young men may wander down to the municipal cemetery late at night after a few drinks to display their disdain of ghosts. They take with them a hammer and a nail or spike. Huddling drunkenly, they drive the nail into the cemetery' stucco wall, reciting in unison the following formula to the rhythm of the blows:

Aquí hinco un clavo	I here drive a spike
del tío monero	before goblin or sprite
venga quien venga	and whatever appear,
aquí lo espero!	I remain without fear!

The last man to run away wins the laurels as the bravest. Sometimes adolescents will challenge each other to spend a night in the cemetery, but otherwise hombría is nonconfrontational, since the defiance is displaced onto a supernatural (nonsocial) object. Nevertheless it is competitive and, like virility, needs public proof.

An unusual quality of hombría in western Andalusia is its strong political connotation. It is demonstrated among workers who uphold laborers' rights by refusing to back down in labor disputes—a courageous and manly act during the Dictatorship. Working-class heroes who defy the police are *valiente,* brave, and *muy hombre,* lots of man. They take a stand at personal peril and do not budge, defending their position and that of their fellows before threats of official persecution. Charismatic labor leaders, especially those jailed and tortured under Franco, like Marcelino Camacho, the head of the underground Workers' Commissions, are highly admired in this respect. Incidentally, so are women, like La Pasionaria, who ardently defend class interests at their own risk. These women are also said to be valiente—like strong men; they too have met their obligations as representatives of the working class. These people are admired not because they have dominated others, but because they have made symbolic sacrifices in defense of their class or group, who in turn pledge a loyal commitment.

Economic Performance

Beyond virility and manliness, economic success also figures in the measure of a man. This is gauged differently according to what resources a man inherits and his physical and social qualities. What counts is public *performance.* This is always related to manual labor, to physical work. The correlation is normally positive, but for the upper class it is inverse. For a señorito, work is dishonorable. His self-esteem derives from always hiring others in subordinate positions to rescue him from working (this is presently changing). Leisure for the gentry was historically a class obligation; appearances had to be maintained for the collective sake of class exclusivity. For a mayete peasant, on the other hand, to work hard, though disagreeable, is appropriate and approved. To avoid manual labor is to earn the reputation of *gamberro,* or wastrel, living parasitically off women. However, for the mayete, the work concept, already ambiguous, is further qualified. He thinks of honorable work as consisting of labor exclusively on his own family plot in moral obligation to his dependents. Wage work, that is, working for others, is called "alienated" work *(trabajo ajena);* it is regarded with dread. For the mayete there is no obligation to hire out his labor, and so it is not dishonorable to avoid day work if the family can afford it.

To the worker, however, falls the onerous burden of having to accept despised wage work to feed his family. And here again a worker's *fama* or reputation is closely tied up with the direct satisfaction of female needs and to the fulfillment of conjugal obligations. While it is true that the household is run entirely by women (wives, daughters, mothers-in-law) the worker must, to be virtuous and therefore honorable in the community's eyes, contribute his share of income to keep this feminine machine running smoothly. Marriage is regarded as an unbreakable compact to provide for women and children, and the workers feel this obligation keenly. So a man works to meet his covenant as a provider, because, as they say, *se obliga,* you are bound.

For women, too, of all classes, marriage involves moral obligations in the sense of dyadic contracts and associated responsibilities. The maintenance of feminine shame is predicated upon the fulfillment of clear-cut contractual duties to husband and dependents. A woman who is sexually faithful of course displays shame and is honest and enhances her husband's honor; but likewise a woman who performs her domestic duties well also displays shame and is also honest. Her shame naturally involves chastity as something conjugally owed, but it partakes also of other sacrifices deeply rooted in marital loyalties, as indeed others have noted (Masur 1984). If we regard shame as above all marital fidelity, it becomes clearer why widows may find themselves partly freed from its sanctions. This disinhibition is in fact one of the reasons why widows are viewed in Andalusian male folklore as licentious and promiscuous (cf. Pitt-Rivers 1977:44, 82). One brief example will illustrate.

Maria, fortyish and recently widowed, had begun an indiscreet affair with Juan, a handsome bachelor. Her neighbor, Josefina, a married woman of 50, grew envious; and out of this tension there developed a catty animosity conveyed through evil glances and mutterings. Open words were finally exchanged, Josefina affecting an indignant moralistic tone. Maria initially ignored these escalating provocations. But one night on her way to visit her lover, Maria responded in kind. The two women then confronted each other angrily, while neighborhood gossips watched expectantly behind lace curtains to enjoy whatever might develop. Taking the offensive, Josefina exclaimed, "Why Maria, you shameless, you're nothing but a whore." Unimpressed, Maria stood her ground. Slowly, but regally she uttered the following repartee, which soon became famous throughout the pueblo: "Listen, you cow, I do whatever I want because my husband's dead and my cunt no longer pays taxes *(mi coño ya no paga contribución).*" This ended the argument in Maria's favor, as the neighborhood roared its approval both of the witticism and the message. While Josefina invoked an abstract moral principle, Maria's case was stronger, for it appealed to a community sense of sexuality as governed by ethical obligations, a contract between husband and wife. Once the man dies, the contract between them is annulled, and within reason (she owes restraint to children), the widow is freed of moral constraints and social prohibitions (I am speaking of the plebeians, not the elite).

Politics Again

To summarize thus far: we see everywhere a common moral thread regardless of whether the context is social, economic, or sexual. This is the stress on mutual responsibilities, either with peers or in marriage with spouse and dependents. In every case one acquires an implicit contract: a marriage, a wage agreement, a friendship, a loan, or a representative position. In each case to be "honorable," that is, to be virtuous before the eyes of the community, one pays one's debts in a gracious manner, one "complies." Honor is the respectful adherence to community tradition, conformity to cherished norms. Appropriate behavior is defined by the web of reciprocal loyalties that are accumulated through life, and this web is highly constrained by age, material possessions and marital status. And as I have said, there is a strong element of sexual obligation and performance in a man's status before the group at every stage of his postpuberty life.

There is also a discrepancy of personality evaluations based on the class perspective of the audience, so that shamelessness is a relative obloquy. As we have seen among the peer group of workers, reciprocal obligations are balanced. Casual friends and drinking companions exchange objects in bars on a rotating basis. This symbiotic mutualism is true for all classes, but is often blurred by exogenous political factors in class relations. A worker feels no pressure to reciprocate a favor from a rich peasant or a señorito in a balanced sense. The exchange is generalized and something is owed; but the worker, socialized to be suspicious of employer intentions, frequently finds fault with his superiors, especially if he is politicized, as most are. If he is given a day wage, he "complies." But he complies only if the wage meets his peer-group criteria for fairness, criteria that may differ from those of his employers in this politically volatile region of Spain. Otherwise, he shuffles and stalls, or works perfunctorily. Since both employer and employee rarely agree on the value and equivalency of what they are exchanging, there is often a dissatisfaction or charges of deceit which preclude a spontaneous "honesty" from arising in labor relations. As men of all classes say ironically, "There is no honor in the labor market," and they view their counterparts as dishonest until proven otherwise. In Seville Province there was one exception to this general rule. A certain señorito living in a neighboring town was known to provide a day wage higher than the minimum without being cajoled. He also provided his men with fresh food during their labors—an unusual act of decency—and there were rumors of Republican sympathies. This man was called "The Gentleman of Andalusia." His case was offered as the exception that proves the rule: one honest man among so many dishonorable thieves.

There is another way in which politics intrudes into personality evaluations. This concerns intraclass behavior in labor relations. Class unity is a major preoccupation among day laborers. When a worker accepts a wage contract he is performing a moral duty not only to his family but also indirectly to the community of workers who have toiled and sacrificed for decades to achieve political equality and trade-union rights. He must not accept a wage lower than the minimum, and must not undercut his fellows. A worker who accepts an unfair wage, or who steals work from equally destitute comrades, or who acts as a scab or blackleg is a sinvergüenza and class traitor. They call him a *chivato,* billy goat, and they avoid and persecute him, and they question his manhood. Similarly in labor disputes a man who fails to support his fellows or who betrays them is a sinvergüenzón and a coward. One notorious example was the case of Isidoro, a local man who refused to support a strike during the olive harvest when the employer announced an unfair wage cut. Everyone else walked right off the job, but this traitor stayed, it is said, to curry favor with the señoritos. However, the employers saw things differently. For them, Isidoro acted honestly, and naturally it was the strikers who acted despicably and were the sinvergüenzas. These political and labor issues insinuate into personality judgments, further complicating the question of what honor is and who is honorable. The first thing the observer has to do therefore in western Andalusia is to isolate the parameters of the "moral community," the peer reference group within the population. In Andalusia this necessitates a thorough grounding in class and labor relations and political history.

Conclusions

In western Andalusia, a man's "honor" (for lack of a better word) is chameleon-like. Male prestige takes its coloration from a substratum of social exchange traditions and ethics. A rivalrous sex-linked honor of dominance exists in Fuenmayor, but it is largely overshadowed by the pragmatic and convivial ethic of honesty (honor = virtue in Pitt-Rivers's terms). Honesty is figured relative to class position and to stages in the male life cycle. But it is one component in a broader evaluative schema, including both sexual and economic functioning. Male reputation devolves from performances in all areas of social life, performances that are highly stylized, contributing to a surface cooperation in public life rather than openly conflictive behavior.

Instead of a unidimensional zero-sum model of honor, we might more profitably approach male status in places like Fuenmayor with a transactional or exchange model of social honor. This would be useful for a number of reasons. First, it would permit us to observe the circulation of valuables by which social values are generated. Second, it would enable us better to see the formation of the web of "connectedness" by which men become gradually articulated to their social environment and by which their relative status is determined. Equally important, by focusing on reciprocal obligations we might develop a greater sensitivity to the character-building moral ambivalences experienced daily. As everywhere, these inner tensions produce the moral compromises conducive to character formation and in aggregate to group personality. For example, a man may have to betray his fellows to feed his family in periods of stress. Workers are constantly faced with such moral dilemmas: as they say, they are honorable until they stop being so; you have to make choices. But in every case, to understand what honor or reputation is, it is first necessary to appreciate the encompassing structure of class, employment, and how people perceive mutual needs.

To reiterate: I am not suggesting that male status in the lower classes is achieved through inherently cooperative *motives,* or that cooperation and competition are mutually exclusive categories. As elsewhere, workers in Fuenmayor "compete" for honest reputations, sometimes desperately. Since it wins them public approval, their integrity is self-serving; but the egoistic quest for personal gain is sublimated in Fuenmayor into ritualistic channels that paradoxically encourage surface harmony.

One additional point: we see little utility in this case for the unidimensional model of a male honor counterpoised to a female shame. The reputation of adult men is founded as much upon rectitude in all-male dyadic contracts as upon control over female sexuality. Further, both male and female transgressors are labeled "shameless" on the basis of moral laxness, sexual or otherwise; and for the common man it is shame, not a touchy vanity, that is lost through immoral acts. In effect, among the lower classes in Andalusia what has been called "honor" should be conceived as a more inclusive category encompassing the notion of honor = honesty, and this honor = honesty is based on male shame.

Thus, there is a much more direct connection between male honor and the "shame" principle than is often indicated. Men are under much more direct public scrutiny than the sex-linked model suggests. They are vulnerable to shaming through their own acts, experiencing continual peer pressure for conformity and accountability. This suggests that one area needing further research is the salience of shame as an autonomous psychological mechanism in intrasex relations. Also in need of more work is the rather neglected question of how *male shame* influences other public phenomena. In particular, as I have stressed before (1982), an inquiry into the psychology of shame would greatly enhance our understanding of certain ocular themes in Mediterranean culture, for example voyeuristic eroticism and the evil eye. For shame is above all *visual* and *public*. Unlike guilt, shame requires an audience: the watchful community. In the psychic mechanism of shaming, it is the "eye" of the community and the related sense of paranoic observation that are assimilated to worldview and to personality.

Finally, what does this case signify for the Mediterranean honor/shame model? It has two implications. First, it strengthens the sensible argument (Herzfeld 1980) that the honor principle needs more detailed ethnographic investigation. But it adds a hypothetical correlation between form and context. It implies a correspondence between the moral discriminations of masculine status and the material constraints of relations and correlative forms of political consciousness and horizontal solidarity. It suggests that any further refinement of the Mediterranean culture paradigm must be wedded to a recognition of variations in class dynamics and community "modes of cooperation." I would add to Herzfeld's warning about national differences the observation that the Mediterranean area consists of a mosaic of regional class formations and labor conditions. It is on this level that Davis's (1977) call for comparative research is most compelling.

To summarize: Mediterranean honor-and-shame consists of layered strata of community morality overlying a basic core of primordial sentiments. Honesty (and hospitality and respect) should not be seen as alternatives to masculine honor, but as components. In this multiplex morality system, some things change, but others, deeply imbedded, remain the same or change little. Honesty and hospitality are responsive to local conditions and are therefore highly variable. These moral and ethical accretions of "personal decency" (Brandes 1980:48) may obscure, but never obliterate, the changeless bedrock of sexual prototypes and masculine competitive jousting which lie tenaciously beneath.

With all this said, then, I believe there is some support here for an informed comparative ethnography of the Mediterranean area. If we shift the analytic focus away from a theatrical unidimensional "honor of precedence"—with all its a priori misconceptions and anachronisms—toward variations on the theme of honor = virtue, on the everyday concerns of Mediterranean men and women, we do find some support for a Mediterranean cultural distinctiveness, at least in terms of what it means to be a man. Male honor in Fuenmayor is subsumed under a pragmatic "honesty," but a man's position derives from a mixture of cultural desiderata, most of which are strongly connected to manly performance. Achieving manliness is a central concern here as elsewhere in the Mediterranean, and even though I would not characterize it as a zero-sum struggle between sexual purity and defilement, its methods remain at least in part conspicuous and competitive display of potency—sexual concerns. "Being a man" may not require cuckolding others here, but a cherished virility nevertheless for all men involves a certain degree of assertive demonstration or narcissistic display, of bravado, of playing to a critical audience. Like all precursors to male prestige in Mediterranean contexts, these public performances are by definition comparative and therefore invidious.

Notes

[1]Adherents of the honor = aggression model have elevated their argument into a global theory of Mediterranean moral codes. They regard competitions for male honor as symbolic displacements for underlying material hostilities. Schneider (1971:17) sees the field of honor as a "substitute for physical violence in the defense of economic interests," in which "women are reduced to currency in the process" (1971:18). In a similar vein, Black-Michaud (1975:194) writes: "Conflicts over honor make it possible for hostile groups to expand their aggressive energies upon each other without drawing in the society as a whole." This is supposed to be functionally related to political instability in weak states, which seems reasonable. But the case of Spain—strongly centralized since the sixteenth century—seems anomalous.

[2]Data were collected between 1972 and 1984. Fieldwork was supported by grants from the National Institute of Mental Health, the Wenner-Gren Foundation, the American Philosophical Society, the National Endowment for the Humanities (Summer Stipend, 1980, and Independent Fellowship, 1985), the Council for the International Exchange of Scholars, and the National Science Foundation. I am grateful to Professors Alfredo Jiménez Núñez and Salvador Rodríguez Becerra and to Señors Cristóbal Martín Caro and Antonio Milla González for their gracious assistance in Spain. My thanks also go to Sarah C. Uhl and Mariko Asano-Tamanoi for helping to organize the symposium upon which this volume is based.

[3]This is reflected in clandestine activity under Franco and in the various election returns since 1976. In the 1977 general elections, the Communists got 26%, the Socialists 22%. In 1979, the Communists received 29%, the Socialists 19%. In the April, 1979, municipal elections, a Communist was voted in as mayor, and a leftist coalition took over the townhall, ending forty-three years of uninterrupted elite dominance. For a brief political history of Fuenmayor, see Gilmore (1980:Chapter 2).

[4]*Honor* and *honra* are not clearly distinguished in Castilian usage. The former has a somewhat archaic or quaint sound; the latter may be more commonly used in modern speech (Pitt-Rivers 1977:174 n.5). For a review, see Caro Baroja (1965:84–86).

[5]Foster (1965:300) describes the Mexican macho as a man who is "strong and tough . . . and who never dodges a fight, and who always wins."

References Cited

Belmonte, Thomas
    1980   The Broken Fountain. New York: Columbia University Press.
Black-Michaud, Jacob
    1975   Cohesive Force: Feud in the Mediterranean and the Middle East. New York: St. Martin's Press.

Blok, Anton
    1981   Rams and Billy-Goats: A Key to the Mediterranean Code of Honour. Man 16:427–440.
Boissevain, Jeremy
    1979   Toward an Anthropology of the Mediterranean. Current Anthropology 20:81–93.
Brandes, Stanley H.
    1980   Metaphors of Masculinity. Philadelphia: University of Pennsylvania Press.
Campbell, J. K.
    1964   Honour, Family, and Patronage. Oxford: Clarendon Press.
Caro Baroja, Julio
    1965   Honour and Shame: A Historical Account of Several Conflicts. *In* Honour and Shame. J.
            G. Peristiany, ed. Pp. 79–137. London: Weidenfeld and Nicolson.
Davis, John
    1973   Land and Family in Pisticci. London: Athlone Press.
    1977   People of the Mediterranean. London: Routledge and Kegan Paul.
Foster, G. M.
    1965   The Folk Society and the Image of the Limited Good. American Anthropologist 67:293–
            315.
Gilmore, David D.
    1975   Friendship in Fuenmayor. Ethnology 14:311–324.
    1978   Varieties of Gossip in a Spanish Rural Community. Ethnology 17:89–99.
    1980a   The People of the Plain. New York: Columbia University Press.
    1980b   Nonmigrant Labor Patterns in Andalusia, 1973–77. Human Organization 39:170–175.
    1982   Anthropology of the Mediterranean Area. Annual Reviews in Anthropology 11:170–205.
Hart, David
    1976   The Aith Waryaghar of the Moroccan Rif. Tucson: University of Arizona Press.
Herzfeld, Michael
    1980   Honor and Shame: Problems in the Comparative Analysis of Moral Systems. Man 15:339–
            351.
    1985   The Poetics of Manhood. Princeton: Princeton University Press.
Lison Tolosana, Carmelo
    1968   Social Factors in Economic Development (Spain). *In* Contributions to Mediterranean So-
            ciology. J. G. Peristiany, ed. Pp. 325–338. The Hague: Mouton.
Luque Baena, Enrique
    1974   Estudio Antropológico Social de un Pueblo del Sur. Madrid: Tecnos.
Masur, Jenny
    1984   Women's Work in Rural Andalusia. Ethnology 23:25–38.
Murphy, Michael
    1983a   Emotional Confrontations between Sevillano Fathers and Sons. American Ethnologist
            10:650–664.
    1983b   Coming of Age in Seville. Journal of Anthropological Research 39:376–392.
Peristiany, J. G.
    1965   Introduction. *In* Honour and Shame. J. G. Peristiany, ed. Pp. 9–18. London: Weidenfeld
            and Nicolson.
Pitt-Rivers, Julian
    1965   Honour and Social Status. *In* Honour and Shame. J. G. Peristiany, ed. Pp. 19–77. London:
            Weidenfeld and Nicolson.
    1977   The Fate of Shechem. New York: Cambridge University Press.
Schneider, Jane
    1971   Of Vigilance and Virgins. Ethnology 9:1–24.
Schneider, Jane and Peter Schneider
    1976   Culture and Political Economy in Western Sicily. New York: Academic Press.

SHAME, FAMILY, AND STATE
IN CATALONIA AND JAPAN

Mariko Asano-Tamanoi

Introduction

The "honor and shame" complex has long been regarded as the most important unifying cultural theme of Mediterranean societies (Peristiany 1966; Wolf 1969; Schneider 1971; Blok 1981; Gilmore 1982). This does not mean, however, that the Mediterranean region has a monopoly on honor and shame. Peristiany (1966:10) may have gone too far when he commented that

> as all societies evaluate conduct by comparing it to ideal standards of action, all societies have their own forms of honour and shame.

But there are indeed cultures in which people constantly resort to similar values of honor and/or shame as central moral precepts, and Japanese culture is one of them.

In this article, I will compare a village in a part of the Mediterranean littoral, Catalonia, and a village in Japan, through the notion of shame as an analytical common denominator. As the native terms for the English gloss "shame" differ between the two villages, the meanings they confer upon it in various contexts differ, and it is these differences in meaning and their implications that I will explore here. In terms of *comparability*, however, the reader may perhaps raise the question of whether or not it is worthwhile to make an extra-Mediterranean comparison: after all, even within the Mediterranean region, honor and shame remain ambiguous and "polysemous" concepts (Gilmore 1982:191). Instead of dealing directly with this question, I would like to explain briefly the circumstances, both personal and intellectual, which gradually led me to this comparative study.[1]

Although I carried out fieldwork in both Catalonia and Japan, my original research plan was by no means simply to investigate the concept of shame in each village, nor was it to compare these two villages or to contrast Catalonian and Japanese cultures through the notion of shame. Rather, throughout my fieldwork experiences in both localities, I began to place unavoidably in comparative terms a certain local notion to which people in both villages give the utmost importance. This notion was the concept of household continuity; that is, people in both cultures felt strongly that the household should be continued through a single heir in each generation and such continuity should ideally be maintained indefinitely. And it was around this notion of household continuity that people in both villages frequently resorted to the native terms for shame, *"vergonya"* in Catalonia and *"haji"* in Japan. Hence in this study, I will start, as Leach puts it (1961:104), "from a concrete reality," in this case natives' remarks making reference to shame, "rather than from an abstract reality," the concept of shame itself. But the ultimate purpose of this analysis is to compare the concepts of shame, which surround the notions of "household continuity," at the level of the meanings people themselves confer upon it in constructing a moral universe. The continuity of the household is equally valued in Catalonia in general (Prat 1973, 1975; Hansen 1977; Iszaevich 1980, 1981) and in Japan in general (Fukutake 1949; Nakane 1967). Hence, while the comparison will specifically be made between two determinate communities, it can be extended more generally between Catalonian and Japanese cultures. This article, then, addresses both methodological and theoretical questions.

Methodologically, my principal purpose is to illuminate the value of shame in a part of the so-called Mediterranean culture area (cf. Davis 1977; Gilmore 1982) by comparisons with similar values in a culture far outside of the Mediterranean and without historical connections of any significance (cf. Blok 1978).[2] In this respect, I initiated this extra-Mediterranean comparison not so much as a student of the Mediterranean but as a student of Japan who is cognizant of the limited horizons of Japanese ethnography. For example, Moeran (1984:2–3) recently commented that

> those studying Japanese rural society have rarely managed to make comparisons or deductions of theoretical interest to anthropologists in general. Rather, they have at times appeared to form as close-knit and introverted a clique as do the very communities they have studied.

My intention is thus to break through this provincialism in the anthropology of Japan by analytically linking rural Japan and rural Catalonia through the shared notion of shame. Perhaps this isolationism could have been equally overcome by comparing Japan with its neighboring nations (cf. Mori 1971).[3] Similarly, the present study does not deal with the question of how the notion of shame in rural Catalonia differs from similar values in other parts of the Mediterranean. Indeed, impartible inheritance, long practiced in Catalonia as well as in Basque areas (cf. Douglas 1969; Greenwood 1976), makes this part of Spain different from the rest of the country, where the practice of partible inheritance is the norm. But, unlike in the anthropology of Japan, circum-Mediterranean comparisons (Davis 1977; Boissevain 1979; Gilmore 1982), and even within-nation and within-region comparisons (Corbin 1979; Driessen 1981) have been undertaken by various anthropologists working in the Mediterranean area. And if circum-Mediterranean comparisons have led to a critical reassessment of the category "Mediterranean" itself (Herzfeld 1985:778), extra-Mediterranean comparisons should equally lead to the critical reassessment of the same category. This study then suggests a possible new globalist direction of the study of honor and shame concepts, as indeed some social historians have urged (cf. Wyatt-Brown 1982).

Theoretically, I have four major points of comparison, around which the subsequent discussion will evolve. First, shame in each village has multiple meanings, and the concept is polysemous even in the context of a single village. In its relation to household continuity, then, shame in each village seems to carry a variable "surface" as well as an immutable "deep" meaning. Hence, this article aims to analyze these layered meanings of the shame notion in comparative perspective. Second, in these two villages, shame, and not honor, is the predominant concern of the people in their everyday life (cf. Wikan 1984). This does not mean, however, that shame in each village does not have a counter notion. It is always coupled with some notion of honor or public esteem, but such a notion has to be carefully analyzed in each culture and in each context, rather than simply bringing in the English gloss "honor" (cf. Herzfeld 1980). When Peristiany pointed out the universality of honor and shame, he did not have the slightest doubt that they always constitute a reciprocal pair. I argue here that different meanings of shame may have different notions as moral partners. Third is the question of "sexuality." Nobody will deny the prominence of sexuality in the Mediterranean codes of honor and shame, as Gilmore stresses in his introduction. In this study, sexuality will be considered in terms of its relation to the ideal of household continuity, for the latter is, after all, dependent upon the birth of an heir in each generation; that is, upon social reproduction and the socialization of sexuality. What should be remembered, however, is that sexuality is always expressed as a cultural construct, and so is the way men and women adapt to sexual morality. How, then, does their adaptation differ between the two villages, and how are such differences, if any, expressed in the notions of shame? Lastly, if there are such differences, why, or what factors explain them? To address this question, I will analyze how the household has been incorporated into the state during the capitalistic expansion of Spain and Japan. As others have argued (Schneider and Schneider 1976; Ortner 1978; Davis, this volume), statecraft is a critical independent variable in the evolution of moral codes.

I have to make it clear, though, that this article largely deals with women's perspectives. This is not only because I am a female anthropologist but also because, in both villages, it was largely women who evaluated, through gossip, each household's continuity by resorting to sentiments and sanctions related to shame. This does not mean that men never gossip: they do, for example, during the weekly gathering on the plaza on a market day or the occasional outings to town (Catalonia), or during *sake* drinking parties or men's annual village outings (Japan). These male gossip circles were largely closed for me. However, the information that these men exchange, particularly the information about household matters, largely comes from women, who pass it to their husbands and sons at home. In a sense, then, intersexual communication takes place at home, and the information gained flows away from the household through two separate channels of men and women, who may evaluate what they hear according to different values and sentiments. Here I present the female side of these values and sentiments. Since this study is based on my own field work in Belunya (pseudonym) in northern Catalonia and in Mino (pseudonym) in central Japan, some sense of place is necessary.

The Settings

As one travels from the south of Spain to the northeast frontier, near the border with France, one is struck by the differences in social environment and in the spatial arrangement of the villages. The segregation of landowners and tenants exists, but in a form different from that in the south: tenants do not form a "class"; rather, each tenant and his family maintains a separate and isolated relationship with his landowner (Asano-Tamanoi 1982, 1983). Even the so-called "southern" volatility in sexual matters, and the consequent segregation of the sexes, seems to be lacking, as men and women work together smoothly both within and around the house and in the fields. Catalonians feel more "European" than other Spaniards and are fond of saying so: indeed phrases like "We Europeans and those Andalusians" and even "We Europeans and those Spaniards" are heard frequently in Belunya in everyday conversation. The visitor may also feel overwhelmed by numerous stone-constructed farmhouses, which surround the nucleated town. So impenetrable and forbidding do they appear, that one feels finding out what is going on inside is a hopeless task. Even within the nucleated town, each house or apartment is complete in itself. Here, the sense of "household" as an isolated unit is pervasive. In Mino, each house seems to be more penetrable or inviting to the sojourner, perhaps because of the light materials used, such as wood, paper, and thatch. Except for the newly constructed ones, most houses are nucleated, and interhousehold relationships are expressed in various cooperative activities for agricultural production. But each house is surrounded by a fence of trees, wood, or stones, and going inside the fence is like penetrating an enclosure. Here too, as in Belunya, the sense of household as a most important unit prevails.

The household units in Belunya *(casa)* and in Mino *(ie)* (by which I mean the residential group and not the physical dwelling) have various surface similarities. But the most important of all is the fact of household continuity at the structural level and the importance people attach to it at the level of perception and values. In other words, both *casa* and *ie* should ideally be reproduced in each generation. This should be done through selection of a single heir or heiress. The reproduction of the household implies the transmission of property at a purely material level, but the property itself does not dictate the norm and ideal of household continuity. Rather, the notion of continuity implies instead a formalized ideal state, or traditional "sense" of continuity. In other words, propertied individuals as well as those with little or no property embrace the same ideal of household continuity. In neither village is this goal of continuity necessarily limited to the patrilineal line, nor even to the consanguineal kin group (Nakane 1967; Iszaevich 1981). Perhaps the eldest son of a patrilineal line may be the most preferred heir, and the idea of primogeniture prevails as an ideology in both villages. But in reality, inheritance and succession show a variety of selection criteria; the younger son may succeed as an heir, but so may the daughter or the adopted outsider, depending on the circumstances. Hence the people of both villages share a similar perception of household boundaries based on permanence rather than biological considerations: the positions of successor and his or her spouse are clearly differentiated as "permanent" members of the household, distinct from the positions of nonsuccessors, who are "temporary" members (Plath 1964; Kitaoji 1971; Iszaevich 1981; Bachnik 1983).[4] While permanent members are those who stay, temporary members are those who leave, ties of kinship notwithstanding.

But how is such a household continuity assured? People employ a series of strategies and make a variety of decisions to secure this central goal (Bourdieu 1976; Bachnik 1983); and it is around these strategies and decisions that people in Belunya and in Mino resort most often to the notion of shame. At this point, to convey this connection most vividly, I will share some field notes which express shame. The statements that follow were recorded in various female gossip circles.

Belunya

Pere (pseudonym) does not have *"vergonya"* (shame). He keeps having affairs with Nuria (pseudonym). What kind of woman she is! A *"puta"* (whore)! Pere's father told him that he would not get his share of the property if he continues to see her, but that does not seem to have much effect on that man (spoken by a middle-aged woman to neighbors in Belunya).

Belunya's population has been increasing since the 1940s (Asano-Tamanoi 1982). Many peasants have stopped farming during the past twenty years, but the local industries that have flourished in and near Belunya could absorb them, and thus most households have somebody who could succeed the families. Pere is one of those apparent heirs who lives with his widowed father. He is still under the influence of his father, who is soon to relinquish a major portion of his property to Pere, a married man with two children. Nuria is also married and has two children. Pere often visits her when her husband is away. In the present case, his father is threatening him by implying punitive intentions concerning Pere's share of the inheritance as a way of discouraging extramarital affairs. According to the standard understanding of Mediterranean "honor and shame" (Pitt-Rivers 1966, 1968), Pere should not have much to lose. His sexual aggressiveness should be praised, at least among his male friends. But in Belunya, where the household is the most important unit, such a group of men is not a significant shaper of public esteem or honor. Instead, my neighbors' criticism were directed not only at Nuria but also at Pere, since man and woman both neglected their respective obligations to their *casa*. Pere apparently lost his *"respecte"* (respect). The village people became skeptical about his ability to succeed his household business (the family manufactured and sold confectionery). And one day, when Pere's wife ambushed him on the street at dawn, my neighbors applauded her courage.

On the surface, then, shame seems to relate to the role performance of an individual as a household member (Davis 1977:99) in upholding and managing the patrimony. Fathers and mothers who do not fulfill their obligations vis-à-vis their children, husbands who do not fulfill their obligations vis-à-vis their wives and vice versa, or heirs who do not fulfill their obligations vis-à-vis their households as groups, are thus people without shame and their conduct is shameful. As Gilmore points out for similar sentiments in Andalusia (this volume), these role obligations are always seen in relational terms. But the gender polarity in fulfilling such role obligations is not so salient in Belunya, as both men and women form integral parts of the household.

In Belunya's past, such role obligations had also been seen in terms of the relationship between the heir and his or her siblings (Iszaevich 1975; Roca 1977). In other words, the ideal of household continuity was partly institutionalized through the custom of dowry, in which the heir took the responsibility of his or her siblings who had to leave. There are still some elderly bachelors and spinsters who live with one of their siblings and his or her family in Belunya. This indicates that the heir chose to take care of them at home rather than to pay a large dowry—a common decision. Thus, in those days when the dowry custom was important, those who ignored their obligations vis-à-vis their siblings were severely criticized as being without shame, which, in this context, seems largely contingent upon fulfillment of customary contract. Even today, when there are conflicts between brothers, village gossip often centers on one brother's shameful neglect of his obligations vis-à-vis his siblings. But the sanction of shame guarding these horizontal relationships seems to be much less salient today, as growing work opportunities have enabled nonsuccessors to establish their own households. Furthermore, the dowry, whether in cash or land, can no longer sustain a single household over a long time period, and the custom itself is rapidly disappearing in Belunya (Roca 1977:48).

At this level of its meaning, then, the Catalonian precept of shame can be coupled with *"respecte"* (respect) primarily in the sense of respect for customary obligation or contract. Men and women who fulfill their respective role obligations as household members are given respect and their conduct is *"respetuoso"* (respectful). Wilson (1969:78), referring to Caribbean societies, comments on a similar sense of respect:

> Men . . . are completely involved in a value system based on "reputation" but with age and social maturity, measured by economic security, marriage and so forth, move into a value and status system based upon respectability.

In Belunya, where the household and its continuity have supreme importance, men, as heads or future heads of households, seem to know the value of respectability even before they establish their own households.

However, this surface understanding of shame and respect becomes somewhat problematical when one considers the vertical line of a cherished household continuity. Parents do carry obligations vis-à-vis their children: to feed, clothe, and shelter them, to socialize, to nurture, and so forth. And if they neglect this, they are shamed before the eyes of the community. But in the above quoted remarks, the gossip's criticism seems to go deeper. To understand it, one perhaps has to bring in the question of sexuality. I argue that what these women are really assessing is the fact that both Pere and Nuria brought "illegitimate sexuality" into their respective homes. And, as this woman's remarks suggest, if the criticism of Nuria is sharper, that is because as a woman Nuria brought this menacing illegitimacy directly into her home, where her children were subject to its destructive power. H⌐re, what these women question is not simply Pere and Nuria as father and mother, but more trenchantly the same Pere and Nuria as a man and a woman, or, using Pitt-Rivers's terminology (1968:505), as "physical persons," who carry the symbolic functions attached to their respective body and blood.

In order to maintain household continuity, then, a stranger could be brought in as a son-in-law or as an adopted daughter through legitimate means; but the heir's marriage and the subsequent procreation of the future heir should take place between legitimate partners. The "illegitimate sexuality" of illicit liaisons should never be allowed to intrude in the household sphere. In other words, the household continuity should be the extension of contacts between legitimate partners as "physical persons." Such a legitimized continuity does not have to be through the same blood but through the culturally "legitimate" blood. The sanction of shame is resorted to whenever illegitimate blood is brought in the sanctity of the household sphere, and is conferred upon both men and women, since such blood could equally be brought in by both sexes. But if libertine women are regarded as more shameful, that is not because women are "of the devil" by nature (Brandes 1981:219) as in Andalusia, but because they bring more powerfully negative effects to the household sphere once they engage in illegitimate sexuality. It is women who primarily nurture and socialize children.

The Catalonian ideal of household continuity does not have a concrete symbol to express it. The family name is perpetuated only patrilineally, so that if the household is continued through daughters and adopted sons, the associations of the household with the family name "tends to be lost in the long run" (Iszaevich

1980:318). Each household carries a so-called housename (*renom* or *motiu*) in Belunya, which can be perpetuated by any successor, be it son, daughter, or the adopted. But, only a handful of wealthy households take the continuity of house-names seriously. What is important for Catalonian household continuity, then, is that each stage of continuance (between a pair of parents and their children) should be "legitimate." What is of focal importance is thus an actual and concrete conjugal relationship between a man and a woman in each generation. One oc-casionally comes across a name which has only a matronymic. This tells one that its bearer is an illegitimate child whose father is perhaps unknown. He or she is thus a product of "illegitimate sexuality" and is thus shameful. Although he or she can be a successor, the resultant continuity of the household, if realized, is far from complete in moral terms; in that sense it is imperfect, a failure. (The contrast to Japan here is interesting, and I will shortly return to this point.)

Shame of illegitimacy, then, is subsumed under the stigma of neglecting one's role performance as a household member. It is based on the notion of men and women as "physical persons," not on the notion of them as carriers of specific family roles. Catalonian shame of illegitimacy, then, constitutes the deeper mean-ing of shame. At this level, shame is aptly coupled with *"honra"* (honor). Al-though to father *many* children is often regarded as a sign of a man's virility in many Mediterranean societies, what gives a man honor in Belunya is to father "legitimate" and thus "good" children, rather like in Delaney's Turkish village (this volume). Likewise, to mother "legitimate" and "good" children gives a woman an equally pure honor. Honor is thus given to both men and women, who mutually form the household. But if the honor of men appears more salient in this sense, it is only because men, as representatives of the households, carry a more public honor.

One has to note that it is not shameful at all not to have a successor, but only in cases of moral dereliction. In Belunya, an elderly couple who were left without a successor arouse only a sense of *"lament"* (pity) and not of shame among the village people. Although household continuity is important, it is only pitiful if it cannot physically be accomplished: after all, a successor should be conceived through the contact of legitimate bodies and blood, but this is not always physi-cally possible. We now turn to Japan.

Mino

The mother of the household *Keito* (housename) is really arrogant.[5] They are one of our branch households, and, as a member of the main household, I introduced several young women as pro-spective brides for her son. But she [his mother] refused them all, saying that he graduated from the best local high school and that all these women do not have appropriate backgrounds. True, he went to a good school, but he did not go to a college. It is *"haji"* (shame) if this branch household does not continue; it is *haji* both for them and for us. [spoken by an elderly woman to me in Mino]

The population in Mino, like in Belunya, has been increasing since the end of the war. While most of the households now combine farming with wage-work at nearby factories or business offices, newcomers to Mino commute to local towns to work there. With the growing opportunities to work, many non-heirs (sons), upon marriage, set up their new households within and near the village. They usually maintain some sort of relationship with their main households, a phenom-enon which cannot be seen in Belunya. However, each household is still the most important unit.

Another difference between the Japanese *ie* and the Catalonian *casa* is also important. Although both have been analyzed as corporate units by anthropologists (Embree 1939; Befu 1962; Beardsley 1965; Nakane 1967; Iszaevich 1981), the *ie* has a dimension which is lacking in the *casa:* the *ie* is not only a group maintaining a shared patrimony but also a group with a common ancestor from whom all the present household members claim descent. The Catalonian *casa* often has its own sacra or icons, but what makes the Japanese perception of household continuity unique is the utmost importance people give to a *chef d' enterprise* who pays homage to the household ancestor. In other words, what is important is not so much *who* becomes the successor but *to fill* the position of successor itself.

In the snippet above, this branch household has only one son, the heir. But he is not yet married, although he is close to forty. Two daughters have been married out and live in Tokyo. Hence, if the son remains single, the house cannot have successors and cannot continue. What the speaker finds shameful, then, seems to be the fact that their household cannot continue and that no one will remain to pay proper homage to their ancestors (note that this is only pitiful but not shameful in Belunya). And since the speaker is the grandmother of the main houseold, she seems to take this fact as her shame too. In other words, shame in its nominal form is not a deplorable attribute attached to actual men or women, nor to their conduct, but to a state of domestic discontinuity. And we so often come across this abstract notion of shame in the Japanese village studies. "Not having a successor is the severest *haji* in the community," so said a (male) Japanese farmer (Kahoku-Shimpōsha 1973:174, my translation).

Curiously enough, shame at this abstract level of meaning is coupled with the equally abstract notion of *"na"* (name), which refers to the formal ideal of household continuity.[6] *Na,* in the village context, refers to the family name of the household. Every Japanese carries a single family name, paternal (if one's father is a successor) or maternal (if one's mother is a successor). Unlike Catalonia, where the family name is perpetuated only patrilineally, in Japan it is transmitted by any incorporated successor. To maintain the family name, any individual who is married or adopted into the new household and who thereby becomes a "permanent" member, simply adopts the family name of the household, losing his or her original family name. Whoever succeeds the household, as well as his or her spouse, should bear the same family name, and the change of family names is always recorded in the official family registry. In this respect, household continuity is symbolized and expressed in the continuity of the same family name, irrespective of *who* bears it.

All of this also suggests that the household continuity of Japanese families can be maintained by a *manipulation* of family names through official channels. For example, a widower in Mino, whose only daughter had been married out, "adopted" his grandson as an heir: but this does not mean that he actually moved to his grandfather's house as his legitimate son. On the contrary, he still lives with his own mother. What this widower did was simply to change his grandson's family name to his. When he grows up and marries, he and his spouse will succeed his grandfather's household no matter where they choose to live; thus, this widower could continue his own household by a slight of hand.

Na in the noun form implies that *"na ga aru"* (there exists *na*). This in turn suggests the fact of household continuity. *Na,* then, has a peculiar characteristic: it bounds the household members through a device of onomastic extension. *Na* should be maintained and perpetuated, but its perpetuation can also be manipulated. Thus, I argue that the abstract concept of *haji* (shame) can be coupled with the equally abstract notion of *na* (Mori 1971). The latter, like the former, is not rooted in the actual person of men or women, nor in their conduct, but in symbolic relations.

But if both concepts remain aloof from the physical person, to what extent does morality of conduct enter into the picture? In other words, how should the obligation of each household member be fulfilled so as not to cause shame for the household? To address this question, we can go back to the main household's grandmother's remarks.

Although the speaker finds the state of household discontinuity shameful, what she is most critical of is the arrogance of the branch household's mother. In her eyes, the mother is responsible for the household discontinuity, because she refuses to arrange her son's marriage, acting out of arrogance and selfishness. In other words, the speaker, while leaning on the abstract notion of shame, does root this notion in the conduct of actual men and women, the branch household's mother in this case. Indeed, women in Mino often criticize their neighbors behind their backs for *hazukashii* (shameful) conduct. In casual gossip, they set aside the abstract notion of household continuity, and are busy assessing actual men and women, their conduct, and their way of thinking. Their targets are various: a group of siblings who fight over the question of who takes care of the elderly parents; a young wife who refuses the care of her mother-in-law; a mother-in-law who constantly demands; a husband who keeps a lover in the local town, and so forth. In other words, they are critical of those who fail to fulfill their respective obligations for the sake of the household and its continuity.

The question of sexuality, which is so prominent in the Catalonian notion of shame, is subordinate to the question of an individual's fulfillment of his or her obligations as a carrier of multiple roles. Women's evaluation of each individual's sexual conduct is a relative case-by-case assessment, and is not dependent upon universal criteria of moral principles. Dore (1978:168), who lived in a Japanese village, writes:

> Adulterous philandering was rarely the trouble. The men, it was taken more or less for granted, occasionally had women when they went off on weekend outings. . . .

In Mino, a village woman commented, "a man, if he hands his whole salary over to his wife, is allowed to have a lover." But the moment such "adulterous philandering" interferes with his role as a household head, father, or husband, it becomes the target of gossip. Equally, a woman who has illicit liaisons, could arouse sympathy among her fellow women, if, for example, her husband's conduct is more morally deplorable. In other words, one's "sexual role" (Davis 1977:77) is only one among many other roles one should perform in the web of one's personal relationships.

Tada (1958:236) argues that the Japanese household provides a "shame-free zone" for all its members, as every effort is made to conceal family disgrace from disclosure. Occasionally such disgrace makes the ideal of household continuity difficult. In Mino, there is a household whose sole son is mentally ill. This family adopted a stranger as successor, while retaining the son at home. According to Tada's argument, the disgrace is to have the mentally ill son, which is concealed by the family who adopted the stranger. But everybody in Mino knows this fact.

Among the gossip circles, then, what is really disgraceful or shameful is the fact that the father of this household has ignored the care of his own son. In this respect, the household by no means provides a "shame-free zone": the gossip encroaches on the household and recreates the family moral order.

It is at this level of the meaning of shame where the notion of *"meiyo"* (honor) enters as a counternotion. We have seen that the abstract concept of shame can be coupled with the notion of *na,* which refers to the ideal state of household continuity. We have also seen that *na* is at the same time manipulable. Japanese has various expressions regarding *na: "na o ageru"* (to raise one's name), *"na o kegasu"* (to pollute one's name), or *"na o sute jitsu o toru"* (to give up one's name and to take its substance), and so forth. All these *na* forms refer to the family name or names of groups one belongs to. These expressions then suggest that the quality of *na* is mutable: it can be "raised," "polluted," or it can become "superficial without any substance." And if the quality of *na* can change, the quality of household continuity expressed by *na* can also change. Such qualities depend upon the moral conduct of men and women who constitute the household. Thus, *"rippana na"* or *"meiyo-aru na"* (honorable or honored name) refers to the state of household continuity that has been realized through honorable conduct of its members. Honor is subsumed under the notion of *na* but makes its appearance only when people, through gossip, evaluate men and women's conduct in terms of their respective obligations as household members. Honor, then, like shame, is conferred upon both men and women, as they integrally constitute the household.

So far, we have seen that in both Belunya and in Mino, shame has not one but various meanings, and is associated with different reciprocal notions at different levels of meaning. But we have also seen that the meanings of shame in its relation to the ideal of household continuity differ between Belunya and Mino. In Belunya, shame at one level is attributed to those men and women who do not fulfill their respective obligations as the household members. It is coupled with respect, which is conferred upon those who do fulfill such obligations. At another level, shame is attributed to those men and women who, as "physical persons," bring "sexual illegitimacy" into the household sphere. The concept of sexual legitimacy constitutes the guiding principle for human conduct, and honor is conferred upon those who stick to this principle.

In Mino, shame at one level is totally abstract, and refers to the state or the possibility of household discontinuity. *Na* is its counternotion, signifying the state of household continuity. Both concepts transcend the individual and his or her conduct. The ideal of household continuity, then, constitutes the principle, or the "universalistic element" (Befu 1962:40), to which the will of actual men and women is subordinate. However, this "universal element" is superseded at another level of the meaning of shame, which is attributed to those who do not fulfill their respective obligations as household members. There is no single, monolithic principle here. The evaluation of each individual's conduct is made in terms of the commonly shared understanding of his or her obligation as a carrier of multiple family roles. Honor is given to those men and women who do fulfill such obligations, leading to the "honorable name" of the household. In both villages, gossip, particularly among women, seems to play an important role in assessing various meanings of shame.

The question then arises why all these differences exist. This leads us to a discussion of how the household has been incorporated into the wider society. Comparison at the national level, however, is still speculative; but this article would not be complete without at least addressing this inevitable "why" question (Bois-sevain 1979). Here, I specifically focus upon the period of capitalistic expansion of Spain and Japan during the period when differences in the state-household relationship between these two nations appear most dramatically. However, such differences can be observed throughout the history of both Catalonia and Japan. After all, Catalonian history is largely the story of an uneasy relationship with the Spanish state, and the rural Catalonians have always been skeptical of the central government. Contrary to this, rural Japan has always been well incorporated into the state since the time of its formation. I would like the reader to bear this in mind while reading the following discussion.

State, Family, and Shame

Perceived in the context of recent national history, an intriguing similarity emerges between *casa* and *ie:* impartible inheritance encouraged nonsuccessors to migrate, providing an important economic resource in the urban sector (Kawashima 1957:11; O'Brien 1975:666). But this similarity is only in the context of the city: the difference is more conspicuous between rural Catalonia and Japan.

Catalonia had never been well incorporated into the Spanish state, and hence the state never fully penetrated into rural Catalonia. Even during the Franco regime, when various government apparatuses were brought into Belunya, the villagers' suspicion of the public authority did not fade away. Coupled with the strong sense of Catalonian nationalism, the people in Belunya have always guarded themselves against the state.

The situation is entirely different in Mino. During Japan's capitalistic expansion, the Japanese government utilized every element of the household as integral parts of the nation's well-integrated system. In a sense, Japanese history of the late nineteenth and early twentieth centuries was a process in which the state recreated the household as a unit in conformity to the society's structural needs (Sakuda 1967:15).[7] Perhaps the manner in which the household had thus been incorporated into the total system is worth describing.

First, since the system of agricultural production largely remained intact, production by a single household remained a norm. The excess labor force ("temporary" members of households) had been absorbed by the industrial sector during the course of Japanese industrialization (Kawashima 1957:11; Nakamura 1978:182). But factory owners could always send the employees back to their households when they became sick or were dismissed (Nakamura 1978:182). In other words, the state committed itself to a policy maintaining the continuity of each household (Itoh 1982). This policy reached its pinnacle in the late nineteenth century when the state created the fiction that every household was a branch household of the Emperor's family: Japan thus became one single *ie* (Irokawa 1970). Accordingly, the ancestor of the Emperor replaced the ancestor of every household (Itoh 1982). Thus, both men and women, as integral parts of the household, had been incorporated into the nation's capitalistic expansion.

The traditional notion of household continuity and the state's family policies during industrialization meshed in a particular way in Japan, mutually reinforcing each other. But then, had the Catalonian notion of household continuity been left as an orphan or as a mere regional custom? Indeed, in its relation to the state, the

Catalonian household seems to have been constituted as an impenetrable entity. It is true that the household contributed nonsuccessors to the industrial sector. But it did not allow the public authority to penetrate into its private domain, as in Japan. Schneider (1971) argues that the absence of effective state bureaucracies in the Mediterranean societies generate pressures toward family solidarity, and that "honor as ideology helps shore up the identity of a group" (1971:17). The Catalonian model of household continuity, then, could be understood as the reflection of a regional suspicion of centralizing authority, which was located far away in Madrid and was regarded as both foreign and predatory.

But what Schneider neglects in her argument is a force that has unmistakably penetrated deep into the household sphere, namely, the ideology of state religion. And the idea of "legitimate sexuality," which underlies the notion of shame in Belunya, has always been a part of this ideology (Ortner 1978; Delaney, this volume). It is largely through women that such an ideology has been brought into the household sphere. Catalonian women attend mass regularly; they are the center of the family gatherings, which have always something to do with the church, such as baptismal occasions, weddings, or funerals. In Belunya, some adult men do not attend mass regularly or at all. But this does not mean that they do not accept Catholic ideology. Rather, they do seem to accept it passively, and it has penetrated deep into their own households. And the Catalonian notion of household continuity, which men also cherish, has been constantly reinforced by the ideology of state religion. If the men do not embrace it enthusiastically, it is women who bring their conduct before the eyes of the public and force them into passive acquiescence through their powerful gossip.

What penetrated deep into the Japanese household sphere, then, is the state ideology, which aimed to maintain the household continuity. Men, as the public representatives of each household, responded to such an ideology, and felt duty-bound to maintain household continuity. In other words, the state ideology forced them to give the utmost importance to the fact of household continuity, irrespective of sentiments of individual men and women. Today, the new Constitution promulgated after the war makes it a rule to divide the household property equally among all the children. But as the widower's complex manipulation of *na* suggests (above), people in Mino and in rural Japan in general (Nōsei Chōsa Iinkai 1963; Itoh 1982) still cling to the idea of household continuity, and particularly men's desire for it is strong. In addition, the postwar land reform, which created the homogenous population of small-scale owner-cultivators, further reinforced the ideal of household continuity, adding a material dimension to it.

However, rural women, although they have also been incorporated into the state ideology as a part of the household, seem to have been always removed from this value system. In other words, Japanese women always seem to have attached more importance to actual sentiments of individual men and women than to the cause of state ideology (Kanō 1972). In Mino, there are a few elderly couples and widows whose sons died during the war. The formal explanation, which is almost always given by men, is that it is honorable to have a son who served the nation. But their wives do not give any value judgments and express nothing but sorrow, and some even criticize the state (cf. Smith and Wiswell 1982; Nolte 1983).[8] Of course this does not mean that men do not feel any sense of sorrow, but that they repress such sentiments, at least publicly. And it is women who bring the actual human feeling to the surface.

In short, while women represent the total social system in Belunya, men represent it in Mino; but in both villages, women are the main evaluators of honor and shame through their powerful gossip.

Conclusion

Finally, how does this extra-Mediterranean comparison contribute to the central theme of this volume: Mediterranean "honor and shame?" Does this comparison result in reinforcing the concept of Mediterranean unity? The important task of comparing this Catalonian case with the other Mediterranean cases still has to be done. Perhaps the reader, having perused discussions of honor and shame in Andalusia, Turkey, or Greece, will make a spontaneous mental comparison of the Catalonian version of honor and shame with similar values in other parts of the Mediterranean. Because of space limitations, I must leave this comparative task to the reader. Catalonia, where the household appears as the critical unit, may be unique. Although "amoral familism" (Banfield 1958) has often been believed to be universal in the Mediterranean region, the importance attached to lineal household continuity may be unique to Catalonia. The reason why both sexes could equally have honor and shame can perhaps be attributed to this critical notion of household in Catalonia. And yet, the Catalonian concept of honor and shame seems to share something with other similar concepts in the Mediterranean region.

I argue that this "something" is the principle underlying the notions of honor and shame in many Mediterranean societies, the principle of "sexual legitimacy." Hence the prominence of "sexuality" in the Mediterranean moral codes. This is, then, what has been made clear by introducing the Japanese versions of honor and shame, which seem to lack such a principle and in which "sexuality" does not loom large. This does not mean that the notion of "sexual legitimacy" does not exist in Mino but that it does not exist as *the* moral principle. It is only one among many other factors to be taken into account when an individual's conduct is evaluated in the light of a person's position as a carrier of multiple roles. Lebra (1976:87) comments:

> Sexuality for Japanese seems foremost a role concept. To be a woman means to play a woman's role in relation to others. . . . It may be speculated that the Japanese individual's sexual identity, so caught up with role playing (and status maintaining), does not become as internalized at the unconscious level of the personality as happens in a culture that identifies sex with intrapsychic passion.

In terms of the ideal of household continuity, a woman cannot be a woman alone. She is not only a woman but also a wife, a mother, a daughter, or a mother-in-law. She is caught up with playing a multiplicity of roles. In short, the notion of "physical person," which looms above the notion of any role obligation in the Mediterranean region, does not exist in Japan.

Because of this very lack of a single bedrock principle, Japanese honor and shame cannot be internalized, while the Mediterranean versions can be, as they are based on the principle that both men and women internalize. This is, as Pitt-Rivers commented (1966:21), why Mediterranean honor is not only "the value of a person *in his own eyes*, but also in the eyes of his society" (emphasis mine). One experiences one's honor and shame in the light of one's understanding of the principle of sexual legitimacy. But one's honor and shame are also evaluated by others, who cherish the same principle. Honor and shame in Japan, then, are primarily in the eyes of the society. One's conduct and personality are evaluated by the community, which takes into account all the possible relationships one could have as a carrier of multiple roles. Moeran (1985:221), describing his experience while living in a Japanese village, writes:

> There is no such thing, then, as Rationality—with a capital R and in the singular form. There are merely rationalities—as many rationalities, perhaps, as there are relationships between people.

Japanese honor and shame exist in these webs of personal relationships and are thus distinct from the Mediterranean variant of honor and shame.

The state-household relationship may perhaps explain these critical differences. The ideology of state religion, the main tenet of which is the notion of "sexual legitimacy," is shared by many Mediterranean societies (Ortner 1978; Delaney, this volume). The rural people's suspicion of the government and the lack of effective state ideologies as well as bureaucracies are also shared by many Mediterranean societies (Schneider 1971). And the household, as an impenetrable entity and last private sanctuary, is a dominant idea in the Mediterranean region. Japan, then, presents a totally distinct state-household relationship. Japan's effective state ideologies have penetrated deep into the household sphere, having made it an integral part of the national system. Mediterranean societies and Japan are thus radically different in this regard, and yet in both cultures, women are the main evaluator of shame, either by conforming to the ideology of state religion (Mediterranean) or by detaching themselves from the state ideology (Japan).

Within-Mediterranean comparisons have invigorated anthropology of the Mediterranean. My hope is that extra-Mediterranean comparisons will equally animate anthropology of the Mediterranean. This study only marks the beginning of such a global direction.

Notes

[1]The original version of this article was presented at the annual meeting of the American Anthropological Association in 1983, before I conducted fieldwork in Japan over the two summers of 1984 and 1985. This version is based on the original paper, rewritten substantially in the light of fieldwork experience in Japan. The research in Catalonia was supported by the American Association of University Women and Northwestern University, and the research in Japan was supported by the United Nations University. My thanks to each of these organizations. Numerous people read and commented on this article at various stages between 1983 and 1986, but special thanks go to D. Gilmore, P. Carrasco, H. Befu, K. Tomio, J. Fajans, and three anonymous reviewers for their valuable criticism.

[2]Blok argues that, since the case for comparative analysis depends on problems and questions one wants to investigate, "research in the Mediterranean will lead us to comparisons with institutions in other parts of the world" as well (1978:485). In addition, several anthropologists have remarked the necessity of comparing Mediterranean with Japanese cultures (Freeman 1973; O'Brien 1975; Blok 1978; Iszaevich 1980, 1981), arguing that central themes of the analysis of both cultures, particularly in rural settings, are largely the same.

[3]Mori's work (1971) is relevant here: he analyzed the notion of shame in China based on his detailed analysis of the major works of the Confucians and the Taoists. He argues that the Japanese notion of shame, although originating in the Chinese concept of shame, is different from the latter because of the long period of feudalism in Japan.

[4]Iszaevich (1981) does not use such terms as "permanent" and "temporary" members. Instead, he uses the "cognitive distinction made in Catalan culture" between "a main inheritor, who marries and stays in the household retaining the bulk of the property, and the minor inheritor, who must leave upon adulthood" (1981:277, 284). The term "minor" refers to the fact that these inheritors are usually given a part of the property in the form of dowry.

[5]A housename is a name attached to each domestic group and is frequently used both in Mino and in Belunya in order to identify an individual as a member of a specific household. A housename is thus another expression of the importance attached to the household. However, in both villages, a housename does not express the ideal of household continuity itself.

[6]As far as I know, Mori (1971) is the only scholar who argued for the coupling of shame with *na,* although his argument was largely confined to the Chinese notion of shame. In Japan, shame was taken up as a subject of academic concern after the publication of Benedict's *The Chrysanthemum and the Sword: Patterns of Japanese Culture* (1946). Naturally, various studies that appeared in response to Benedict (who cited Japanese culture as a typical example of "shame culture") dealt with shame as a counterconcept to "guilt."

[7]Obviously, not every household conformed to the society's needs. In the beginning of the Meiji era (1868–1912), a brief period of liberalism was created by rural elites, and there was an outbreak of rebellions among landless peasants. However, as many of these rural elites became parasitic landlords, this liberalism died out, and peasants became firmly controlled by the state under the Emperor system (Irokawa 1970).

[8]Wiswell, wife of anthropologist John Embree, who stayed in a Japanese village between the two world wars, describes the village women welcoming the soldiers' return (Smith and Wiswell 1982:80): "After lunch the hamlet women gathered in several different houses to dress up. They wore school girls' skirts and middies, kimono turned inside out, soldiers' uniforms, firemen's uniforms, and all kinds of men's clothing—pants, coats and hats. . . . They generally acted in complete accordance with their presumed sex, making passes at all the girls and women. The girls squealed loudly and jumped off the road into the fields to avoid being pinched on the buttocks. One old lady got hold of a young woman, and later a man, and held them against the walls imitating the movements of intercourse. The crowd roared with laughter, while the poor victims ran away as fast as they could when released." The village women were actually organized in the National Women's Association and were supposed to show their sense of patriotism (1982:24–26). But what was described here cannot be seen as their support of state ideologies. Rather, by using symbolic expressions, they demonstrated their protest of the political order (cf. Nolte 1983).

References Cited

Asano-Tamanoi, Mariko
  1982   The Changing Peasant Society in Catalonia: The Transformation of the Masoveria System. Ph.D. dissertation. Northwestern University.
  1983   Reconsidering the Concept of Post-Peasantry: The Transformation of the Masoveria System in Old Catalonia. Ethnology 22:295–305.
Bachnik, Jane
  1983   Recruitment Strategies for Household Succession: Rethinking Japanese Household Organization. Man 18:160–182.
Banfield, Edward C.
  1958   The Moral Basis of a Backward Society. New York: Free Press.
Beardsley, Richard K.
  1965   Cultural Anthropology: Prehistoric and Contemporary Aspects. *In* Twelve Doors to Japan. J. W. Hall and R. K. Beardsley, eds. Pp. 48–120. New York: McGraw Hill.
Befu, Harumi
  1962   Corporate Emphasis and Patterns of Descent in the Japanese Family. *In* Japanese Culture: Its Development and Characteristics. R. J. Smith and R. K. Beardsley, eds. Pp. 34–41. Chicago: Aldine.
Benedict, Ruth
  1946   The Chrysanthemum and the Sword: Patterns of Japanese Culture. Boston: Houghton Mifflin.
Blok, Anton
  1978   Review of People of the Mediterranean by John Davis. Man 16:427–440.
  1981   Rams and Billy-goats: A Key to the Mediterranean Code of Honour. Man 16:427–440.
Boissevain, Jeremy
  1979   Towards a Social Anthropology of the Mediterranean. Current Anthropology 20:81–93.
Bourdieu, Pierre
  1976   Marriage Strategies as Strategies of Social Reproduction. *In* Family and Society. R. Forster and O. Ranum, eds. Pp. 117–144. Baltimore: Johns Hopkins University Press.

Brandes, Stanley
    1981 Like Wounded Stags: Male Sexual Ideology in an Andalusian Town. *In* Sexual Meanings:
        The Cultural Construction of Gender and Sexuality. S. B. Ortner and H. Whitehead, eds. Pp.
        216–239. Chicago: University of Chicago Press.
Corbin, John
    1979 Social Class and Patron-Clientage in Andalusia: Some Problems of Comparing Ethnogra-
        phies. Anthropological Quarterly 52:99–114.
Davis, John
    1977 People of the Mediterranean: An Essay in Comparative Social Anthropology. London:
        Routledge and Kegan Paul.
Driessen, Henk
    1981 Anthropologists in Andalusia: The Use of Comparison and History. Man 16:451–462.
Dore, Ronald P.
    1978 Shinohata: A Portrait of a Japanese Village. New York: Pantheon.
Douglass, William
    1969 Death in Murelaga. Seattle: University of Washington Press.
Embree, John
    1939 Suye Mura: A Japanese Village. Chicago: University of Chicago Press.
Freeman, Susan T.
    1973 Studies in Rural European Social Organization. American Anthropologist 75:743–750.
Fukutake, Takeshi
    1949 Nihon Nō-son no Shakai-teki Seikaku [Social Character of the Japanese Village]. Tokyo:
        Tokyo University Press.
Gilmore, David
    1982 Anthropology of the Mediterranean Area. Annual Review of Anthropology 11:175–205.
Greenwood, Davydd
    1976 Unrewarding Wealth: The Commercialization and Collapse of Agriculture in a Spanish
        Basque Town. Cambridge: Cambridge University Press.
Hansen, Edward C.
    1977 Rural Catalonia under the Franco Regime: The Fate of Regional Culture since the Spanish
        Civil War. Cambridge: Cambridge University Press.
Herzfeld, Michael
    1980 Honor and Shame: Problems in the Comparative Analysis of Moral Systems. Man 15:339–
        351.
    1985 Of Horns and History: The Mediterraneanist Dilemma Again. American Ethnologist
        12:778–780.
Irokawa, Daikichi
    1970 Meiji no Bunka [The Meiji Culture]. Tokyo: Iwanami.
Iszaevich, Abraham
    1975 Emigrants, Spinsters and Priest: The Dynamics of Demography in Spanish Peasant Socie-
        ties. Journal of Peasant Studies 2:292–312.
    1980 Household Renown: The Traditional Naming System in Catalonia. Ethnology 19:315–325.
    1981 Corporate Household and Ecocentric Kinship Group in Catalonia. Ethnology 20:277–290.
Itoh, Mikiharu
    1982 Kazoku Kokka-kan no Jinruigaku [Anthropology of the State as a Household]. Kyoto: Mi-
        nerva.
Kahoku-Shimpōsha
    1973 Mura no Nippon-jin [Japanese in the Village]. Tokyo: Keisō Shobō.
Kanō, Masanao
    1972 Nihon Kindaika no Shisō [Some Thoughts on the Japanese Modernization]. Tokyo: Ken-
        kyusha.
Kawashima, Takeyoshi
    1957 Ideologii to shiteno Kazoku-seido [Household System as an Ideology]. Tokyo: Iwanami.
Kitaoji, Harunobu
    1971 The Structure of the Japanese Family. American Anthropologist 73:1036–1057.
Leach, Edmund
    1961 Rethinking Anthropology. London: Athlone Press.
Lebra, Takie Sugiyama
    1976 Japanese Patterns of Behavior. Honolulu: University Press of Hawaii.

Moeran, Brian
    1984   Lost Innocence: Folk Craft Potters of Onta, Japan. Berkeley: University of California Press.
    1985   Ōkubo Diary: Portrait of a Japanese Valley. Stanford: Stanford University Press.
Mori, Mikisaburō
    1971   Na to Haji no Bunka [Culture of Shame and Name]. Tokyo: Kōdansha.
Nakamura, Kichiji
    1978   Ie no Rekishi [History of *Ie*]. Tokyo: Nōsan Gyoson Bunka Kyōkai.
Nakane, Chie
    1967   Kinship and Economic Organization in Rural Japan. London: Athlone Press.
Nolte, Sharon
    1983   Women in a Prewar Japanese Village: Suye Mura Revisited. Peasant Studies 10:175–190.
Nōsei Chōsa Iinkai
    1963   Nōka Sōzoku to Nōchi [Inheritance Practices of Farming Households and Farm Land]. To-
            kyo: Nōsei Chōsa Iinkai.
O'Brien, John
    1975   Systemic Effects of Inheritance Processes in Northern Spain. Current Anthropology 16:666.
Ortner, Sherry B.
    1978   The Virgin and the State. Feminist Studies 4:19–35.
Peristiany, J. G.
    1966   Introduction. *In* Honour and Shame: The Values of Mediterranean Society. J. G. Peristiany,
            ed. Pp. 7–18. Chicago: University of Chicago Press.
Pitt-Rivers, Julian
    1966   Honour and Social Status. *In* Honour and Shame: The Values of Mediterranean Society. J.
            G. Peristiany, ed. Pp. 19–77. Chicago: University of Chicago Press.
    1968   Honor. Encyclopedia of the Social Sciences 6:503–511.
Plath, David W.
    1964   Where the Family of God is the Family: The Role of the Dead in Japanese Households.
            American Anthropologist 66:300–317.
Prat, Joan
    1973   Estructura y Conflicto en la Familia Pairal. Ethnica 6:131–180.
    1975   La Posición Social de la Mujer en el Israel Bíblico y Cataluña: Notas para una Aproxima-
            ción. Ethnica 10:79–151.
Roca, Encarna
    1977   Qui és Català [Who is Catalan]. Barcelona: Dopesa.
Sakuda, Keiichi
    1967   Haji no Bunka Saikō [Reconsideration of Shame Culture]. Tokyo: Chikuma Shobō.
Schneider, Jane
    1971   Of Vigilance and Virgins: Honor, Shame and Access to Resources in Mediterranean Soci-
            eties. Ethnology 10:1–24.
Schneider, Jane and Peter Schneider
    1976   Culture and Political Economy in Western Sicily. New York: Academic Press.
Smith, Robert J. and Ella L. Wiswell
    1982   The Women of Suye Mura. Chicago: University of Chicago Press.
Tada, Michitarō
    1958   Haji to Taimen [Shame and Prestige]. *In* Kōza: Gendai Rinri [Readings: Contemporary Eth-
            ics], vol. 6. Pp. 227–248. Tokyo: Chikuma Shobō.
Wikan, Unni
    1984   Shame and Honour: A Contestable Pair. Man 19:635–652.
Wilson, Peter G.
    1969   Reputation and Respectability: A Suggestion for Caribbean Ethnology. Man 4:70–84.
Wolf, Eric R.
    1969   Society and Symbols in Latin Europe and in the Islamic Near East: Some Comparisons.
            Anthropological Quarterly 42:287–301.
Wyatt-Brown, Bertram
    1982   Southern Honor: Ethics and Behavior in the Old South. New York: Oxford University Press.

REFLECTIONS ON HONOR AND SHAME IN THE MEDITERRANEAN

Stanley Brandes

Introduction

Ever since Julian Pitt-Rivers published *People of the Sierra* (1961) and John G. Peristiany edited the volume on *Honour and Shame: The Values of Mediterranean Society* (1965), anthropologists have associated the honor and shame theme with Mediterranean studies. Indeed, these two books seem to have played a pivotal role in the emergence of this geographic subspecialty. Twenty years ago, there was barely sufficient anthropological research on the Levant, North Africa, and Southern Europe to justify lumping these regions together into a recognizable culture area. Nowadays, few scholars would question the rationale of a graduate student who declares an interest in the anthropology of the Mediterranean or the legitimacy of a jobhunter who names this area as his or her regional specialization. In social anthropology, culture areas become academically acceptable not only with the proliferation of relevant, high-quality scholarship, but also through the definition of distinctive problems and themes. Julian Pitt-Rivers and John Peristiany were among a handful of pioneers—a group that also included John Campbell (1964) and Julio Caro Baroja (1965)—who succeeded in impressing upon the profession the centrality of honor and shame to Mediterranean peoples. They thereby helped to shape a new field.

David Gilmore and the essayists that he has brought together in this volume are heirs to this intellectual legacy. They demonstrate the continuing fruitfulness of honor and shame as organizing principles for research. There is no doubt, as Peristiany pointed out long ago (1965:10), that qualities like honor and shame manifest themselves in one form or another among peoples throughout the world. These qualities seem to play an especially overt role in face-to-face societies, which function as moral communities by evaluating their members according to a single set of relatively unambiguous standards. It is also true, as Herzfeld convincingly argues in this volume, that honor-and-shame concerns vary widely from one language group to another, from one moral community to another, and that no single model is capable of capturing local subtleties and complexities.

Nonetheless, when taken as a whole, the articles in this volume seem to reveal, however tentatively, a specifically Mediterranean variety of the honor-and-shame syndrome, a substratum of beliefs and attitudes that many peoples in this small, but highly diverse, part of the world share. For one thing, honor—which might best be translated as esteem, respect, prestige, or some combination of these attributes, depending on local usages—is treated throughout the area as a sort of limited good, in George Foster's sense (1965). Wherever we look, Mediterranean honor appears to be related to control over scarce resources, including, of course, land and property, political power, and, perhaps most notably, female sexuality, with its procreative potential.

The connection between honor or esteem, on the one hand, and social masculinity on the other, is also an inescapable part of the Mediterranean value system. As Gilmore convincingly argues in the introduction to this volume, even where the concern for expressing virility and masculine prowess coexist with other evident aspirations, like generosity, political power, or material prosperity, a man's performance in the nonsexual domain confers upon him a coveted manliness. To be respected is to achieve gender-specific goals. Success or failure, in whatever area, is likely to be perceived and expressed in terms of anatomical or behavioral sexuality. Moreover, in a region like the Mediterranean, where male-female differences provide the metaphoric basis for other types of differentiation, it is understandable that gender should be a built-in, structural feature of language. Indeed, the Romance and Semitic tongues split the world into masculine and feminine domains, thereby facilitating—if not actually producing—the vision of a universe so divided. Honor and shame, as measures of prestige, esteem, respect, and self-worth, do not everywhere derive equally from sexual identity and behavior. But, likewise, there is no place in the Mediterranean for which these matters do not loom large, whether in and of themselves or as models for interpreting other aspects of existence.

Throughout the rest of this chapter, I hope to underscore a few of the theoretical advances in honor-and-shame research that are represented in this volume. I wish not only to pinpoint several of the many important contributions, but also to suggest fruitful issues for continuing research. In so doing, I rely in part on insights derived from my own Spanish data, and therefore also use this opportunity to relate some of my own unpublished field material.

Separating Honor from Shame

Probably the single most significant contribution of this volume to Mediterranean studies is that it challenges—demystifies, as contemporary academic parlance would have it—some of the more standard ways of thinking about Mediterranean value systems. One such heretofore inviolate assumption is that honor and shame are inextricably linked, tied to one another in cognitive as well as affective terms. Many of us, for example, have long assumed that there exists a sex-linked, binary opposition in which honor is associated with men and shame with women. This belief no doubt can be traced to Pitt-Rivers's original formulation, derived from his Andalusian research (1961). We have also, in somewhat contradictory fashion, tended to define honor and shame as interdependent aspects of the same phenomenon. Who of us, in lecturing on the topic to undergraduates, has not casually explained that in Mediterranean countries an honorable person is amenable to being shamed, while the person who is oblivious of other people's opinions, and thereby incapable of feeling ashamed, can have no honor? Anthropological analyses of honor and shame—particularly the classic studies, if they can be called that—have made it difficult for us to separate these concepts. In more ways than one, honor and shame have become the bread and butter of Mediterranean studies.

And yet, as a number of the papers in this volume wisely demonstrate, we should accept this conceptual linkage skeptically, if at all. A careful reading of these articles, as well as previous research, reveals at the very least that some linguistic groups focus on shame, while others on honor. Gilmore's essay on "Honor or Honesty?" is the first analysis of this topic in the Spanish context to describe terminological usage as I have experienced it. A sense of honor is no doubt important to Spaniards, as it is to people anywhere. Is there any known group that is indifferent to personal pride? But, as Gilmore notes, the term *honor*, in its several Castilian forms, is heard rarely in Spain, and then usually in a literary or historical context; contemporaneously, it is unlikely to emerge during the course of unreflective, daily conversation. Shame, by contrast, is an enormously salient term that anybody would encounter at least a dozen times a day. It is therefore reasonable to draw upon this concept to explain Spanish values and social relations; emically and etically it makes sense as an organizing principle.

With Greece, the situation appears opposite. Greeks, no less than Spaniards, would seem to be guided by the force of public opinion, by the spectre of being shamed. And yet the term shame seems to enter very little into published analyses of Greek values and psychodynamic life. Campbell, after all, wrote about *honor*, family, and patronage. And Herzfeld, in the chapter published here, challenges the way the term *filotimo* has been employed anthropologically; he substantiates the specialized geographic distribution of terms that I am talking about by making honor, rather than shame, his frame of reference.

If we turn to the Arabic Mediterranean, the situation seems similar to Greece: for Marcus, honor, not shame, is the analytical focus. And, while not exactly central to Davis's Libyan example, honor rather than shame is the concept relevant to it. Is this terminological convergence merely coincidental, or does it reflect North African reality? This issue is complicated by the fact that both Marcus and Davis base their analyses on literary texts, an epic poem on the one hand, a political treatise on the other.

All this is merely to point out that whether from the scientific or native perspective, whether from oral or literary evidence, the concern with honor seems to predominate in some regions or linguistic groups, the preoccupation with shame in others. Where anthropologists have discussed both concepts among the same people, we must suspect the almost inevitable imposition of our own ideas about honor and shame upon the group in question.

In this volume, most authors demonstrate a kind of linguistic sensitivity that was often absent from earlier treatments of honor and shame. As Herzfeld points out, we should be concentrating our attention on native categories, and understanding them on their own terms. We must beware of discovering honor and shame, as such, everywhere simply because we have learned that they are by definition Mediterranean. Until now, scholars felt duty-bound to encounter manifestations of these moral Bobsy twins when carrying out fieldwork any place in the Levant, North Africa, and Southern Europe. Hence, it is not surprising that these concepts occasionally emerge in the anthropological literature in almost unrecognizably transmuted form. The papers here increase our awareness of this difficulty; they thereby operate as a guard against ethnocentrism.

The Importance of Crosscultural Contrasts

In addition to increasing our awareness of native categories and interpretations, this volume reminds us that honor and shame are significant organizing principles elsewhere than the Mediterranean. It implicitly cautions us not to exaggerate the significance of these concepts to Mediterranean peoples, when in fact they may be no more pronounced here than in other parts of the world. Mariko Asano-Tamanoi's chapter is the most striking in this regard. It demonstrates that general utility of crosscultural comparisons. For example, she shows that, when considered crossculturally, the concepts of honor and shame can place certain otherwise elusive features of social organization in relief. Hence, from an analysis of Catalan and Japanese value systems, the structural significance of the house in both locales is impressed upon us. The salience of this social unit in each locale emerges through the simultaneous consideration of two seemingly diverse, but actually quite similar, milieux.

Professor Asano-Tamanoi's essay is innovative on many counts, but especially because it jolts us out of certain customary comparative frameworks, namely those that compel us to consider similarities and differences only among societies that share a longstanding historical-linguistic tradition. Mediterraneanists have overlooked the fact that insights sometimes derive from comparisons among vastly different cultures; when Davis (1977) and Boissevain (1979) criticize their colleagues for failing to compare and contrast, what they have in mind is the kind of controlled comparison that Fred Eggan advocated (1954) and that Nadel (1952) and others practiced to excellent advantage several decades ago. But these scholars were inquiring about the origins of particular elements of social structure and value systems. The careful description of such elements, and in particular the underlying structural relationships among these elements, were of less concern. Surely if structural anthropology and applied psychoanalysis have taught us anything, it is that the features of one society may echo and thereby reveal those of another vastly separated from the first in space and time.

Hence, it is noteworthy that anthropological analyses of the Mediterranean code of honor fail to mention Marcel Mauss, whose essay on *The Gift* (1967[1925]) dwells on the importance of honor to Melanesian, Polynesian, and Northwest Coast exchange systems. Davis (1977), Boissevain (1979), Wolf (1982), Silverman (1979), and others are quick to attack anthropologists for not utilizing the documents at their disposal, for not taking account of written history. Perhaps they are right. At the same time, however, anthropologists of the Mediterranean have been equally guilty of ignoring the anthropological resources at hand. They have been fearful of straying too far afield geographically, as if common historical heritage provided the only key to truth. If we are to comprehend honor in Libya, Greece, or Morocco, the understanding we can derive from Polynesia and Japan can be at least as illuminating as that we might hope to gain through documentary research. The type of understanding that emerges in each case is different. But each kind is equally valid and important.

Lexical and Evolutionary Contrasts

One simple, but critically necessary, goal that is achieved through comparisons across space and time is to place our own data in the perspective of human experience as a whole. Only in this fashion can we hope to reduce the ethnocentrism that inevitably pervades our work. Hence, I would claim that the anthropology of Spain, and by extension the Mediterranean, has been unduly influenced by Anglo-Saxon models and perspectives. When anthropologists of the Mediterranean—be they themselves of the region or not—describe the villages and towns that they study, they tend to focus on features of the social structure and value system that they perceive to be most different from their own. In anthropology, after all, we learn through contrast. Hence, codes of honor and shame, however they may be defined locally, stand out when compared with those in London and New York.

And yet are they really so different? There are several issues to be considered in this context. The first is linguistic. Do the actual terms honor and shame in English or any other language necessarily indicate an enhanced sensitivity to those qualities? In my own dialect of English, for example, the words honor, honorable, and derivatives of these rarely occur, while shame, shameful, ashamed, and the like are considerably more frequent. If we can judge by Shakespeare's plays, Elizabethan usage was the reverse; Spevack's concordance (1974) indicates that honor and its derivatives occur precisely 989 times in the Shakespearean corpus, more than double the 470 citations of shame and its derivatives. Do these presumed changes in word frequency necessarily indicate a lesser concern with honor among contemporary middle-class Americans than among Elizabethans? I suggest, rather, that the terminology by which we refer to the certain qualities has changed, while our concern with honorable status and conduct has not.

Even if, for argument's sake, we declare that terminological usage directly reflects psychological concerns, linguistic evidence from the Mediterranean lends no great support to the idea that people in that region are possessed with gaining, retaining, or competing for honor. Herzfeld's paper in this volume is a case in point: the term *filotimo,* which glosses "honor," occurs infrequently in Greek discourse—and Greece is probably the single European country that has produced the most honor-related literature. The Italian *onore* evokes vague associations with Sicily and the Mafia, but Giovannini appears capable of writing a fine essay about female chastity codes in that part of the world without citing the term. As for Delaney's insightful consideration of village Turkey, we are presented with a lexical distinction in Turkish between different types of honor, but never learn whether or how these terms are used at the folk level. The same situation apᵢ to Davis's essay, in which we are informed of the (Arabic? Libyan?) word ɪor honor, but in which its actual everyday usage remains a mystery. In fact, the more evidence at our disposal, the less certain we can be that there exists any marked lexical contrast between English speakers and Mediterranean peoples.

This circumstance by no means negates the notion that honor is more critical to peoples of the Levant, North Africa, and southern Europe than to ourselves. After all, we might well be dealing with a contrast between rural and urban, or between pre- and postindustrial, settings. Here is yet another dimension to the issue that the present volume highlights, albeit perhaps less explicitly than the linguistic matter. The standard anthropological treatments of honor and shame have dealt overwhelmingly with rural and/or preindustrial milieux. To quote one recent formulation, "The honor and shame constructs . . . are rooted in a model of rural social organization that by no means appears to be always applicable to city life" (Kenny and Kertzer 1983:14). It is therefore to be expected that analyses of this topic, like those presented in this volume, should similarly derive from village contexts in specifically nonindustrial settings.

But can we be so certain of the incompatibility of honor and shame with urban industrial milieux? After all, we are still influenced in anthropology by antiquated rural-urban stereotypes. The absence of a concern for honor and shame in Mediterranean cities reflects all too well the Redfieldian notion (1941, 1947) that urbanites are relatively free from the shackles of customary law; in the anonymous urban setting, Redfield believed, people develop individualistic behavioral codes and operate independent of public opinion. Under such circumstances, it would be impossible for a value system like that of honor and shame, which is based almost entirely on popular reputation, to exert its influence in cities.

The religious dimension of the folk-urban continuum also reinforces the conventional wisdom that honor and shame are rural, rather than metropolitan, concerns. Rightly or wrongly, Mediterraneanists have portrayed honor and shame as deriving largely, if not entirely, from religious tradition (see e.g., Brandes 1980; Dwyer 1978; Goody 1983; Guichard 1973; Mernissi 1975). It is, of course, impossible to deny the influence of Christianity and Islam in producing—or at least reinforcing—many of the sexual attitudes that are often associated with the honor-shame complex. If we then continue to believe that rural people are more influenced by sacred morality than are urbanites, we have a good explanation for the apparent centrality of honor and shame to villagers as opposed to city dwellers.

There are several problems with drawing such a conclusion, however. First, we cannot assume that people who share a religious tradition necessarily adhere to identical values. Hence, anthropological analyses of honor and shame pervade the literature on Catholic Spain and Sicily, not Ireland or Mexico; of Islamic Morocco and Turkey, not Malaysia or Indonesia. Obviously more than religion is needed to explain why Mediterraneanists are so good at uncovering manifestations of honor and shame in the villages and towns of their area. Second, we should not take for granted that rural people are more influenced by religious practices and ideas than are urbanites. In fact, evidence from Seville (Linz and Cazorla 1969) demonstrates that some rural people are less devoted religious practitioners than those in nearby cities. Thus, if villagers are relatively more bound by codes of honor and shame—which is by no means certain—it is not because they are bearers of a more sacred tradition.

What I am suggesting is that research on the honor-shame complex reinforces longstanding rural-urban stereotypes. In this literature, villagers appear anachronistic, with their small-town religious mentality and their honor-shame hangups. Urbanites, through implicit contrast, are portrayed as relatively rational, free of the exotic moral and psychological concerns that plague their rural counterparts. Johannes Fabian might well point to this aspect of Mediterranean scholarship as an example of how anthropology "strives to constitute its own object— the savage, the primitive, the Other" (Fabian 1983:1)—the Other in this case consisting of the Mediterranean peasantry and rural workers. It is hardly coincidental that discussions of honor and shame derive from observations in villages and small towns. These are the settings that anthropologists have selected to differentiate Mediterranean peoples from themselves. Urbanites presumably provide less striking differences.

We must repeat, however, that research on honor and shame among residents of Milan, Athens, and Barcelona has yet to be carried out. The question is not whether urbanites, who speak the same language as their rural counterparts, actually employ the terms honor and shame in the same fashion and with the same frequency as those in the countryside. Rather, we must try to discover how and to what degree prestige, respect, and self-esteem are anchored to distinct notions of masculinity and femininity. We need to know whether city dwellers understand their world in terms of a sexualized, gender-based idiom, as is so common throughout the rural Mediterranean. Until such urban research is carried out, it will be impossible to state whether anthropologists working in Mediterranean cities fail to report the existence of this value system because of its actual absence, or because their intellectual interests and observations lie elsewhere.

Evidence from Becedas and Monteros

Having discussed the concepts of honor and shame in Mediterranean societies generally, I now turn to the way these values manifest themselves in Becedas and Monteros, the two Spanish communities I know best. I take up this topic for several purposes: as a way of introducing recurrent themes in the honor-shame literature that I have not yet discussed, as a means of relating insights and observations that Mediterraneanists seem to have overlooked, and as a framework for suggesting future comparative research.

First there is the matter of honor and socioeconomic standing. Previous analyses of honor, particularly by Caro Baroja (1965) and Pitt-Rivers (1965), dwell on the ways in which honor has depended upon wealth and social status, especially in past historical epochs. Evidence from Becedas and Monteros, as well as from the bulk of the papers published in this volume, demonstrate the opposite, whether by implication or explicit declaration. That is, to the degree that a concept of honor exists—and let us, for purposes of discussion, take honor to mean good reputation and respected community standing—it is based on a radical sense of equality, the likes of which most of us in the United States, for example, do not possess. Certainly this situation pertains among the people of Becedas and Monteros. As I have described it (Brandes 1975), Becedas is a socially and economically homogeneous farming community of small peasant proprietors in Old Castile. Monteros, by contrast (Brandes 1980), is a typical Andalusian agrotown in which class and status distinctions are not only evident but also dominate people's consciousness. Members of both communities are habitually aware of matters bearing on family and personal reputation. But in neither place does the essence of individual or collective worth, pride, esteem, respect, or whatever, seem to depend on material resources. In other words, access to these qualities is independent of wealth, and that is as true of economically stratified Monteros as it is of egalitarian Becedas. The ingredients for maintaining a good reputation certainly differ in the two places; what they share is a rejection of the idea that wealthy, powerful people are, by virtue of their economic circumstances, inherently superior. In Herzfeld's terms, there exists "a nominal equality of access to moral resources" (this volume).

However, there is one way in which money does help, according to my Spanish informants. Given favorable financial circumstances you can leave the community at will to pursue sexual adventures. You have access to birth control information and devices (a highly restricted matter during the Franco era when the bulk of my research in these communities was carried out). And you have the physical space, the accommodations, to hide your amorous activities from friends and family. The standards by which community members measure reputation do not vary by social class; it is simply that the rich have the means to maintain pretenses, while the poor do not. The poor are therefore more vulnerable to having their good name besmirched than are the rich, and therefore must maintain correspondingly greater control over their instincts. The equal access to moral resources, at least for the people of Becedas and Monteros, is therefore more hypothetical than real.

There is yet another condition that limits full equality: birth. One's reputation depends largely on the reputation of one's family, so that the behavior of one's parents and grandparents automatically determines to an extent the respect that one can ever hope to command. As previously indicated, the Spanish word *honor* and its derivatives are rarely employed in either of my Spanish field settings. If probed, however, informants will discuss the concept. One Monteros man, for example, told me the legend of a person who visited a *sabio,* or wise man, to ask whether honor would be difficult to recapture, once lost. Replied the *sabio,* "It would be like putting piles of chicken feathers on the doorsteps of all the houses on your street at night, having a storm blow all the feathers away, and then having to replace them the next day exactly as they were the night before." And not only does a dishonorable person remain so throughout life, but this reputation also attaches to his or her family. Marriage, a primary means of mobility in stratified, state societies (Ortner 1978), is what is ultimately at stake.

In the two Spanish settings that I know best, the word shame and its lexical derivatives emerge frequently in natural conversation, and are by no means sex exclusive. Hence a person who controverts social norms without concern for reprisal is said "to lack shame" *(no tener vergüenza)* or to be a "shameless one" *(sinvergüenza).* These qualities are applied either to men or to women, with no notable preponderance for one gender group or the other. To be shameless automatically affects one's reputation adversely and, over the long run, might well ruin the good name of one's whole family.

Over the long run: here is an important qualification that highlights a much-neglected dimension of the Mediterranean value system that is evident in the communities where I have worked. There, the nouns *vergüenza* (shame) and *sinvergüenza* (shameless one) are usually applied to concrete actions and events that have occurred in the immediate past. To convey one of the most frequent uses of the term *vergüenza,* I might cite an occasion when I was watching a bullfight on television with some neighbors in Monteros. The bullfight was broadcast live, and, in front of the entire national audience, one of the bullfighters—Rafael Torres—began crying visibly. He had had the good fortune of fighting a brave, energetic bull, and had done a superb job until the very end. His problem was that no matter how many times he pierced the animal with his sword, it refused to fall dead; only after countless attempts did the bull finally reel over and die. Rafael Torres had inexplicably botched the performance. A clean kill, with one swift, artful, finely calculated stab, would have boosted his prestige. Instead, Rafael Torres was publicly reduced to the role of common butcher. The culmination of the fight, said my neighbors, was a *vergüenza* for him, and that explained his emotional outburst. Far from ridiculing him, the neighbors seemed to sympathize with his plight. But they also pitied him his unlucky fate. And to any Andalusian, to be pitied is shameful.

But the shamefulness of this situation, like countless similar ones, was transitory. Later in the afternoon, with Rafael Torres's second bull, he had better luck and killed the beast with a single, swift jab. He again cried, but this time from joy, said the neighbors, because he had redeemed himself. Similarly, a child who is caught lying will be scolded by his parents and called a *sinvergüenza.* Any fieldworker in Spain is likely to encounter this circumstance at least several times a day. But the appellation "shameless one" has no enduring meaning. It does not affect the child's reputation, much less that of his family. Should the child turn into a permanent, pathological liar, however, and the condition persist into adulthood, the reputation of the child and his family would be affected; their ability to command respect and be taken seriously by the community at large would be vastly reduced. In this eventuality, however, the terms *vergüenza* and *sinvergüenza* would probably be insufficiently strong to describe their reputation, and some substitute, like *malo* (bad, evil), would be employed.

The term *vergüenza* and its derivatives are usually employed as mechanisms of social control. For the most part they describe either disrespectful behavior or hapless circumstances that evoke pity. In both cases, the situations are perceived as impermanent. The individual who has been shamed, or who has acted shamelessly, has sufficient command over his or her life to be able to overcome the temporarily shameful condition. Shame, therefore, is an individual quality that defines the relationship between a single man or woman and his or her society. It concerns public opinion. The person, like Rafael Torres, who is shamed *(avergonzado)* is momentarily victimized by bad luck and thereby pitied by society at large; the shameless one *(sinvergüenza)* or the person who is lacking in shame *(no tiene vergüenza)* defies public opinion, is scornful of it, as in the case of the child who lies. Both personal conditions are ephemeral and reversible. They are also both potentially instructive to society at large as well as to the individuals who evoke negative images.

The element of control or choice is thus critical to understand the Spanish conception of shame. The shamed or shameful person has to be perceived as existentially in command of his or her actions, regardless of temporary lapses. This explains why analysis should always consider the life cycle when describing what shame means to any given people. In Becedas and Monteros, infants and toddlers are often teased jokingly when they engage in behavior over which they themselves are seen to have no control, but which would be considered shameful and disrespectful in older children. Hence, in changing an infant's diaper and cleaning the unpleasant mess from the buttocks, a mother will smile and call the son or daughter a *sinvergüenza*. Similarly, a father will laughingly and gently protect himself from the slaps of his angry two-year old son, all the while calling him a *sinvergüenza*. But the term is used in these cases affectionately, as a mark of endearment. To call these babies shameless is to affirm their antisocial behavior. However, the playful manner in which the term is uttered indicates a realization that these small ones have no control over their actions.

Socialization practices change at around age six or seven. From this time, which coincides approximately with First Communion and the official declaration that children are morally responsible for their own behavior, boys and girls begin to be perceived as amenable to social control. They are now said to have *sentido* (sense or judgment), and therefore have the capacity to alter their behavior in accordance with acceptable norms. If an eight-year old raises his hand to his father, there might well be a beating, accompanied by loud accusations that the child "lacks shame" *(no tiene vergüenza)* or that he is a *sinvergüenza*. This time, however, no air of playfulness will be detected. To the contrary, the punishment and name-calling are designed to teach the child conformity at a stage of life when he is capable of following the rules.

Not only the life cycle, but also mental health must be taken into account when analyzing the Spanish conception of shame. In the communities where I have resided, schizophrenics and other people with grave emotional disturbances are evident. Their behavior is abnormal. Yet in no instance have they or would they be called shameless. The category is simply irrelevant to their permanently helpless, hapless state. They are perceived as having no control over their actions; hence, the term *vergüenza,* which is employed above all as a sanction against deviant behavior, could not possibly affect them. Nor would using the term in reference to the mentally ill serve in any way as a reminder to others, who are themselves capable of conformity. The conceptual gulf between those who can take responsibility for their own comportment and those who cannot is simply too great.

Once a person is old enough and mentally fit enough to know the difference between appropriate and inappropriate behavior, conformity to the basic cultural rules becomes mandatory. This includes rules of all kinds, not just those pertaining to sexual conduct. Deviation results in accusations that the transgressor— male or female—is shameless, that is, scornful of public opinion. In the short run, shameless behavior or a shamed state of being can be overcome; it is transitory, reversible, correctable. Over the long run, however, persistent transgressions lead people to believe that something in the very biological constitution of the deviant individual leads him or her to act inappropriately. In this case, the individual acquires a bad reputation *(mala fama),* which adheres to his or her close relatives as well. From the emic perspective, the person's condition can no longer be described as shameful; it is, rather, inherently perverse, and thereby potentially hereditary.

From the developmental perspective, we might say that small Spanish communities like Becedas and Monteros use the concept of shame to cultivate what Howard Gardner has called "the personal intelligences" (Gardner 1983:237–276). Spaniards try to teach their children *"the ability to notice and make distinctions among other individuals* and, in particular, among their moods, temperaments, motivations, and intentions" (Ibid:239; emphasis in the original). This type of intelligence, to the Spanish, manifests itself not only in carefully modulated behavior appropriate to different categories of people in one's social universe. It also becomes evident through one's sensitivity to the way others react, and through concern for their opinions. The absence of such concern results in shamelessness.

It would appear that societies like Becedas and Monteros can emphasize shame as a mechanism of social control because within these communities prevail what Elizabeth Bott terms close-knit networks (Bott 1971). They are face-to-face communities in which people know one another in multiple capacities, as neighbors, relatives, work companions, and friends. Gossip is the prevalent means of social control. Bott has described the atmosphere in which close-knit networks operate thusly:

> One has little privacy in such a situation. But if one wants to reap the rewards of companionship and small acts of mutual aid, one must conform to local standards and one must be expected to be included in the gossip. Being gossiped about is as much a sign of belonging to the neighborly network as being gossiped with. If one refuses contact with neighbours one is thought odd and eventually one will be left alone; no gossip, no companionship. [Bott 1971:67]

In those words, Bott was of course describing some of her informants in London. But the ideas she extracted from them are similar to the opinion of one of my own friends in Monteros, who said to me that living in a *pueblo* is simultaneously the best and the worst fate that can befall anybody; it is the best because of social support and companionship, the worst because of the tyranny of public opinion. The two dimensions of village life are inextricably bound. Individuals are brought into line through the threat of being put to shame, but it is only through compliance to this sanction that anybody can reap the benefits of belonging to the group. Only by caring about what others think, by being amenable to the impact of shame, can a person derive public, hence self, esteem.

The similarities between Bott's Londoners and people I know in Becedas and Monteros bring us back to the issues of geographical distribution and rural-urban distinctions. On the basis of present suggestive evidence, we may speculate that the honor-shame complex or its equivalents flourish wherever there are close-knit networks, be it in London, Becedas, Athens, or rural Sicily. Neither the culture area nor the size and density of the population would seem to have as much determining influence as the quality of interpersonal relationships in any given setting. Honor and shame are above all mechanisms of social control that operate through the manipulation of personal images and reputations. Wherever public opinion reigns, a moral system of approbation-opprobrium, conceptually related to an honor-shame complex, will be present.

Nonetheless, the evidence to date points to a specific version of this syndrome that is characteristically Mediterranean. This version, if not unique in all its dimensions, would seem to distinguish the Mediterranean idiom of social control from similar systems elsewhere. In southern Europe, North Africa, and the Levant, several qualities recur often in anthropological considerations of honor and shame. It is to these that we now turn.

Moral Systems in the Mediterranean: An Overview

If we accept Elizabeth Bott's understanding of face-to-face communities, in which close-knit networks prevail, it follows that the members of any such society are going to share a discernible set of moral values. In fact, membership in the community may more or less be defined according to acceptance of and adherence to those values; shame, dishonor, and eventual ostracism normally fall upon flagrant, persistent deviants. Preoccupation with honor and shame may thus be perceived, wherever it is found, as a measure of social belonging, as a barometer of concern for one's secure place within the group. Bott's discovery is a crosscultural truism.

At the same time, Mediterranean communities, as they have been analyzed anthropologically to date, display particular moral concerns—a more or less predictable array of ideas about right and wrong, good and bad—which arise from shared historical and ecological circumstances. First, as we have observed throughout this volume, morality and human belonging within Mediterranean communities are closely tied to gender. In this part of the world, women and men are supposed to be endowed biologically with particular, sex-specific personality traits. These traits, in turn, impel women and men to behave in certain ways, which are virtually beyond individual control. Community-imposed sanctions, applied according to established codes of honor and shame, need to be mobilized in order to assure the relative harmony of social life within any given community. Virtually all the papers collected here speak to the issue of how honor and shame operate as mechanisms of social control. Delaney's chapter (this volume) is particularly useful in showing that honor and shame represent a sex-based symbolic, or even "genetic," code, which structures social relations, governs both inter- and intragender behavior, and gives rise to certain concepts of sexuality, procreation, and family organization.

This leads us to a second issue: the particular family organization that characterizes Mediterranean peoples, and that constitutes the major arena within which codes of honor and shame are played out. Naturally, if we examine the evidence carefully, we are going to discover numerous variations in family structure not only spatially but also temporally within the Mediterranean world. But it is also true, taking a bird's eye view, that the Mediterranean family—at least when compared with much of Oceania, Asia, and sub-Saharan Africa—is atomistic and isolated. Across the northern rim of the Mediterranean, nuclear families predominate, and maintain only precarious ties to the bilateral kindreds of husband and wife. Along North Africa and the Levant, as well as throughout most of Yugoslavia, patrilineages prevail, and yet these are for the most part genealogically shallow institutions, commanding only ephemeral loyalties from their constituent nuclear families. As Jane Schneider long ago pointed out (1971), scarce ecological resources throughout the Mediterranean have probably been largely responsible for the historical development of a competitive ethos among small kinship units, which see life as a struggle for prestige, power, even sheer survival. The plight of the Mediterranean family has been further exacerbated by outside powerholders—colonial exploiters, entrenched agrarian elites, predatory capitalist states, and as Goody emphasizes (1983), the Church—which have left the nuclear unit isolated and vulnerable.

One result of all these pressures has been the emergence and persistence of male competitiveness. By elevating female chastity to a symbolic virtue, women could readily become pawns in the struggle for family honor. Chaste women were transformed into a resource, which could be exchanged for wealth, power, and prestige. Christianity, Islam, and Judaism, the three great Mediterranean religions, probably aided this development by providing scriptural justification to male dominance and patriarchy; under their influence, female sexuality could be domesticated, tamed. The shamefulness attached to the uncontrolled Mediterranean woman enforced female comformity to the dominant value system. It is likely that these core sexual values became metaphors in terms of which other realms of life might be conceived. Hence, hospitality, honesty, and other desirable qualities came to be measures of masculinity and femininity. The symbolic emphasis on these harmonious qualities within Mediterranean communities also must have occurred in part as a compensatory response to competitive pressures, as mechanisms through which aggressive tendencies might be ameliorated. In the Mediterranean, historically as well as contemporaneously, there has always existed a tension between cooperation and competition. Each of these opposing qualities is sexually tinged, regardless of the areas of life in which it manifests itself. It is this pervasive sexuality that is particularly characteristic of Mediterranean value systems, of Mediterranean codes of honor and shame. In this, the codes may be distinguished from parallel moral systems elsewhere (see Asano-Tamanoi, this volume).

Despite this common substratum among moral codes throughout the Mediterranean, the intricacies, subtleties, historical changes, and local variations among them allow for rich, multifaceted scholarly analyses. This volume demonstrates, above all, the benefits of diverse approaches to the topic of honor and shame. Represented here are psychoanalytic (Gilmore), feminist-materialist (Giovannini), semiotic (Herzfeld), diachronic (Marcus, Davis), comparativist (Asano-Tamanoi), and cultural particularist (Herzfeld, Delaney) points of view. All of these dimensions reinforce the central importance of honor and shame to the Mediterranean value system, and, in fact, remind us that these moral qualities are essential defining features of the Mediterranean culture area. The approaches do not compete. Rather they emerge as distinct, though mutually necessary and compatible, avenues to the total comprehension of a complex phenomenon. Economic, psychological, cognitive, and social structural perspectives appear in this volume as mutually enlightening ways to perceive this critical feature of Mediterranean culture.

But what about the future? Insofar as it is possible to identify pressing research needs, I would count the investigation of honor and shame in urban, industrial settings the most important. The folk-urban continuum continues to exert a subtle but profound influence on the kinds of questions we ask and the types of information we collect, and this bias should be overcome. The second most important priority is the investigation of honor and shame in human development. We need to know how children come to acquire their sensitivity to public opinion, in what conceptual terms they phrase this sensitivity, and how their concern for reputation changes throughout the life span. Finally, there is the ever-present matter of change; we know all too little about how the honor-shame complex becomes transformed when cities grow or villages die, or when migrants move here or there, with or without their families. Only after such matters are addressed can we hope to identify with greater exactitude than at present causes for the emergence, persistence, and disappearance of values as varied and potentially elusive as honor and shame.

References Cited

Boissevain, Jeremy
    1979   Towards a Social Anthropology of the Mediterranean. Current Anthropology, 20:81–93.
Bott, Elizabeth
    1971   Family and Social Network: Roles, Norms, and External Relationships in Ordinary Urban
        Families. Second Edition. New York: Free Press.
Brandes, Stanley
    1975   Migration, Kinship, and Community: Tradition and Transition in a Spanish Village. New
        York: Academic Press.
    1980   Metaphors of Masculinity: Sex and Status in Andalusian Folklore. Philadelphia: University
        of Pennsylvania Press.
Campbell, John
    1964   Honour, Family, and Patronage. Oxford: Oxford University Press.
Caro Baroja, Julio
    1965   Honour and shame: an historical account of several conflicts. *In* Honour and Shame: The
        Values of Mediterranean Society. John G. Peristiany, ed. Pp. 79–138. London: Weidenfeld and
        Nicolson.
Davis, John
    1977   People of the Mediterranean: An Essay in Comparative Social Anthropology. London:
        Routledge and Kegan Paul.
Dwyer, Daisy
    1978   Images and Self-Images: Male and Female in Morocco. New York: Columbia University
        Press.

Eggan, Fred
    1954   Social Anthropology and the Method of Controlled Comparison. American Anthropologist 56:743–763.
Fabian, Johannes
    1983   Time and the Other: How Anthropology Makes its Object. New York: Columbia University Press.
Foster, George
    1965   Peasant Society and the Image of Limited Good. American Anthropologist 67:293–315.
Gardner, Howard
    1983   Frames of Mind: The Theory of Multiple Intelligences. New York: Basic Books.
Goody, Jack
    1983   The Development of the Family and Marriage in Europe. Cambridge: Cambridge University Press.
Guichard, Pierre
    1973   Al-Andalus: Estructura Antropológica de una Sociedad Islamica en Occidente. Nico Ancochea, transl. Barcelona: Barral.
Kenny, Michael, and David Kertzer, eds.
    1983   Urban Life in Mediterranean Europe: Anthropological Perspectives. Urbana: University of Illinois Press.
Linz, Juan, and José Cazorla
    1968/69   Religiosidad y Estructura Social en Andalucía: la Práctica Religiosa. *Anales de Sociología* 4:75–96.
Mauss, Marcel
    1967   The Gift: Forms and Functions of Exchange in Archaic Societies. Ian Cunnison, transl. New York: Norton. [First published 1925].
Mernissi, Fatima
    1975   Beyond the Veil: Male-Female Dynamics in a Modern Muslim Society. Cambridge, Mass.: Schenkman.
Nadel, S. F.
    1952   Witchcraft in Four African Societies: An Essay in Comparison. American Anthropologist 54:18–29.
Ortner, Sherry
    1978   The Virgin and the State. Feminist Studies 4:19–37.
Peristiany, John G., ed.
    1965   Honour and Shame: The Values of Mediterranean Society. London: Weidenfeld and Nicolson.
Pitt-Rivers, Julian
    1961   The People of the Sierra. Chicago: University of Chicago Press.
    1965   Honour and Social Status. In Honour and Shame: The Values of Mediterranean Society. John G. Peristiany, ed. Pp. 19–78. London: Weidenfeld and Nicolson.
Redfield, Robert
    1941   The Folk Culture of Yucatan. Chicago: University of Chicago Press.
    1947   The Folk Society. American Journal of Sociology 52:293–308.
Schneider, Jane
    1971   Of Vigilance and Virgins: Honor, Shame, and Access to Resources in Mediterranean Societies. Ethnology 10:1–24.
Silverman, Sydel
    1979   On the Uses of History in Anthropology: the *Palio* of Siena. American Ethnologist 6:413–436.
Spevak, Marvin
    1974   The Harvard Concordance to Shakespeare. Cambridge, MA: Harvard University Press.
Wolf, Eric
    1982   Europe and the People Without History. Berkeley: University of California Press.

CONTRIBUTORS

Mariko Asano-Tamanoi was born in 1951 in Japan and educated at the Tokyo University of Foreign Studies, Tokyo University, and Northwestern University (Ph.D., Anthropology 1982). Having completed fieldwork projects in both Japan and Catalonia, Spain, she is currently Research Associate at the Center for the Study of Industrial Societies, University of Chicago. Dr. Asano-Tamanoi has published several articles on both Spanish and Japanese society and culture.

Stanley Brandes was born in 1942 in New York City and educated at the University of Chicago (B.A., 1964) and the University of California-Berkeley (Ph.D., 1971). Having completed extensive fieldwork in both northern and southern Spain, as well as in Mexico, he is currently Professor of Anthropology at the University of California-Berkeley. Author and editor of several volumes including *Migration, Kinship, and Community: Tradition and Transition in a Spanish Village* (1975) and *Metaphors of Masculinity* (1980), his most recent book is *Forty: the Age and the Symbol* (1985).

John Davis was born in 1938 in London and was educated at Oxford University and the London School of Economics (Ph.D., Anthropology, 1969). He has carried out field projects both in southern Italy (1964–66) and in Libya (1975–79) and is currently Professor of Social Anthropology and Director of the Centre for Social Anthropology and Computing, University of Kent at Canterbury. Among numerous other works, Prof. Davis is the author of *Land and Family in Pisticci* (1973), *People of the Mediterranean* (1977), and the forthcoming *Libyan Politics: the Zuwaya Tribe and the Revolution* (Routledge and Kegan Paul).

Carol Delaney earned her doctorate at the University of Chicago in 1984, having conducted anthropological field research in Turkey between 1979 and 1982. She returned to Turkey briefly in 1986. Dr. Delaney first went to Turkey in 1975 when she was a student at Harvard Divinity School in order to visit Harran, allegedly the home of the prophet Abraham, as part of a research project on contemporary uses of the story of Abraham. Currently she is Assistant Director of the Center for the Study of World Religions and Lecturer in Anthropology at Harvard University.

David D. Gilmore was born in New York City in 1943 and educated at Columbia College (B.A., 1965) and the University of Pennsylvania (M.A., English, 1967; Ph.D., Anthropology, 1975). He did fieldwork in southern Spain at various times between 1971 and 1984 and in northwestern Morocco (1979–80) and is currently Associate Professor of Anthropology at the State University of New York-Stony Brook. Among his publications are *The People of the Plain: Class and Community and Lower Andalusia* (1980) and the forthcoming *Aggression and Community: Paradoxes of Andalusian Culture* (Yale University Press).

Maureen J. Giovannini was born in Auburn, New York and educated at the State University of New York-Cortland and at Syracuse University where she earned her M.A. and Ph.D. (Anthropology, 1976). She has been on the faculty of Boston University for several years and is currently with Organizational Dynamics, a consulting firm in Burlington, Massachusetts. She conducted fieldwork in Sicily between 1973 and 1974 and again in 1978. Her interests are in gender roles, social and cultural change and industrialization. She has published previously on Sicily in *Man* and the *American Ethnologist*.

Michael Herzfeld received his B.A. from the University of Cambridge (1969), his M.A. from the University of Birmingham (1972), and his D.Phil. from the University of Oxford (1976). He has done extensive fieldwork in the Dodecanese and on Crete, in both rural and urban settings. His publications include *Ours Once More: Folklore, Ideology, and the Making of Modern Greece* (University of Texas Press, 1982; Chicago Folklore Prize cowinner, 1981–82), *The Poetics of Manhood: Contest and Identity in a Cretan Mountain Village* (Princeton University Press, 1985), and *Anthropology Through the Looking-Glass: Critical Ethnography in the Margins of Europe* (Cambridge University Press, 1987, forthcoming), as well as numerous articles. He has guest-edited special issues of *Semiotica* and *Anthropological Linguistics*. He is currently Associate Professor in the Department of Anthropology at Indiana University, Bloomington, where he has taught since 1980.

Michael A. Marcus was born in 1950 and educated at the University of Wisconsin, the American University in Cairo, New York University (Ph.D., Anthropology and Near Eastern Studies, 1983). Having conducted field research in eastern Morocco, he is currently Lecturer in Religious Studies, Central Connecticut State University. Among his publications is the forthcoming book, *Islam and the Moroccan Past Imagined* (Princeton University Press).

A BOOKSHELF ESSENTIAL

The 1986–87 *Guide to Departments of Anthropology,* 25th edition, lists 479 US and foreign anthropology departments in academic, museum and research institutions and government, with details about degrees offered in anthropology, degree requirements, number of students in residence and degrees granted, academic year system, special resources and facilities, faculty/staff names, degrees and subfields, and graduate support available.

Includes over 20 pages of tables showing degree information for individuals, locations of departments and levels of enrollments, and number of degrees granted, both graduate and undergraduate.

Lists 420 recent doctoral dissertations in anthropology.

$15.00 to members, $25.00 to all others
Please enclose payment, in US funds, with all orders

American Anthropological Association
1703 New Hampshire Av NW
Washington, DC 20009

THE ANTHROPOLOGICAL MUSE

"With this book anthropology is moving away from a positivist framework
to a hermeneutic definition of science."—*J Iain Prattis, Editor*

J Iain Prattis, Editor. Foreword by Dell Hymes. Contributions of poetry, art,
and photography by John J Cove, Stanley Diamond, Marcene Marcoux, M
Estellie Smith, Edwin Wilmsen, Alan M Klein, George Park, Kenneth B
Liberman, Roy Wagner, William Bright, Robin Fox, J Iain Prattis, Bruce
Grindal, Ivan Brady, Paul Friedrich, Dennis Tedlock, Nathaniel Tarn,
Regna Darnell, Janie Brady, Anthony Leeds, Robin Ridington, Jean De-
Bernardì, Wilson Duff, Toni Flores, Susan Scrimshaw, Deborah Tannen,
Robert G Williamson, Cecil Helman, Douglas Uzzell, Rosario Morales, Ben
Fuller, Gene Anderson, David Price, Bruce A Cox, Gaisma Kadegis, Inés
Talamantez, Floyd Westerman, Duncan Pryde, Simon Brascoupé, Aqqaluk
Lynge, Francis Thompson, Tukak' Teatret. Finale by J Iain Prattis.

$16 (Members), $24 (all others)
Please enclose payment, in US funds, with all orders.

**American Anthropological Association
1703 New Hampshire Av NW
Washington, DC 20009**

ANThROpoloqy ANd public policy
A diAloquE

ANTHROPOLOGISTS HAVE BEEN RELUCTANT PARTICIPANTS in the formulation of public policy. Critics, yes; analysts, occasionally; but few in our ranks have even aspired to those positions where the courses of action are determined. . . .

—Walter Goldschmidt
from the *Preface*

Edited by Walter Goldschmidt, this volume is a collection of papers from the Forum on Anthropology and Public Policy, held in conjunction with the annual meeting of the American Anthropological Association, December 4, 1985.

The Forum was inspired by the conviction that governmental action must, if it is to effectively preserve human value, be rooted in an anthropological perspective. This means applying an understanding of *culture* as a phenomenon and of *cultures* as the context for all human action. The idea of culture is now universally accepted, but its superficial application does not suffice. For this reason, it is imperative that professionally trained students of culture take their place alongside economists, political scientists, lawyers, and others in the formulation of public policy. [Goldschmidt]

With contributions by Claiborne Pell, U.S. Senator from Rhode Island, Nyle C. Brady, Senior Assistant Administrator for Science and Technology for the U.S. Agency for International Development, David E. Long, Associate Director for Regional Affairs in the Office of Counter Terrorism in the U.S. Department of State, and anthropologists William O. Beeman, Dale F. Eickelman, Walter Goldschmidt, and Barbara Pillsbury.

$4.50 to members, $6.00 to all others.
Please enclose payment, in US funds,
with all orders.

American Anthropological Association
1703 New Hampshire Ave., N.W.
Washington, DC 20009

Number 21 in a series of Special Publications